KING HUSSEIN

KING HUSSEIN:

A LIFE ON THE EDGE

ROLAND DALLAS

FROMM INTERNATIONAL
NEW YORK

For Rita, Sarah and Katharine

CONTENTS

CHRONOLOGY

1893 Sharif Hussein takes family to Constantinople (Istanbul).

1908 Sharif Hussein and family return to the Hejaz.

1916 Sharif Hussein launches the "Great Arab Revolt" against the forces of the Ottoman empire in the Hejaz.

1917 The Balfour Declaration promises a national home for the Jews.

1918 The Ottoman empire, allied to Germany, collapses.

1921 Abdullah arrives with small force in Amman. Meets Churchill in Jerusalem and accepts the amirate of Transjordan, financed by the British.

1924 Abdulaziz ibn Saud drives Amir Hussein and his son, Ali, from the Hejaz.

1935 Prince Hussein, son of Crown Prince Talal, is born.

1948 British mandate to administer Palestine, from League of Nations, ends. The state of Israel is proclaimed and Jewish forces take part of Palestine; Abdullah's forces take the Arab part.

1951 King Abdullah is assassinated, and is succeeded by Talal.

1952 King Talal is declared incapable and is succeeded by Crown Prince Hussein.

1953 Hussein takes the oath of office and becomes king in fact as well as in name. Marries Dina Hamed.

1956 Hussein dismisses Glubb Pasha. The Suez affair erupts. Nationalist left win election, Suleyman Nabulsi becomes prime minister and Hussein faces a political challenge.

1957 Hussein dismisses Nabulsi; survives incident at Zerqa.

1958 Jordan forms Arab Union with Iraq. King Feisal of Iraq is assassinated. Britain sends troops to prop up Hussein's government.

1959   Hussein confers with President Eisenhower in White House.

1960   Prime Minister al-Majali assassinated.

1961   Hussein marries Antonia Gardiner (Princess Muna).

1967   The Six-Day War ends in disaster for the Arabs. Jordan loses West Bank, East Jerusalem to Israel. UN Security Council approves Resolution 242 on the Middle East.

1970   Palestinian *fedayeen* led by PLO try to create a state within a state in Jordan, threatening Hussein, who fails to negotiate agreement with PLO and orders army to expel *fedayeen* from country. Syrian forces enter Jordan, move south, and retreat when attacked by Jordanian army and threatened by America and Israel.

1971   Prime Minister Wasfi al-Tall assassinated at start of Palestinians' Black September terror campaign.

1972   Hussein divorces Princess Muna; marries Alia Toukan (Queen Alia).

1973   Yom Kippur war between Egypt and Israel.

1974   Arab League, in Rabat, approves resolution declaring the PLO to be the sole legitimate representative of the Palestinian people.

1977   President Anwar Sadat addresses Israeli parliament. Queen Alia dies in helicopter crash.

1978   At the end of talks at Camp David, Israel, Egypt and America sign peace agreements and a framework for a settlement on the West Bank.
       Hussein marries Lisa Halaby (Queen Noor).

1981   Sadat assassinated.

1982   President Reagan's peace plan.

1985   King Hussein and Yasser Arafat agree to co-operate; Arafat later withdraws.

1986   King Hussein closes PLO offices in Jordan.

1988   *Intifada* is under way. Arafat recognizes Israel and abjures terrorism. Jordan detaches itself from responsibility for the West Bank.

1990   Saddam Hussein's Iraq invades Kuwait.

1991 American-led coalition forces expel Iraq from Kuwait. Middle East peace conference held, clearing way for bilateral Arab-Israeli contacts.

1993 Secret Israel-PLO peace negotiations in Norway end with a Declaration of Principles and Interim Agreement.

1994 Jordan and Israel sign peace treaty.

1995 Yitzhak Rabin, prime minister of Israel, assassinated. Hussein delivers eulogy at funeral.

1996 Benjamin Netanyahu elected as prime minister of Israel. Peace process begins to disintegrate.

1997 General election held in Jordan is boycotted by the opposition.

1998 Hussein treated at Mayo Clinic in Rochester, Minnesota, for cancer.

1999 After more treatment at the Mayo Clinic, Hussein is flown home, where he dies on February 7th.

MAPS

I The Hejaz in the Ottoman world

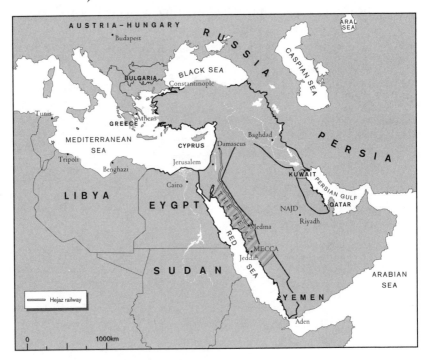

2 Jordan and the Middle East

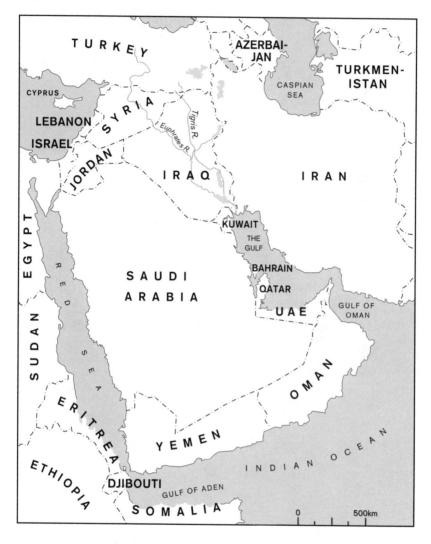

3 Jordan and Israel in 1949

LEBANON

SYRIA

Safad

GOLAN
HEIGHTS

Acre

Haifa

SEA OF
GALILEE

Nazareth

MEDITERRANEAN
SEA

Nablus

Jordan R.

Tel Aviv
Jaffa

WEST
BANK

Jerusalem

Amman

Hebron

DEAD
SEA

Gaza

GAZA
STRIP

Beersheba

Rafah

ISRAEL

JORDAN

EGYPT

Area under Egyptian control

Demilitarised zone

1948 ceasefire line

International borders

Aqaba

0   40 miles

4 Israel and Occupied Territories after the Six-Day War of 1967

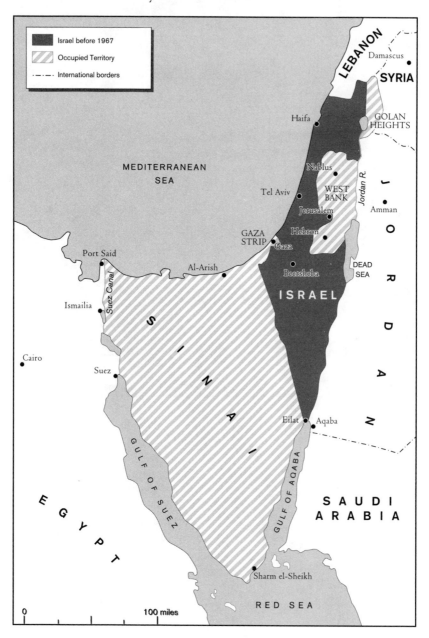

Israel before 1967

Occupied Territory

International borders

LEBANON

Damascus

SYRIA

Haifa

GOLAN
HEIGHTS

MEDITERRANEAN
SEA

Nablus

WEST
BANK

Jordan R.

Tel Aviv

Jerusalem

Amman

GAZA
STRIP

Hebron

Gaza

J   O   R   D   A   N

Port Said

Al-Arish

DEAD
SEA

Ismailia

Suez Canal

Beersheba

ISRAEL

S   I   N   A   I

Cairo

Suez

Eilat   Aqaba

GULF OF SUEZ

E   G   Y   P   T

GULF OF AQABA

SAUDI
ARABIA

Sharm el-Sheikh

0   100 miles

RED   SEA

5 Jordan today

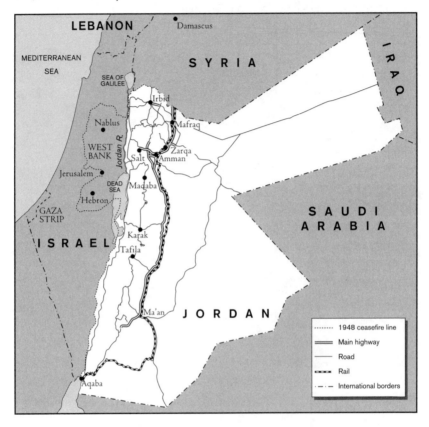

LEBANON

Damascus

MEDITERRANEAN
SEA

SYRIA

IRAQ

SEA OF
GALILEE

Irbid

Nablus

Mafraq

WEST
BANK

Jordan R.

Zarqa

Salt Amman

Jerusalem

DEAD
SEA

Madaba

SAUDI
ARABIA

Hebron

GAZA
STRIP

Karak

ISRAEL Tafila

Ma'an

JORDAN

.... 1948 ceasefire line
━━━ Main highway
─── Road
▄▄▄ Rail
─·─· International borders

Aqaba

THE HASHEMITE FAMILY TREE

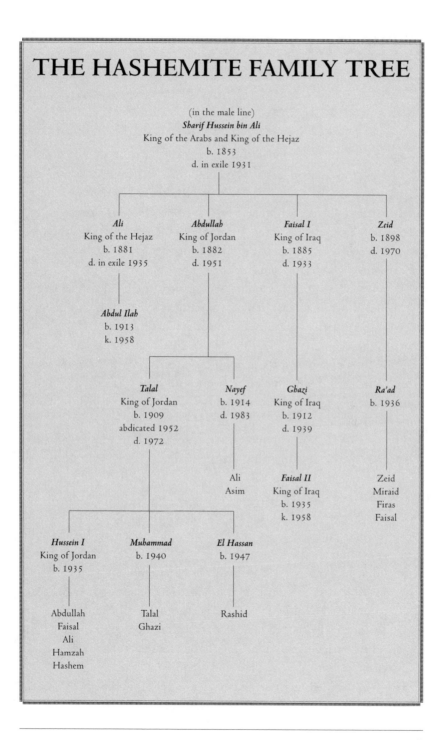

(in the male line)
Sharif Hussein bin Ali
King of the Arabs and King of the Hejaz
b. 1853
d. in exile 1931

Ali	*Abdullah*	*Faisal I*	*Zeid*
King of the Hejaz	King of Jordan	King of Iraq	b. 1898
b. 1881	b. 1882	b. 1885	d. 1970
d. in exile 1935	d. 1951	d. 1933	

Abdul Ilah
b. 1913
k. 1958

Talal	*Nayef*	*Ghazi*	*Ra'ad*
King of Jordan	b. 1914	King of Iraq	b. 1936
b. 1909	d. 1983	b. 1912	
abdicated 1952		d. 1939	
d. 1972			

	Ali	*Faisal II*	Zeid
	Asim	King of Iraq	Miraid
		b. 1935	Firas
		k. 1958	Faisal

Hussein I	*Muhammad*	*El Hassan*
King of Jordan	b. 1940	b. 1947
b. 1935		

Abdullah	Talal	Rashid
Faisal	Ghazi	
Ali		
Hamzah		
Hashem		

INTRODUCTION

He was described as a *macho* and his relations with his four wives were uneven. Although widely admired in the West, he was a strongman, albeit a benevolent one, at home. He was supported by a personality cult. He was intensely ambitious. He believed that he was a man of destiny. Yet Hussein bin Talal, third king of Jordan, was a man of substance who had lessons to impart.

This strongman had few political prisoners (he would argue that he had none). He ran a quasi-democracy with a fairly sound economy and he got along, with some ups and downs, with Jordan's Islamists – in sharp contrast to his fellow Arab rulers. His personality cult was less extreme than many. And there is no law against being intensely ambitious. If he had adopted mottoes, two would have suited him: "Moderation, stability and tolerance forever" and "My Hashemite family forever". He would see no contradiction.

Hussein of Jordan was an extraordinary figure on the world stage, most notably for his longevity in office. Among serving heads of state and government prior to his death, nobody had held office longer except Britain's Queen Elizabeth. Hussein assumed his constitutional powers as king on reaching the tender age of 18 on May 2nd 1953. He faced his first political crisis on May 4th 1954, when he dismissed his first prime minister at the age of 19.

The first American president with whom he had dealings was Dwight Eisenhower, whose personal intervention saved his regime. A British prime minister, Harold Macmillan, performed a similar service. The king also knew Charles de Gaulle. Long after all three statesmen had departed from the international spotlight Hussein was still there, dealing with Bill Clinton, Tony Blair and Jacques Chirac.

Hussein's record was not just one of survival, although that is the politician's first art. His record was, however, remarkable. He survived attempted poisoning. The aircraft in which he was flying was almost forced out of the sky. He was nearly killed in an ambush and an air raid. Radio stations of "brotherly" Arab governments, especially Egypt's, urged Jordanians to assassinate their king; Hussein's grandfather, King Abdullah, was gunned down at the great al-Aksa mosque in Jerusalem on July 20th 1951. The murder was witnessed at close hand by Hussein, then a schoolboy, and the future king prepared himself to suffer the same fate – while doing his utmost to prevent it.

Hussein's regime almost tottered when his cousin, King Feisal of Iraq, was assassinated in Baghdad, but it was propped up by Britain and indirectly by Israel. The Israelis seized the West Bank in the six-day war of 1967. Palestinian guerrillas led by Yasser Arafat almost created a state within a state in Jordan and were talking of overthrowing Hussein's regime when, almost at the last minute, the king moved against them. Syria invaded and was turned back by the joint efforts of Hussein's armed forces, the United States and Israel.

Parallel with his struggle for survival was a struggle for recognition. Rightly or wrongly, many Arabs did not regard the king and his Hashemite ruling family as genuine representatives of Arab nationalism. His difficulties had their roots in history. First, the Hashemite family is not Jordanian at all: it comes from the Hejaz, a province of the Ottoman empire comprising the holy cities of Mecca and Medina and the port city of Jeddah. The Ottoman sultan appointed King Hussein's great-grandfather, also named Hussein, as amir of the Hejaz (the local ruler, usually a direct descendant of the Prophet Muhammad with the honorific title of Sharif).

Second, Sharif Hussein was ousted from the Hejaz by fanatics loyal to the founder of the al-Saud dynasty in Saudi Arabia, Abdulaziz ibn Saud, thereby losing much of his and the Hashemite family's legitimacy. Third, the sharif's son, Abdullah, was made amir of Transjordan (the territory on the East Bank) by none other than Winston Churchill, then colonial secretary, in 1921 and was paid a subsidy to keep order in the area with the assistance of a British-officered armed force, the Arab Legion.

Fourth, Amir Abdullah acquired the West Bank as a result of a secret deal with Jewish leaders, notably Golda Meir, that was supported by the British foreign secretary, Ernest Bevin. Both Abdullah and the Jews agreed that after the British mandate for Palestine expired in 1948 and British forces abandoned the area, the Jews would take their share of Palestine, as laid out in an international partition scheme, and Amir Abdullah would take the Arab share. The deal worked. Abdullah convened two meetings of Arab notables from the West Bank who agreed that their territory should join Transjordan, which subsequently became Jordan under the promoted King Abdullah. This exercise in *realpolitik* made sense. The other Arabs were a shambles and Abdullah's rival, the mufti (titular Islamic leader) of Jerusalem, was a diehard rejectionist who was blind to the reality that Israel was there to stay. King Abdullah's and King Hussein's energies were thereafter spent trying to accommodate their governments and peoples to this reality. It may have been the only way forward, but it did not give the Hashemites much legitimacy in the Arab world.

This analysis runs counter to the official history, which recounts that Sharif Hussein was a true Arab nationalist hero for having raised the banner of the Great Arab Revolt against the Ottoman empire (which was collapsing before and during the first world war). He did so with arms and money supplied by the British. But it can be argued that while the British were using the Hejazi Arabs in their campaign against Turkey, Sharif Hussein was using the British to advance Arab interests. In return for helping the British and French against Turkey, he received promises (later proved to be false) that the allied powers would grant independence to loyal Arabs after the war was over.

In the same way, it can be argued that Amir Abdullah "saved" the West Bank for the Arabs in 1948 by sending in his Arab Legion, commanded by Lieutenant-General Sir John Bagot Glubb (Glubb Pasha) to take over the Arab part of partitioned Palestine. Had he not done so, the Jews would have been sorely tempted to move into the West Bank and nobody else could have stopped them. However, Amir Abdullah's critics thought he was motivated by personal ambition rather than the defence of Arab interests. Much as Abdullah took money from the

British and the Jews without batting an eyelid, King Hussein cheerfully took money from the British and the Americans as well as from the Saudis, Kuwaitis and other Arab autocrats. The Hashemites thought they were using the money-givers, and *vice versa*. But the willingness of the king to ask Britain and America, and possibly Israel, for help when *in extremis* did not exactly enhance his claim to be an Arab nationalist.

Like the issue of Arab legitimacy, another geological fault-line ran through Hussein's kingship that caused dangerous tremors and one earthquake: Hussein's relationship with Yasser Arafat, chairman of the Palestine Liberation Organization (PLO) and subsequently president of the Palestinian Authority. This relationship was consistently bad. The two men were rivals for influence over the West Bank. There was no room for compromise. Hussein regarded Arafat as devious, unreliable, elusive and unscrupulous; Arafat thought, not without good reason, that if the king were given the opportunity to replace him, he would seize it. The situation cried out for close co-operation between the two men. It did not happen.

Israel has been the beneficiary. For Hussein it was a no-win situation. After the Palestinian guerrillas formed a state within a state in Jordan, threatening Hussein's throne, Jordanian forces drove them into Syria and Lebanon with considerable loss of life. The king won, the Palestinians called it Black September and hijacked some airliners to Jordan in its memory; supporters of the king called it White September. But the king also lost – and lost badly. Without considering the consequences, sentimental Arab leaders, unwilling to fight Israel themselves, declared that Arafat's PLO was the sole legitimate representative of the Palestinian people. Hussein was denied the right to govern the West Bank, land that was once part of Jordan, or to negotiate about its future with the Israelis (who with the Americans would have accepted him as a reliable negotiating partner).

Thereafter, the king was a political leader seeking a role. He could enter the negotiating game only if the PLO agreed. More than a decade was wasted by the Arabs in trying to work out a formula satisfactory to all concerned. The situation played straight into the hands of the Israelis, who built hundreds of *kibbutzim*, other settlements, housing estates and military bases throughout the West Bank. The situation would have been entirely different if Hussein, who was acceptable to both Israel and the United States, had been authorized by the Arabs to represent the Palestinians. But he was not, and the Arabs have only themselves to blame.

Finally, the king played a key role in the convening of the Madrid peace conference, but then had to confine himself to negotiating peace between Jordan and Israel – while letting PLO-sponsored negotiators and the Israelis handle the future of the West Bank. During the subsequent talks in Oslo, the king was kept totally in the dark. In the years that followed the king continued to seek a role. Increasingly it was that of elder statesman, adding his voice whenever he was asked or thought it was needed during a crisis. He had not given up all hope of regaining influence over the West Bank and – more importantly – the Holy Places in Jerusalem.

Apart from Arafat, another leader stood in the way of Hussein's ambitions: Benjamin Netanyahu. Hussein had long dreamed that peace with Israel would bring prosperity to the Near East. There would be motorways, railways and airline services linking capitals; there would be international networks of oil, gas and water pipelines; there might be a free-trade area and numerous joint projects; investments would pour in; and the security risks would shrivel into insignificance. This dream was shared by Israel's Shimon Peres, among others. After Oslo, it seemed possible – even inevitable. After Netanyahu was elected as prime minister of Israel, however, the dream ended; Netanyahu did his best to ditch Oslo and to put Israel back into its former security-obsessed Middle Eastern ghetto. Hussein was in despair: his life's work was unravelling. His own peace treaty with Israel was becoming deeply unpopular among Jordanians. His new role became one of putting vigorous pressure on Netanyahu.

Other aspects of the king's long reign are more positive. His relations with Jordan's Islamic fundamentalists are an example to the Arab world. In most Arab countries, fundamentalists are jailed, exiled, muzzled or driven underground; many turn violent. Not so in Jordan. Following in his grandfather's footsteps, the king kept on good terms with the Muslim Brotherhood, the main Islamist organization, while promoting moderate Islam and a better understanding among Jordanians of Christianity and Judaism. He authorized one of his prime ministers to appoint fundamentalists as cabinet ministers and several held office in a relatively short-lived government. He appealed to the Brotherhood to take part in the 1998 general election. It refused, but not over anything concerning Islam: the Brotherhood thought the king's election rules would rig the result in favour of independent pro-government candidates representing tribes or extended families.

There was no suggestion that the Muslim Brotherhood was about to turn violent. It was indeed difficult for Hussein to be criticized on religious grounds: he appeared to be a devout Muslim; he claimed to be directly descended from the Prophet Muhammad; and he scattered pious phrases such as "God be praised!" through his public statements.

By Arab standards, Hussein's Jordan was open, free and democratic and a model for the Middle East and the Maghreb. Only the government of King Hassan of Morocco could claim to be in the same league of democratic achievement. By Western standards, however, Jordan had a long way to go. It was ruled by a somewhat autocratic monarch who hired and fired prime ministers as he wished and who handled key aspects of foreign policy himself. For most of his reign, after Hussein in political importance in Jordan came the king's brother, Crown Prince Hassan, not the prime minister. But in January 1999 Hussein's son, Abdullah, was named as crown prince. As king, he may be as autocratic, and as popular, as his father.

However, Hussein did try to keep his ear close to the ground. His security service kept him fully briefed on the mood in the street. Thus he did not hesitate to go against the West and most of the Arab world in seeming to side with Iraq's Saddam Hussein after Iraqi troops marched into Kuwait. He was reflecting the euphoria among Palestinians in Jordan after Saddam Hussein offered to withdraw from Kuwait if Israel would withdraw from the West Bank. Hussein knew that if he joined the chorus of condemnation of Saddam Hussein, he would have to deal with angry demonstrations. He subsequently mended his fences in the West and the Arab world, and he was again given a respectful hearing wherever he went.

At the time of the king's death, Jordan's economy was in quite good shape although poverty remained widespread. Hussein had lent his support to structural reforms, the dinar was freely convertible and the foreign-exchange reserves were respectable. Many Palestinians who were expelled from the Gulf had moved to Amman and built their home there, and the capital had experienced a construction boom. There was talk of turning Amman into a financial centre. Amman's hospitals and universities were of a fairly high standard and attracted foreigners. By any reckoning, these were substantial achievements.

But everything depended on the peace process, which Hussein had done so much to help – even push – along. His death left great uncertainty.

1 MURDER AT THE MOSQUE

The American ambassador begged the king to drop his plan of praying at Jerusalem's great al-Aksa mosque and instead pray at the mosque in Amman, where he would be among friends.

"I have heard there may be an attempt on your life," he said. King Abdullah of Jordan replied: "Even if it were true, I would go. I will die when I am destined to die."

Abdullah knew his expedition was dangerous. "I have asked many people to come with me to Jerusalem tomorrow," he told his 16-year-old grandson, Prince Hussein. "It is very strange. Some of them don't want to come. They seem afraid of something. I have never heard so many feeble excuses in my life."[1]

Arab East Jerusalem in July 1951 was tense. On July 16th a prominent Lebanese politician, Riad al-Sulh, had been murdered there. King Abdullah had wanted to pray at al-Aksa for two reasons, one official and the other top secret. The official reason was that the king regarded al-Sulh's murder as an attempt by his Palestinian enemies to destabilize his kingdom. Abdullah wanted to show that he was not afraid of them and that he remained in charge.

The secret reason was that the king had arranged, while in Jerusalem, to hold a clandestine meeting about possible terms for a peace agreement between Jordan and Israel with Reuven Shiloah and Moshe Sasson of the Israeli foreign ministry in a Jerusalem house on Saturday July 21st (according to Sasson).[2]

The 69-year-old king was going against all the odds. Israel was being difficult about concessions. Sentiment among Palestinians, including hundreds of thousands turned into refugees by the creation of the state of Israel in 1948, was fiercely opposed to peace with the Jews, who were regarded as cruel usurpers and oppressors. Many Palestinians, dreaming that somehow they might return home after Israel was destroyed on the field of battle, feared that Abdullah planned to betray them. "I know that I am hated," he told a visitor. But peace with Israel was the only sensible solution that he could envisage.

His grandson had been surprised a few days before the Jerusalem trip by Abdullah's words, which came out of the blue. "I hope you realise that one day you will have to assume responsibility," he said solemnly. "I look to you to do your very best to see that my work is not lost." Then Abdullah asked his grandson to accompany him to al-Aksa and, unexpectedly, to wear his military uniform. The grandson, who hero-worshipped his grandfather and liked nothing better than to sit in his tent and listen to him talking to visitors, immediately agreed.

Before leaving Amman, his capital, Abdullah was chatting to some acquaintances about life and death. "When I have to die, I would like to be shot in the head by a nobody," he said. "That's the simplest way of dying."

On Friday July 20th, amid tight security, the old king and the young prince arrived at al-Aksa. A guard of honour presented arms. The king rebuked them: noisy military ceremonies should not be held in holy places, he said. Abdullah entered the *haram* (large courtyard), paid his respects at the tomb of his father, King Hussein of the Hejaz, and entered the mosque, where the Koran was being recited to about 1,000 of the faithful and being broadcast live. As his grandson recalled it later, the king turned to enter, and when he had taken about three paces inside the main doors, a man came out from behind the great door to his right. He did not look normal. He had a gun in his hand and, before anyone could react, he fired. The man was only 6 feet away but Abdullah never saw him. The king was hit behind his right ear and fell to the ground. His turban rolled away.

The man fired more shots, one of which (by Hussein's account) struck a medal on his chest and ricocheted away. He later decided that his grandfather's insistence that he wear his uniform had saved his life.

The shots were heard by listeners to Jerusalem Radio. So were the shots of Abdullah's soldiers, who killed perhaps 20 people and injured some 300 in panic and fury.

The king's party went from the mosque to Jerusalem's airfield where a Scottish wing-commander in Jordan's air force, Jock Dalgleish, came up to the young prince and offered to fly him back to Amman in a two-seater Dove. He accepted the offer. "I little thought that two years later Dalgleish would teach me how to fly," he wrote, "and that seven years later Jock and I, in similar aircraft, would be fighting for our lives, attacked by Nasser's Syrian MiGs. The next day I carried a gun for the first time in my life."

Who killed the king? A nobody, thus fulfilling his wish: a tailor's apprentice from Jerusalem with a criminal record who was a member of "Holy War", a paramilitary group led by Haj Amin Husseini, the mufti of Jerusalem. The men behind him were, according to the findings of an investigation, Abdullah al-Tall, who had served as an aide of the king but had changed sides and lived in Cairo, and two relatives of the mufti. By one account, the investigators concluded that 60,000 Palestinian pounds, a huge sum of money, had passed hands. It was assumed, writes the Israeli historian Avi Shlaim, that the mufti, King Ibn Saud of Saudi Arabia and the Egyptian government had all played a part in instigating and financing the murder.

Reactions were mixed. The French consul in Jerusalem, no friend of the pro-British Abdullah, said: "There are 600,000 Palestinians who are delighted with his death."[3] The British felt the main prop of their Middle East strategy had been knocked out from under them. Prince Hussein was devastated. "He of all men had the most profound influence on my life," he wrote later, after becoming king of Jordan. "He loved me very much, that I know, and I loved him to the point where I no longer feared his rather austere outward appearance. To him I think I was a son."

On November 6th 1995, giving the eulogy at the funeral in Jerusalem of Yitzhak Rabin, the assassinated Israeli prime minister, the 60-year-old King Hussein recalled his grandfather's fate in Jerusalem in 1951 and added, with Abdullah's fatalism: "When my time comes, I hope it will be like my grandfather's and like Yitzhak Rabin's." He did not enjoy that final luxury.

2   GROWING UP

Prince Hussein may have been a well-loved "son" to his grandfather, but life in the Jordanian royal family was tense and difficult. Hussein's father, Crown Prince Talal, was showing signs of emotional instability and his father, Amir Abdullah of Transjordan (as the king was first known) treated Talal with contempt.[1] As a strong and healthy man, Abdullah could not appreciate what mental illness was. Talal suffered acute mood swings: at times gentle and sensible, he was also subject to withdrawal and fits of violence that were eventually diagnosed by Swiss specialists as dementia praecox (schizophrenia).

It was a sad fate for an intelligent man in his 40s who had prepared carefully for kingship at the British military academy at Sandhurst, as a cavalry officer in Jordan's Arab Legion and as a judge of the tribal courts. Abdullah, who had dreamed of having a brave, intrepid Bedouin son as his successor, thought Talal was awkward, difficult and above all weak and indecisive. "My own son hates me," Abdullah complained. Talal was the son of Abdullah and his first wife, Musbah, who was also his first cousin.

Talal's illness did not, however, prevent him marrying and fathering five children. When he was well, he entranced them as a story-teller. He seemed kind and gentle, quite unlike the bluff, stern Abdullah. Talal's wife, Zain, evoked her son Hussein's strongest adjectives when he described her: she was not only very beautiful but also very wise, tender and loving and full of advice and encouragement – "a major factor in my life".

Hussein credited his mother with helping his father to step in after the death of King Abdullah and rule Jordan, if only for less than a year. Talal could have not done it without her.

As a small boy, life was a strain for Hussein. Talal was poor: his allowance was of only £1,000 a year. The family lived in a five-room house with one bathroom. The crown prince's growing schizophrenia and differences with his father must have been an acute strain. At one point the family was so short of cash that, at his mother's request, Hussein said he made a painful sacrifice for a small boy: to sell the bicycle that his cousin, Crown Prince Feisal of Iraq, had given him as a farewell present at the end of a visit to Baghdad. It had been his pride and joy.

Before the age of 16 Hussein had gone to seven schools, in Amman and the Egyptian city of Alexandria. He seems to have been sent to schools and withdrawn from them at the whim of his grandfather and father; Abdullah favoured English and Islam while Talal stressed Arabic. At his first school, a Christian mission in Amman, he was not a top-of-the-class student.

Hussein was happiest, in the period before his grandfather's assassination, at Victoria College in Alexandria, Egypt, where he learnt not only Arabic and English but also "football, cricket, books and companionship". He pleased his grandfather by taking lessons in fencing. He loved being treated like the other boys and making friends. But he added wistfully: "I never had any who were really close."[2] By another account, this small, solemn schoolboy was bullied.

Having decided that Talal would not make a worthy successor, Abdullah pinned his hopes on young Hussein, who was Talal's eldest son. When home on holiday from Victoria College in the last year of Abdullah's life, Hussein was woken up at 6 am and taken to the king's palace by 6.30 am. In a room set aside for studies, the young prince read Arabic and religious texts with a tutor. Occasionally he had breakfast with his grandfather: a cup of cardamom-flavoured coffee with some flat bread-cakes without butter or jam. Sometimes Hussein acted as his grandfather's interpreter when he dealt with English-speaking visitors (Abdullah said he spoke only Arabic and Turkish though in fact he also understood English and probably could speak it).

Most evenings Prince Hussein dined with his grandfather. "I would listen to him talking about the subtleties and pitfalls of the hazardous profession of being a king," he wrote later. "Or I would sit at meetings with notables, or watch him dictate or play chess."[3] Hussein's preparation for government, reminiscent of that of William Pitt the Younger at the hands of his father, the Earl of Chatham, could not have been bettered. During the period between his grandfather's death and his own accession to the Hashemite throne he did not forget what he had learnt.

Hussein acquired a bitter streak. He would never forget the sight of his grandfather's supposed friends abandoning him and scurrying for safety after he had been shot, and the rapacious politicians subsequently fighting for the crumbs of office. "If life is cheap, man is cheaper yet," he thought.

After Abdullah's assassination, Hussein wanted to return to Victoria College in Alexandria. However, because of tension in relations between Egypt and Jordan, this was impossible for the crown prince. So Hussein had to start again, this time at Harrow, one of Britain's most prestigious private schools, where his cousin Feisal, later to become king of Iraq and to be savagely assassinated, was already a student.

Harrow was difficult. Hussein found that his English was not as good as he had thought: it was hard to understand not only the British aristocratic accent (he thought it was a "gabble") but also the unwritten laws of private-school behaviour. Hussein's best subjects were history and English literature, but it was an effort to understand and learn at the same time.

At first his fellow-schoolboys struck him as snobbish, arrogant and remote. But he eventually made friends, learnt how to play rugby and, predictably for a boy short in stature, played scrum half. His housemaster said: "At the beginning of term he went out to play rugby for the first time. He had never seen the game before, and was a bit lost to start with. But before the end of the game he was tackling low like an old hand." [4] One of Hussein's recollections, symbolizing his acceptance at Harrow, was the glow he said he felt on the rugby pitch when a boy threw him a long, low pass shouting: "Get going, Hussein! It's all yours!" Later, when he was king in 1962, Hussein said that he was very proud to have been at Harrow, numbered many Old Harrovians as friends and loved to wear his Harrovian tie.

On one occasion when both Hussein and Feisal were at Harrow, a senior British official asked how the young princes were getting on. Feisal, said the headmaster, was well-behaved, quiet and unassuming and might make an excellent constitutional monarch if allowed the opportunity. Hussein, on the other hand, was more vigorous, headstrong and determined, likely to be a strong ruler. However the future king's house matron found him to be highly strung and sometimes lonely.[5] She also said he was "a very philosophical fellow, but a simple soul at heart", who wanted to chat about his worries about his father.[6]

It was while he was at Harrow that Hussein acquired his love of fast cars. At first he had a blue Rover, then a maroon Bristol which could hit 90 mph with ease. It was looked after by a garage manager who became a friend, Maurice Raynor. Later, Raynor came to Amman to look after the king's stable of fast cars, one of which was a traditional Morgan sports model.

Much later, in 1997, King Hussein made a gift of a large undisclosed amount of money to Harrow to pay for the refurbishment of the school's Vaughan Library. It was doubtless appreciated by the old boys in the Harrow Association, some of whom are members of Britain's establishment. In 1997 the king was elected as president of the association and flew to London for its annual dinner, a black-tie affair in the elegant Merchant Taylor's Hall in the City. The *Harrow Record 1997* reported: "In a most moving speech, His Majesty replied that he had only been at Harrow for a short time, but it had been an important time in his life and it made a great impression on him."

While Hussein was studying at Harrow, Talal was deteriorating. By one account, King Abdullah was partly to blame. He had intimidated his son by his domineering manner and scathing criticism, which destroyed Talal's self-confidence. There had also been some incidents when Talal was at Sandhurst, the British army academy, described as "some sort of bullying". The king and crown prince scarcely spoke to each other. In 1940, Abdullah had signed a secret decree taking Talal out of the line of succession (it was subsequently rescinded). First in line was Naif, his half-brother, who was regarded by the British as a lazy lightweight who would not damage British interests. Talal, by contrast, had been described in 1940 by the British minister in Amman, Sir Alec Kirkbride, as "intemperate in his habits, untrustworthy and at heart deeply anti-British".

By the end of the war, Talal had managed to cut back on his drinking, which had become a problem, and behave in a friendly manner. But it did not last. In 1948 and 1949 British diplomats referred to his "fits of irritability" and his "unpredictable and violent temper".[7]

In May 1951, shortly after his father left for a state visit to Turkey, Talal had a mental breakdown. Doctors persuaded him to take treatment in Beirut, where the specialist blamed Abdullah for his son's condition and said he needed a long convalescence. But he was back at home in June, suffered another breakdown and went this time to Switzerland.

Talal was in Switzerland in 1951 when King Abdullah was assassinated and his half-brother Naif was appointed as regent. However, the notables from Jordan's leading families preferred to take a chance on the unpredictable first-born than on his younger brother, who some thought was lazy. They were encouraged to take this view by a report by the respected notable Said al-Mufti, who saw Crown Prince Talal in Geneva on what must have been one of his good days. He concluded that Talal appeared to be sane. Two doctors were sent to Geneva and diagnosed, contrary to their better judgment and perhaps with the encouragement of al-Mufti, that Talal was only depressed and had no mental disease. At the same time Naif lost support for having tried to manoeuvre his way to the crown and, at the last minute, for having considered a coup attempt.[8]

Talal returned home to a warm welcome from people who hoped he might bring a breath of fresh air to the old regime and clear out many of the late king's cronies.

The new king and his prime minister, Tawfiq Abul Huda, made several concessions that King Abdullah would not have appreciated. They engineered a reform of the constitution so that it no longer proclaimed that all power resided with the king; it appeared to create something akin to a constitutional monarchy with respect for human rights. There were, however, some significant loopholes.

Talal visited the Hejaz, the land of his grandfather, King Hussein, and his father, King Abdullah, which had been conquered by Abdulaziz

Ibn Saud of Saudi Arabia. He flew in a Saudi aircraft. Thus Jordan symbolically acquiesced in the conquest of the Hashemite lands (including Mecca and Medina) by Ibn Saud. Talal also signed the Arab League's collective security pact. King Abdullah had refused to do so because the league had refused to recognize his takeover of the West Bank in 1948; now Talal and Abul Huda shrugged their shoulders.

Until January 1952, Talal, aided by Abul Huda, performed well, more or less, as a constitutional monarch. Gradually, however, the schizophrenia returned, perhaps caused by the pressures of high office. On one occasion after giving lunch to an ambassador, Talal swept the table-cloth from the table together with glasses and cutlery and struck his wife and daughter. On a trip to Paris he was found wandering in the street.[9] Queen Zain and her family, including Crown Prince Hussein, observed the deterioration – and the threat to her life – at close quarters while on a European holiday. Zain kept quiet about the symptoms, hoping they would go away. However, Abul Huda soon became aware of the change: the king, reverting to the authoritarian mode of his father, insisted that the prime minister dismiss two high officials whom he regarded as his enemies. A British diplomat reported more frequent and more violent attacks by Talal on his wife and children.[10]

The finale was played out with painful publicity. In May 1952, the prime minister asked his three most senior ministers to try to persuade Talal to take medical treatment abroad. Talal would agree only to take a "holiday" and to set up, in June, a "throne council" to act on his behalf during his absence.

While this was going on, the queen and her family (excluding Hussein, who was at Harrow) remained in a hotel in Lausanne, Switzerland, unwilling to return home to Amman and face the unstable Talal. It was this decision that pushed the crisis to a conclusion. The queen said she would return only if Talal was moved elsewhere, possibly to Egypt or Cyprus. As the climax approached, she told Hussein to come to Lausanne from Harrow. Talal flew to Switzerland, ostensibly to bring the queen home. (During this period Talal had also said he intended to travel by liner to the United States and, later, to abdicate and devote himself to a life of prayer in the Hejaz.)

The succession, which could have provoked a collapse of the young state, was remarkably smooth. The discreet but decisive Kirkbride and the British commander of Jordan's Arab Legion, Lieut-Gen Sir John Bagot Glubb (Glubb Pasha), played their part; so did the Jordanian notables. All took a long-term bet on Hussein.

It was clear what had to be done: Talal had to be declared incapable and either abdicate or be deposed, and be succeeded by Crown Prince Hussein. The Swiss authorities refused to help. So the prime minister, Abul Huda, obtained a diagnosis from Egyptian and Jordanian doctors of Talal's incapacity and convened a special session of both houses of parliament on August 11th. The members voted unanimously to depose Talal and to crown Hussein. One man can take the credit for the smooth transition, and the preservation of the house of Hashem: the prime minister, Abul Huda, astute manipulator of power in Jordan.

Talal was moved to Egypt and, in 1953, to a nursing home in Turkey. He remained there, visited annually by Zain and Hussein, until his death in 1972.

It is not difficult to imagine the impact of such a family drama on a teenage boy. Writing in 1962, he said little about this period except to record that his father's schizophrenia deteriorated and, like any wife and son, "my mother and I hoped, until all hope was gone, that he would recover". Hussein must have been profoundly upset about what had happened to his father and fearful that Talal's schizophrenia might run in the family. He must have been permanently on his guard against his father's mood swings; he may well have become acutely embarrassed by Talal's behaviour when dealing with people outside the family, and he was certainly protective towards his mother, Queen Zain.

At this time, Hussein seems already to be somewhat introspective. He spent much of his time away from the family at boarding schools yet did not wholly fit in at these schools, where he stayed for only short periods. Two figures dominated his youth: King Abdullah and his mother. He seems to have acquired a sense of cool objectivity: while he was angered and disturbed by his father's behaviour, he treated him with filial respect and, when looking back on his short reign, felt sorry for him.

On August 12th 1952, the young prince's life changed forever. A page-boy came to the door of his room at Lausanne's Beau Rivage hotel bearing an envelope on a silver salver. It was addressed to "His Majesty King Hussein" and it explained to him what had happened in Amman. Hussein promptly returned home, where he was pleasantly surprised by what he saw as a spontaneous and enthusiastic greeting. He did a grand tour of the country to show himself to the population. But there remained six months before the inauguration. How would he spend them? His uncle, Sharif Nasser bin Jamil, and the prime minister suggested Sandhurst, about 35 miles southwest of London. Hussein leaped at the opportunity; Glubb Pasha fixed the details.

Hussein loved it. At Harrow he had been treated like a boy; at Sandhurst he felt he was accepted as a man, although he was only 17 years old. He took a crash course but not the soft option offered to foreign dignitaries. That decision meant he took part in night assaults on rugged terrain and a lot of drill. He appears to have received no special treatment. Sergeants at Sandhurst liked to shout at the officer-cadets: "I call you Sir, and you call me Sir! The only difference is you mean it and I don't!" A drill-sergeant is reputed to have screamed at Hussein, when he took a wrong step on one occasion: "What an idle little king we are today, Sir!" Sandhurst's regimental sergeant-major Lord used to address him, with his customary bellow, as: "Mr King Hussein, Sir!" (Later, Hussein made a surprise appearance on British television, reminiscing about his Sandhurst days, when Lord was the subject of the programme "This Is Your Life".)

Fellow-cadets showed him no reverence, and *vice versa*. After his bicycle's tyres were let down by practical jokers before he needed to use it to get to a lecture, he made a point of unscrewing the tyre-valves of 30 other bicycles at night. "I might have been suspected," he said later. "But nobody ever proved who did it."

Hussein also related the story of going to London's Central Criminal Court, the Old Bailey, to sit with the judge and observe British justice at work. He was acutely embarrassed when his wristwatch alarm, a prize possession, went off during the proceedings. It had been set for midday by a practical joker.

On another occasion, Officer Cadet Hussein intervened after all students were confined to barracks because one of their number had set off the college fire-alarm at night and would not admit to it. Hussein himself admitted guilt. The college commander asked him how he could have done the deed since he had been celebrating his birthday in London at the time. Hussein agreed and said the commander's point applied to many cadets. The commander accepted Hussein's logic and let off all cadets who were in London.

The young king's car became known as the people's car because, he says, he gave many lifts in it to cadets who were weekending in London. These were happy days, full of youthful enthusiasm as well as worries and uncertainties, and they made Hussein an Anglophile. He retained close links with Sandhurst and in 1996 he gave a very fine piece of silver which is awarded as a prize for the Most Improved Overseas Student. Sandhurst has no old boys' association, like Harrow, but it has twice bestowed its own accolade on the king. He represented Queen Elizabeth at the officer cadets' passing-out parade (equivalent to graduation as an officer) in 1981 and 1993, a remarkable and unparalleled honour.

But the carefree times were ending. On May 2nd 1953, after a procession past cheering crowds to the parliament building in Amman, Hussein assumed the powers and responsibilities of king. It was a simple oath of office: "I swear by the name of God that I will preserve the constitution and be faithful to my people." He then prayed at his grandfather's tomb and went home to receive the congratulations of his mother, who told him not to let power go to his head.

In this way a long and dramatic reign began. It was to see Jordan ranged at times against Syria, Egypt, Saudi Arabia and the PLO. The legitimacy of the Hashemite dynasty was to be questioned, especially over its close links with Britain and subsequently with the United States. For many people, Jordan would seem to be a Western puppet. And for many years Hussein would follow the strategy of his grandfather and keep in close and secret touch with the adversary of the Arabs: Israel. Like his grandfather, the young king would adopt a pragmatic approach to Israel. The Jewish state was, he thought, a reality that had to be accepted and dealt with: no amount of terrorism or speechi-fying would make it go away. Indeed, help from Israel was on at least three occasions vital in preserving the Hashemite government. And Hussein, like his grandfather, would be a target for assassins.

Before beginning an account of Hussein's reign, however, it is essential to dig into its Hashemite roots in the Hejaz, a province of the Ottoman empire that comprised Mecca, Medina and Jeddah, and to describe the dramatic events which led to the rise and fall of the kingdom of the Hejaz, leading to the rise of the Hashemites in Transjordan and the West Bank.

3   SHALLOW ROOTS

The house of Hashem, King Hussein's extended family, does not come from Jordan. Its roots are in the Hejaz, which is now part of Saudi Arabia. The Hejaz includes the holy cities of Mecca and Medina, where the Prophet Muhammad lived, wrote and taught, and the city of Jeddah.

At the turn of the 20th century the Hejaz was a *vilayet* (province) of the Ottoman empire. It was ruled in part by the sultan and his representative, the governor (*vali*). Usually, the vali deferred to a local leader, the amir, who was appointed by the Ottoman rulers in Constantinople (subsequently renamed Istanbul). By tradition the amirs were widely respected because they claimed to be direct descendants of the Prophet Muhammad. This qualified them and their descendants for the title of sharif.

The sharifs' fitness for office was judged on how they handled the annual pilgrimage (*haj*), during the last month of the Muslim lunar calendar, on its final stage through tribal lands to Mecca. It was a profitable business for the amir: licences, duty and other taxes helped to cover his running costs each year.

King Hussein's great-grandfather and founder of the Hashemites as a ruling dynasty, Hussein ibn Ali, was born in Constantinople in 1853. His cousin Abdiye bore him three sons, Ali, Abdullah and Feisal. At that time, two families were the centuries-long rivals for the post of amir: the Awn family and the Zaid family. Awn al-Rafiq was amir from 1882 to 1905. He became embroiled in a quarrel with his nephew, Hussein, who was summoned by the sultan to Constantinople with his sons, Ali, Abdullah and Feisal, in 1893 to keep them out of trouble. The family lived there, in a house overlooking the Bosphorus, for 16 years. These were formative years for Abdullah, from the ages of 11 to 27. He learnt fluent Turkish as well as Arabic but the children's tutor found him to be "mischievous".

In 1908, the sultan recognised Hussein's claim to be amir of the Hejaz. Ali Haydar, the Zaid family's contender, claimed to have a more direct descent from the Prophet Muhammad than the Awns. He was told by the Ottoman prime minister: "In politics, such matters are of no significance."[1] Hussein was the older man and therefore the senior claimant, and that was that. It is likely that Hussein gave the prime minister private assurances of his loyalty and reliability.

What sort of family was it? T.E. Lawrence (Lawrence of Arabia), writing much later, described Sharif Hussein (then about 60 years old) as clean and gentle-mannered and seemingly weak. "But this appearance hid a crafty policy, deep ambition and an un-Arabian foresight," he added. "His Circassian mother had endowed him with qualities foreign to both Arab and Turk."[2] (Circassians are a non-Arab Muslim people who lived in the Caucasus region of western Asia until Russian expansion in the 19th century forced them to emigrate. Many arrived and settled in what is now Jordan, starting in 1878. Since then Circassians have made a contribution to Jordanian society out of proportion to the size of their community.)

Sharif Hussein and his boys had had a training at the court in Constantinople in deviousness that stood the sharif in good stead until he was overcome by ambition. When the boys returned to the Hejaz with their father, "as young *effendis* in European clothes and with Turkish manners, the father ordered them into Arab dress; and to rub up their Arabic, gave them Meccan companions and sent them out in the wilds with the Camel Corps", Lawrence wrote. "Soon they hardened and became self-reliant."

Abdullah, the sharif's second son, recalled later that on his arrival back in the Hejaz from Constantinople, he felt he had come home "in honour and dignity". His father was treated with respect and even reverence by his rough-and-ready new subjects.[3] After all, was not Hussein a member of the noble house of Beni Hashem, of the Prophet's own tribe, the Quraish? Sharif Hussein claimed descent in the male line from the Prophet's daughter, Fatima. As such, he took precedence over the Turkish governor, the *vali*.

In 1910, Abdullah was back in Istanbul, having been "elected" to one of the two Hejaz seats in the new Ottoman constitutional parliament. Until 1914, the "member for Mecca" spent winter and spring in Istanbul, in parliament (but not notably excelling at anything) and the rest of the year in the Hejaz.[4]

In this way Abdullah acquired an intimate understanding of the relations between an imperial power and a poor colony. He acquired a mind-set that was far from being nationalist. He dealt pragmatically with the existing international power structure and would quickly adapt to any changes in it. With such a background, it is not surprising that his guiding light would not be ideology or nationalism but an avid defence of the interests of his family, coupled with the strong conviction that by advancing his own personal ambitions he would be promoting the interests of the Hashemites and also his people.

Soon after returning home, Sharif Hussein made a fatal mistake. He appeared to think his territory was too small and began to look southeast to Najd, a desert inhabited by poor Arabs with little culture, led by Abdulaziz Ibn Saud. Its capital, Riyadh, was a mud-walled village. But its tribesmen, the Ikhwan (brethen), who belonged to the intensely puritanical Wahabi sect of Islam, were religious fanatics who killed ruthlessly and efficiently for their beliefs.

In 1910 the British consul in Jeddah reported that Sharif Hussein had demanded an annual payment from Ibn Saud and had encouraged the Najd ruler's subject tribes to switch allegiance to him and his Turkish masters.

Sharif Hussein sent a military expedition into Ibn Saud's territory and captured, by accident, Ibn Saud's favourite brother, Saad. In return for Saad's release, Ibn Saud had to proclaim his sincere attachment to the Turkish state and make a regular undisclosed payment to the sharif. Ibn Saud thereafter planned his revenge. He was patient but determined.

Sharif Hussein opposed Turkey's entry into the first world war on the side of Germany. He knew that Turkey's distant *vilayets*, such as the Hejaz, would be vulnerable to British attack. So after war was declared between Britain and Turkey in 1914, the sharif, at the instigation of his son Abdullah, approached the British about changing sides.

His case officer was first Lord Kitchener and subsequently Sir Henry McMahon. Sharif Hussein, working with Abdullah, wanted a deal with Britain that would make him master of an independent Hejaz – and possibly much more. The "McMahon letters", as they were later known, were studiously vague but encouraging. More to the point, the British Foreign Office approved payments of £50,000 to Hussein and £10,000 for Abdullah – but "only in return for definite action and if a suitable rising takes place". At the same time the Ottomans were sending him some 50,000 gold pounds a year – not bad for a penniless desert outpost.

The "Great Arab Revolt" started in June 1916. Hussein's sons Ali and Feisal cut the new Hejaz railway from Damascus to near Medina and the next day the Turks were attacked throughout the Hejaz. A force loyal to Sharif Hussein ousted the Turks from Mecca and he moved in.

As the revolt proceeded, Sharif Hussein made his second fatal mistake. In 1916, before an assembly of approving notables, and with the enthusiastic support of Abdullah, the sharif proclaimed himself to be "king of the Arabs".[5] This rash action appeared to Ibn Saud of Najd as another threat to his barren desert. The reality was that the sharif had become the king of the Hejaz (and not of Arabia), and the Hejaz had been transferred from Turkey's sphere of influence to Britain's.

The members of King Hussein's cabinet were an odd lot: the foreign minister of the Hejaz was a professor from the Anglo-Egyptian Sudan; the defence minister was an Egyptian army captain; the postage stamps were printed by a British agency in Egypt; navigation in the Red Sea was controlled by the British; and the head of the British mission to the Hejaz took over the role of the Ottoman *vali*.[6]

Lawrence thought the new king was "pitifully unfit for the rough-and-tumble of forming a new administration out of the old Turkish system". Of his sons, thought Lawrence, Feisal and Zeid were trustworthy, Abdullah was "an intriguer" and Ali "a religious fanatic".[7]

The British took a dim view of the new king while supporting the efforts of his sons to dislodge the Turks. The British and French, in the top secret Sykes-Picot agreement of 1916 (named after Sir Mark Sykes of Britain and Georges Picot of France), set aside the vague promises to the sharif of an independent Arabia. Instead, they divided up the post-war Near East into zones of influence: France would get what is now Syria and Lebanon while Britain would get Iraq and Transjordan. Palestine would be administered internationally.

This was followed by a very public declaration by Sir Arthur Balfour, the foreign secretary, in November 1917. Balfour said: "His Majesty's government view with favour the establishment in Palestine of a national home for the Jewish people and will use their best endeavours to facilitate the achievement of this object, it being clearly understood that nothing shall be done which may prejudice the civil and religious rights of existing non-Jewish communities in Palestine." At the time the population of Palestine was put at 600,000 Arabs and 80,000 Jews.

The Sykes-Picot agreement and the Balfour declaration amounted to a stab in the back for the sharif. The British and French were not about to hand over land and power to a weak and untested Arab ally. They were, however, prepared to go through the motions. Eventually the British would show their gratitude to the Hashemites while keeping ultimate control of their area of influence.

By the end of the first world war in 1918, Turkish rule had collapsed: Medina and Aqaba had fallen; the army, led by the sharif's second son, Prince Feisal, and T.E. Lawrence entered Damascus.

Prince Abdullah led a leisurely siege of Taif and recorded, possibly with some embellishments, his encounter with the *vali*, who was a Turkish general. "He seemed pleased to see me, and after several moments he said: 'This is a great catastrophe – we were brothers and now we are enemies.' I felt bolder in his presence now that our positions were reversed but said, as gently as I could: 'The master has become master again, and is freed from slavery and the yoke of him whom he enlightened.' His face became as white as a sheet, but he recovered himself and said: 'I knew that the Arab nation would separate from us one day, but I never thought it would happen so quickly.'"[8]

While the Hashemites felt triumphant, and awaited their reward from the British and French, Sharif Hussein's nemesis was becoming restive. Ibn Saud felt neglected by the British, who had picked the cosmopolitan Sharif Hussein as their favourite. Ibn Saud was paid a smaller retainer than the sharif. He felt isolated in the remote and unwelcoming Najd. A struggle for power seemed inevitable.

Ibn Saud had an advantage over Hussein: the allegiance of the fanatic Ikhwan. "I have seen them hurl themselves on their enemies," wrote one Arab eye-witness of their exploits, "utterly fearless of death, not caring how many fall, advancing rank after rank with only one desire – the defeat and annihilation of the enemy. They normally give no quarter, sparing neither boys nor old men, veritable messengers of death from whose grasp no one escapes."9

After some minor clashes between the Ikhwan and Sharif Hussein's men, both sides prepared for a pitched battle at Turaba, only 60 miles from Mecca. It did not take place. Instead, on the night of May 25th 1919, the Ikhwan, armed with swords, spears and ancient rifles, overran the sharif's forces, which were led by Prince Abdullah. The prince fled in his nightshirt, according to the British agent and famous Arabist Harry St John Philby.10 Most of his men were killed. The British, worried, told Ibn Saud not to take advantage of his position. He decided to wait. But the non-battle of Turaba was the beginning of the end for Sharif Hussein and the responsibility lay with Abdullah.

In 1920 Prince Feisal attended the Paris peace conference as his father's envoy. There he made contact with the Zionists and discussed the possibility of an alliance against the Europeans. This was fanciful and unrealistic. Feisal also sent an extraordinary letter to a leading American Zionist, Felix Frankfurter, who later became a justice of the American supreme court. He wrote: "We feel the Arabs and Jews are cousins in race, having suffered similar oppressions at the hands of powers stronger than themselves, and by a happy coincidence have been able to take the first step toward the attainment of their national goals together. We Arabs, especially the educated among us, look with the deepest sympathy on the Zionist movement.... We will wish the Jews a most hearty welcome home."11

Subsequently, Prince Feisal reached an understanding with the moderate Zionist leader, Chaim Weizmann, in January 1919 for an accommodation between Arabs and Jews. The idea was for the two peoples to live together without British interference with the Jews living in a sort of province. Nothing came of it. Had they known of its existence, many Palestinians would have treated the idea as treason.

Prince Feisal was offered, and accepted, the kingdom of Syria. Five months later, French forces ousted him and established a republican state there. This unexpected development was followed by rumours that Feisal would be made king of Iraq instead. What did this leave an envious Abdullah? Not much. But the power-hungry prince fixed on the land between the Hejaz, Iraq and Palestine east of the Jordan river. This inhospitable desert had been neglected by the Ottomans and the British and had become noted for brigandage. A few hardy British officers kept watch over it.

With his father's blessing, Abdullah set off from Medina in 1920 with a small band of retainers and tribesmen. After a stop in Ma'an he arrived in Amman in 1921 with the declared intention of invading Syria, putting his brother back on the throne and staking his own claim to the kingdom of Iraq. It was not clear how he would form an army for such an improbable adventure.

This may have been a negotiating position. Abdullah was, after all, no fool and he was well aware of his vulnerability. Moreover, as a historian of the region has written, the British may have denied it but there is "some evidence that Abdullah's arrival may have been pre-arranged with Great Britain".[12]

Abdullah's move coincided with a conference in Cairo chaired by Winston Churchill, then colonial secretary. Churchill had a "sharifian" policy of creating small kingdoms and putting pro-British members of the old sharif's family on the thrones. Churchill had abandoned Syria to French influence and planned to put the unhappy Feisal on the throne of Iraq instead. It was important, therefore, to have a friendly government controlling the land between Iraq and Palestine. Someone would have to rule it. Why not Abdullah?

The solution was simple: let Abdullah stay, provided that he made three concessions: he would have to give up his claim to Iraq; recognize the British "mandate" over Transjordan as part of its mandate over Palestine (granted at the San Remo conference of 1920); and promise not to cause any trouble for the French in Syria. At a half-hour meeting in Jerusalem, Churchill, supported by Lawrence, offered the amirate of Transjordan to Abdullah with the three vital conditions.

Never one to miss a trick, Abdullah made a counter-offer: make me king of Palestine as well as Transjordan. Remembering the Balfour declaration, Churchill declined: its terms would crucially not apply east of the Jordan. But he offered Abdullah the princely sum of £5,000 a month to train and run a police force. Relieved to have the chance of ending a risky political and military adventure, Abdullah agreed to the British terms. By the stroke of a pen on a Sunday afternoon in 1921, as Churchill was later quoted as saying, he had created the amirate of Transjordan.[13]

On September 16th 1922 a League of Nations mandate over Palestine was granted to Britain. It said the "national home" of the Jewish people was to be established in Palestine and the mandatory power was obliged to protect the rights of all the inhabitants. But the Balfour declaration would not apply east of the Jordan river.

In the following year Transjordan was reorganized as an autonomous state with a grant of £150,000 a year from Britain, and would have British "advisers" including Harry St John Philby. At the same time, Feisal was awarded the throne of Iraq.

(Much later, after Abdullah was assassinated, Churchill delivered a revealing eulogy in the House of Commons. "I was myself responsible for...his appointment or creation as amir of Transjordan in 1922," he said. Abdullah had left Mecca to dislodge the French from Syria but "we persuaded him not to take this disruptive step.... He ran every risk to keep good faith with those with whom he worked.... The Arabs have lost a great champion, the Jews have lost a friend and one who might have reconciled difficulties...and we have lost a faithful comrade and ally.")

Meanwhile in the Hejaz events were moving towards a climax. Following the Turkish revolution led by Kemal Ataturk, the caliphate was abolished in 1924. The ousted sultan, ruler of the Ottoman empire, had also held the title of caliph as one of the most senior spiritual leaders of Islam. Now the job was up for grabs. Sharif Hussein, demoted by the British from the title of "king of the Arabs" to the more modest one of "king of the Hejaz", wasted no time.

Hussein, reminding his listeners that he was a descendant of the Prophet Muhammad and also held the high honour of being Guardian of the Two Holy Places (Mecca and Medina), "accepted" the title of caliph during a visit to his son Abdullah in Transjordan. His son Feisal, king of Iraq, hurried to Amman to congratulate the new caliph. Other Arab leaders stayed away. Ibn Saud glowered.[14]

The sharif compounded his error by becoming unpopular at home. By 1920, according to the British agent in Jeddah, C.E. Vickery, the sharif was a man "hated and dreaded by his own subjects, with whom it is literally impossible to work or even to regard as a sane man.... There is no cesspool in the world as foul as the cities of the Hejaz. Sharif Hussein has vetoed every scheme for improvement, has barred all progress."[15]

Ranged against him was Ibn Saud, with his Ikhwan. "He is a man of splendid physique, standing well over six feet, and carrying himself with the air of one accustomed to command," wrote Gertrude Bell, a well-known traveller in remote parts of Arabia. "Though he is more massively built than the typical nomad sheikh, he has the characteristics of the well-bred Arab, the strongly marked aquiline profile, full-fleshed nostrils, prominent lips and a long, narrow chin, accentuated by a pointed beard. Among men bred in the camel saddle, he is said to have few rivals as a tireless rider. As leader of irregular forces, he is proved daring."[16] But under British orders, Ibn Saud kept his hands off the Hejaz.

T.E. Lawrence went there to put the finishing touch to Churchill's sharifian policy: an agreement between Britain and the sharif himself. In return for British protection and a handsome subsidy, Sharif Hussein would accept the system of international mandates and the Balfour declaration. In other words, there would be no independence, and Jewish immigration would continue. The old man refused. Britain's protection and subsidy were removed.

War with Ibn Saud, such as it was, began in 1924. At Taif, Prince Ali and his soldiers, terrified of the Ikhwan, fled before their advance on the town. Those who stayed, some 300, were slaughtered and houses in the town were looted. With Mecca the next target, the old sharif was obliged to abdicate in favour of Prince Ali. He left for exile in Cyprus and later Amman, and died in 1931.

Ibn Saud was persuaded not to give the Ikhwan a free hand in Mecca and the damage when the city fell was relatively light. By 1925, with the towns still loyal to Ali under siege, Ali was persuaded to follow his father into exile. Ibn Saud appointed himself as king of the Hejaz. The destiny of the Hashemites was henceforth to evolve away from home.

4   ARABS AND JEWS

Just as the withdrawal of British support had been fatal to the old sharif, the provision of it became crucial to the survival of Amir Abdullah of Transjordan. On taking his new post, Abdullah had, with British encouragement, incorporated the provinces of Ma'an and Aqaba into Transjordan although they had belonged to the kingdom of the Hejaz. This went down badly with Ibn Saud. So the Ikhwan marched into Transjordan and headed for Amman, Abdullah's capital, in 1924. They were turned back only by the extraordinary intervention of a squadron of the British air force and a detachment of armoured cars.

Thus the amirate started its existence with little independence, under the protection of an alien and seemingly all-powerful country. This perception of Transjordan's position was to last for many years. It made Abdullah's dream of a united Arab kingdom of Syria, Lebanon, Iraq, Transjordan and Palestine (with himself, unsurprisingly, as king of the whole) look unrealistic. Nonetheless, Abdullah believed in it to his dying day.

Transjordan was outwardly unpromising: it amounted to a cultivable strip on the east bank of the river Jordan, a few poor under-developed towns, negligible natural resources, apart from phosphates and potash, and a lot of desert. Its government survived on a British subsidy.

In 1928, Abdullah signed a treaty with Britain under which he recognized the British mandate and British control over foreign and financial policy. In return Britain promised to give Transjordan military help if it was attacked. The treaty also recognized Transjordan's "independence".

It quickly proved to be useful. The Ikhwan launched another attack on Abdullah's southern desert and were turned back by the British air force and the British-trained Arab Legion.

Was Abdullah a puppet? Yes and no. He was a realist. His gift was that he knew the limits of his own power and influence as well as that of the leaders of foreign powers with whom he dealt. It was essential to be a friend of Britain – and dangerous to be an enemy. Within such limits, Abdullah operated with skill. Although he dreamed particularly of one day becoming ruler of Syria, he did nothing about it except promote his cause with discretion (because the British disapproved). But Abdullah used his considerable skill and his alliance with the British to gain control of the West Bank of the Jordan and East Jerusalem (which the British approved).

He was short, plump and physically unimpressive. He lacked the courtly, graceful manner of his brother, Feisal. But he was clever. He took risks yet was cautious; he had a certain dignity yet was flamboyant; he was a skilful raconteur and could easily win over suspicious guests (such as the Israelis) with the genuine warmth of his manner; yet he could with perfect peace of mind deceive people whom he regarded as stupid or unrealistic – or both.

He was no administrator. "Abdullah is a fraud," said one British general. "He spends his money on himself and his friends. He cannot rule for lack of force, ability and energy. We are wasting our money on him and the country is going to wrack and anarchy."[1]

This opinion began to spread among the British. T.E. Lawrence thought he might have to escort Abdullah out of the amirate and into exile. In 1924 Abdullah submitted to an ultimatum from London: the British would henceforth have an idea of where their money was being spent. Thereafter, the grumbles became infrequent.

No events of great note are recorded in the annals of Transjordan for the late 1920s and 1930s. The amirate was quiet under Abdullah with the British, led by the ambiguously named "minister", Alec Kirkbride, making sure that Abdullah made no "mistakes". Still very much the outsider from the Hejaz, the amir concentrated on consolidating his position in Amman.

He did this with success. "From 1932 to 1948, the whole of Jordan was indeed one of the happiest little countries in the world," wrote the man who subsequently became British commander of the Arab Legion and known as Glubb Pasha. This was the heyday of British colonialism, when Glubb could write that nine years commanding the Jordan frontier force between 1930 and 1939 were among the happiest in his life, spent dealing with the Bedouins. "I deeply loved these poor, simple people, and became so intimate with them that among them I felt as if I were at home."[2]

Amir Abdullah, for all his administrative faults and improvidence, was also close to the people, appearing at regular public audiences and endeavouring to solve individual problems, a traditional approach that his grandson would follow when he became King Hussein. It was certainly not Western democracy. Rather it was a form of open authoritarianism, which seemed to suit Transjordan well. Later, King Hussein would adopt his grandfather's approach and acquire Glubb's love of the Bedouin.

The amir could not resist promoting his dream of a Greater Syria stretching from Damascus and Beirut through Palestine to the Hejaz with young Arab nationalists who visited him in Amman. There was no meeting of minds: Abdullah wanted to be the autocratic and conservative monarch of this realm and the young nationalists dreamed of power for themselves – and a republic.

No neighbour welcomed the idea of a Greater Syria. The British favoured a divide-and-rule policy and did not want an all-powerful figure; Ibn Saud wanted nothing to do with the Hashemites; King Feisal in Iraq opposed the expansion of a neighbouring power centre; and the Damascenes and Palestinians looked down their noses at the upstart desert autocrat.

While the inter-war years were fairly quiet in Transjordan, this was not the case across the Jordan river, where the British mandate and the Balfour declaration applied. Jewish immigration proceeded steadily, causing ever greater concern to Palestinians who thought they had a better claim to the land. True, the Jews did rule this area for a brief period in ancient history under King David, said the Palestinians. But we are direct descendants of the Canaanites, who also appear in the Old Testament, they argued, and we have lived here in large numbers ever since.

(The Jews had their eyes not only on the land between the Mediterranean and the Jordan river but also the land to the east of the river. "Trans-Jordan has from earliest time been an integral and vital part of Palestine," said the Zionist leader, Chaim Weizmann. "There the tribes of Reuben, Gad and Manasseh first pitched their tents and pastured their flocks.")

In the Palestine mandate area, three towns were dominant: Jerusalem, the seat of government and headquarters of the Arab Higher Committee, headed by Haj Amin Husseini, and the Supreme Muslim Council; well-to-do Nablus; and the much poorer Hebron. Jerusalem's population under the mandate became roughly 40 per cent Palestinian Arab, 40 per cent Jewish and 20 per cent Palestinian Christian.

In the early years of the mandate, Palestinian leaders tried to persuade the British that they had made a mistake with the Balfour declaration and urged them to withdraw it. This approach, through committees and petitions, failed.

Next, in the late 1920s and 1930s, came trouble. Muslims and Jews clashed over shared or rival claims to religious sites, particularly the western wall of the Temple Mount in Jerusalem and the tombs of Abraham and Sarah in Hebron. Then came guerrilla operations. A religious figure, Izzedine al-Qassam, attracted many poor Palestinians from the coastal slums to his side. He led raids from the hills around Nablus until he was killed by the British in 1935. (Sixty years later, the "Brigades of Izzedine al-Qassam" were trying to honour his name by bombing the Middle East peace process out of existence.)

As usual, however, the Palestinians could not present a common front. Haj Amin Husseini was appointed grand mufti of Jerusalem with the support of the British, who were in search of a "valid Arab spokesman". Haj Amin became an intransigent Palestinian nationalist who tried to acquire more power.[3]

A rivalry developed between two leading Jerusalem families: the Husseinis and the Nashashibis. The Husseinis were more likely to be pan-Arab nationalists; the Nashashibis were pro-British. The Arab Executive, supposedly a representative Palestinian body, squabbled. Meanwhile, the Jews bought up good coastal land and replaced Palestinian farm labourers with Jews. The lines were drawn: Arab nationalists wanted Palestine to be independent of the British and to halt both Jewish immigration and sales of land to Jews; the Jews were determined to press on, successfully holding the British to their commitment in the Balfour declaration.

The inevitable result was the rebellion of 1936–39 which began with a Palestinian general strike. The British refused to accede to Arab demands. The Jews stopped using Arab labour and services. So Palestinian guerrillas derailed trains, blocked or mined ports, brought down power lines and put an oil pipeline out of business.[4] The British cracked down harshly and the strike faded in the cities. It continued in the countryside, but by the time of the outbreak of the second world war in 1939 it was all over. Many leading figures were in jail or, like Haj Amin Husseini, in exile. The Nashashibis stayed out of trouble.

East of the Jordan, Amir Abdullah observed the muddle and the failure. It would have been surprising if this ambitious and restless man did not try to profit from it. Husseini's supporters claimed that indeed there was a secret plan under which Palestine under the mandate would be partitioned between Arabs and Jews, and the amir would be brought in as ruler of the Arab bit.[5]

Abdullah seems to have concluded that the entity of Greater Syria would have to be achieved by stages, of which the first would be to take over Palestine. To do this, he would need the acquiescence of the British, the Jews and the Palestinians. They would all have to be convinced.

Abdullah knew it was in his interests to keep on the right side of the British, and his loyalty was rewarded. The British saw the need to guarantee order and stability in the area without the cost of a standing British army. So they decided to set up a local force under their control. It would be better, they thought, to base it in loyal, dependent Transjordan than in volatile mandated Palestine. The Arab Legion, commanded first by Colonel Frederick Peake and subsequently by Glubb Pasha, was created in Transjordan. In 1948 it was to be deployed in Palestine in the interests of both the British and Abdullah. (Some of its British officers won the undying loyalty of their men; others behaved with crude colonialist arrogance.)

Among the Palestinians, Abdullah deployed his charm, his title and his availability. The Nashashibis wanted him to take over Palestine, but the Husseinis were opposed. To show goodwill and woo the leading families, Abdullah employed well-educated Palestinians as his advisers. But the time was not ripe: mandated Palestine remained under British control.

As for the Jews, Abdullah's grasp of power politics, finely honed during his years in Constantinople, told him they were there to stay and more would come: the British would keep their promise in the Balfour declaration. Unlike the Husseinis, who regarded the Jews as hated intruders to be opposed by all possible means, Abdullah realised he had to do a deal with them – if possible to his own advantage.

The amir thought that "the Zionist threat and avalanche could have been blunted but not entirely thwarted", his grandson, King Hussein, wrote much later. "Morality and power politics do not always match. The tragic undoing and dismantling of the Palestinian people, to which their leadership unwittingly contributed, was that they adamantly refused to understand or accept this unpleasant but elementary fact of life." Amir Abdullah, on the other hand, "perceived the Zionist iceberg and its dimensions while others had seen only its tip. His tactics and strategy were therefore attuned to circumventing and minimising the possible consequences of a head-on collision. Others saw only the tip, and their responses were over-confidence, inflexibility and outright complacency."

What sort of deal could be acceptable to the Jews and be to his advantage? Abdullah envisioned a Hashemite-Zionist alliance. Palestine would be turned into a condominium of Palestinians and Jews, without the dubious benefits of British supervision. The genial, trustworthy Abdullah would be its benevolent monarch. It would be a stage on the road to a Greater Syria.

It was, of course, a non-starter: the Zionists had set their hearts on establishing an independent Jewish state and, not surprisingly, nothing else would do. Abdullah, who had grown up under the multi-racial Ottoman empire and been educated in cosmopolitan Constantinople, may well not have been an anti-Semite. But the Jews asked themselves:

how stable was his government? They had no idea. (An answer came in 1951 when Abdullah was assassinated and eventually succeeded by his realistic grandson: it was stable.)

Links with the Zionists were established early: in the 1920s and 1930s sporadic contacts with Jewish representatives took place. Colonel Frederick Kisch, chairman of the Palestine Zionist Executive, talked to the amir and his father, King Hussein of the Hejaz, who was in Amman on a visit in 1924. However, Kisch's proposal for a joint Arab-Jewish committee fell on stony ground. In 1926 Abdullah was calling for Jewish settlements and investments in Transjordan. "We are poor and you are rich," he said. "Please come to Transjordan. I guarantee your safety." Kisch returned in 1931 and arranged for a Jewish doctor to operate on a cataract in one of the king's eyes. In 1931, Abdullah, having failed to find an Arab farmer for state land that had passed into his domain, did a secret deal with a Jewish firm. After it was revealed, the amir had to abrogate it. This information did much to discredit Abdullah in the Arab world. Later, Abdullah was said to have taken money from the Jewish Agency.[6]

It was during this period that Abdullah committed another indiscretion – and got away with it. He took as his third wife Nahida, a black slave-girl who had been brought to him from Mecca as a playmate for his daughter, Maqbula. But Nahida tickled the fancy of the amir, who bedded her, freed her and eventually married her and built a palace for her. In Amman, Nahida's success (she subsequently went into real estate on her own account) was ascribed by some to witchcraft.

In 1934 Abdullah tried again to launch his proposed condominium of Arabs and Jews under the Hashemite monarchy. He put it to the two Palestinian family factions, the Husseinis and the Nashashibis, as well as to the Jewish Agency. Only the Nashashibis approved. That stubborn nationalist, Haj Amin Husseini, insisted on an end to the British mandate, the abrogation of the Balfour declaration and full independence for the Arabs. He hated Abdullah.

Aware of Abdullah's financial dependence on Britain and his pleasure in spending money, Jewish representatives in 1936 offered him financial assistance in return for allowing Jewish settlements in Transjordan.

Abdullah demurred. But by one Jewish account, Abdullah received Jewish money anyway.[7]

In the following year, a commission under Earl Peel, which had been asked to report on the Arab revolt and make recommendations, published its findings. It favoured partition with the Palestinians keeping about 80 per cent of the territory, the Jews gaining 15 per cent, and a sliver of land between Jerusalem and Jaffa, on the coast, remaining mandated. The Arab part, Earl Peel suggested, should merge with Transjordan under Amir Abdullah and receive subsidies from the Jews and the British.

Abdullah, over the moon, promptly accepted the Peel Commission's report. Arab nationalists, suspicious of the Jews and of the amir and blithely unaware of their own weakness, rejected it. The Zionists hesitated. We can only speculate over what might have happened to the history of the Jews if they had immediately thrown their full international weight behind the report.

The next year it was too late: the British government itself rejected partition and proposed a federation, leading to independence in five years, with limits on Jewish immigration and property ownership. Incredibly, Haj Amin Husseini turned down this strongly pro-Palestinian proposal on the ground that five years was too long. In 1938 he went into exile and spent the second world war in Germany.

The region was affected little by the war although the population did quite well economically. Palestinian products sold at high prices and Palestinians were employed in increasing numbers at British military installations. Abdullah remained loyal to Britain and so did the Jews. Abdullah kept up his contacts. He talked to the Zionist leader Moshe Sharett in 1942 about his recurrent dream of fitting a partly Jewish Palestine into a four-state federation with Transjordan, Syria and Lebanon, with him as king.

After the war the British rewarded the amir for his loyalty. He was crowned king of Transjordan in 1946 and his country was declared to be fully independent although it remained heavily dependent on British money and skills; the terms of the independence agreement gave the British virtually a free run across Transjordan.[8]

In the post-war years, Abdullah's contacts with the Jews grew. His first interlocutor, in 1946, was Elias Sasson, head of the Arab section of the political department of the Jewish Agency, who was fluent in Arabic and supplied Abdullah with money, according to Jewish sources.

The following year saw tension rise: the Zionists insisted on partition and an unimpeded flow of settlers while the Arab League backed the Husseinis and the Arab Higher Committee in Jerusalem in demanding immediate independence for an Arab-led state. Jewish guerrillas began operations against the British.

Abdullah sent secret messages to the British foreign secretary, Ernest Bevin, expressing his willingness to take under his wing the Arab part of a partitioned Palestine if Britain abandoned the mandate, as it said it would. But the king pointed out that he could not say so in public and indeed sometimes had to say the opposite, for fear of appearing ambitious and land-hungry.

Bevin, the canny former trade-union leader, understood immediately. "It seems the obvious thing to do," Bevin told the visiting Transjordanian prime minister, Tawfiq Abul Huda.[9] "But do not go and invade the land allocated to the Jews." Instead of being part of the problem, Abdullah, Britain's trusted retainer and ally, became part of the solution, as he had been for Winston Churchill. He was backed by Sir Alec Kirkbride.

This distinguished colonial officer had gained the respect and trust of the Transjordanian notables and, on occasion, had managed to prevent Abdullah from going off the rails. He viewed the king's peccadillos with equanimity provided that they did not damage British interests. Other Britons serving in the area were less tolerant. One said he was regarded with contempt as a British puppet by other Arab leaders and invariably cheated at chess. Another said Arab leaders mentioned his name with a pitying smile or a shrug of the shoulders.

Abdullah's next job was to work out a deal with the Zionists to carve up Palestine. This was difficult. With the mufti, the Arab Higher Committee and neighbouring governments deeply suspicious of his motives, Abdullah had to play his cards close to his chest. He could never appear to be in league with the Jews. On the contrary, he had to appear to be shoulder-to-shoulder with his Arab brothers against the Zionist menace.

In August 1947 the UN's special committee (UNSCOP) recommended partition. Abdullah, a wiser man than he was at the time of the Peel Commission's report recommending partition, kept quiet in public but persistently advocated partition in private. The proposal was approved.

The crunch was coming. Britain was giving up the mandate, convinced that partition would not work peacefully. Neighbouring Arab governments were arming themselves with the help of the British and might intervene. The Arab League had been formed and might co-ordinate military operations against the Jews to prevent partition. The UN's special committee on Palestine had added its voice to those favouring partition but made no suggestion about who would govern the Arab bit. Abdullah had to move.

On November 17th 1947, the king met Golda Myerson (who later changed her name to the Hebrew Golda Meir), the acting head of the political department of the Jewish Agency.[10] Again he proposed an "independent Hebrew republic in part of Palestine within a Transjordan state that would include both banks of the Jordan, with me at its head". That idea got nowhere with Mrs Myerson. She wanted two states, one Jewish and the other Arab. What would the Jews do, asked Abdullah, if he took the Arab part of Palestine. They would react favourably, she replied, if he did not interfere with the establishment of a Jewish state and provoke military conflict. Abdullah said he would not allow his forces to fight the Jews and would not co-operate with other forces against them. One of the Jews present wrote in an official report: "In conclusion, Abdullah asked us to raise considerably our financial aid."[11] True, in taking Jewish money, Abdullah was compromising his position. But he could argue that he was using the Jews by taking their money to advance his own interest, which was to work in tandem with them.

Writing to the man whom Foreign Office mandarins referred to as "Mr Bevin's little king", the British foreign secretary threw his support behind Abdullah's planned takeover of the Arab bit of Palestine while leaving the Jewish sector, without any trouble, to the Jews. But Bevin coupled this with a stern warning of the danger that one false step might lead to his isolation in the Arab world.

Not surprisingly, as the end of the mandate approached, Abdullah felt he had to ally himself formally with his fellow-Arabs while concealing his real intentions from them (and indeed from his own prime minister). The suspicious Golda Meir worried about rumours that Abdullah planned to double-cross the Jews by joining an Arab invasion of Palestine. Abdullah responded that he was a Bedouin and therefore a man of honour; he was a king and therefore doubly a man of honour; and finally he would never break a promise made to a woman. Mrs Meir and her leader, David Ben-Gurion, were unimpressed.

After fighting had broken out between Jewish forces and Palestinian irregulars, the Jews gained the upper hand. With great skill, Abdullah obtained the Arab League's authorization to send his Arab Legion into Palestine to help the people there. Confusion followed. The Jewish Agency tried to pin down Abdullah in writing to his pledge not to interfere at all in the Jewish areas; Abdullah replied in writing with a nationalist line that might have pleased the mufti. He talked in public of war, perhaps to conceal his plans but perhaps also because he was genuinely shocked by the terrible Jewish massacre of innocent Palestinian villagers at Deir Yassin. The Jewish leaders could not believe that Abdullah's pledge to Golda Meir as a Bedouin, a king and as a man to a woman still stood. But it did.

His promise was reinforced by the determination of General Glubb to keep to his orders from London to ensure that his Arab Legion should stay on the Arab side of the UN's final partition line. These orders suited him: the British general feared a defeat at the hands of the Jews that would wreck his precious little army with unforeseeable consequences. The British government, which wanted to keep the Legion out of war, had failed to send enough arms and ammunition to enable it to fight one. Persistent entreaties for more supplies fell on deaf ears.

5 NOT QUITE WAR

Before the British mandate expired in 1948, amateur Arab military units, some led by incompetent officers, tried to advance into the area assigned by the UN to the Jews. Had they done so vigorously, they might have got somewhere; but they hesitated. Transjordan's Arab Legion made a point of not advancing. Bevin cabled to the American secretary of state, George Marshall, the top secret information that British officers on secondment to the Arab Legion were under orders to withdraw to Transjordan if the Legion became involved in fighting Jewish forces in territory assigned to the Jews.

As Glubb Pasha put it in a message to London, "The Transjordan government never intended to involve itself in any serious military operations at all, and was fully aware from the first that partition was inevitable."[1] However, Abdullah and Glubb succeeded in repelling Jewish probes into Arab East Jerusalem. Glubb claimed that his little force, poorly armed, "saved" Jerusalem. Volunteers in the "Arab Liberation Army", a motley collection of Arab units, certainly did not. "The idea that a mob of bandits and enthusiasts could, in three or four weeks, be made into an army was ludicrous," Glubb wrote afterwards.[2]

The Jews made short shrift of their other potential adversaries from Egypt and Syria. Abdullah, who saw their fellow-Arab units as a barrier to the establishment of permanent Jordanian control of the West Bank, did little to help them. At one meeting with the Israelis, he even wished them well in expelling the Egyptians from Gaza. Meanwhile, the Arab Legion had occupied much of what later became known as the West Bank. Abdullah then made a decisive move.

In September 1948 an "all-Palestine government" was set up in Gaza under the aegis of the mufti as a clear challenge to the ambitions of Abdullah. In the following month it declared independence. Abdullah, alone among the members of the Arab League, refused to recognize it.

Abdullah convened a "Palestine Arab Congress" in Amman a few days later. It was attended by several thousand Palestinian notables. They denounced the mufti and refused to recognize the Gaza "government", claiming they were the true representatives of the Palestinian people. They asked that the Palestinian homeland be placed under Jordanian "protection".

To make the point perfectly clear, Abdullah convened a second conference of notables in the West Bank town of Jericho in December. It passed a resolution calling for the union of Transjordan and Arab Palestine under the Hashemite crown. The resolution also expressed no confidence in the Arab Higher Committee and other hardliners. At the Jericho meeting were the mayors of Hebron, Bethlehem and Ramallah as well as some military commanders and former supporters of the mufti. It was a great success for Abdullah. But it would have to be accepted by the Jews.

David Ben-Gurion had announced the creation of the state of Israel on May 14th 1948, and President Harry Truman promptly recognized it in the name of the United States after the first pro-Israeli lobby in Washington had exercised its muscle and, for the first time but not the last, angered an American president. American policy had been to create a homeland for displaced Jews from Europe. "Many Jews, however, chose to believe that our Palestine policy was the same as the Zionist programme for the state of Israel," Truman wrote afterwards. "Whenever it failed to conform, they would charge that we had turned pro-Arab...I do not think I ever had so much pressure and propaganda aimed at the White House as I had in this instance. The persistence of a few of the extreme Zionist leaders – actuated by political motives and making political threats – disturbed and annoyed me. Some were even suggesting that we pressure sovereign nations into favourable votes in the General Assembly."[3]

King Abdullah, who recognized power when he saw it at work, was tempted to strike his own deal with the new state, regardless of what his fellow-Arabs did. He was dissuaded by the British from doing so. Nonetheless, talks went on. The most active yet shadowy figure on the

Jewish side during the entire period was the Arabist Elias Sasson. A young colonel, Moshe Dayan, was present at some meetings. Reuven Shiloah, an eccentric figure in the foreign ministry who was his own man, had an important part to play.

The distinguished Israeli historian Avi Shlaim describes one unusual encounter between Abdullah, Sasson and Dayan. Dayan was baffled that, by the end of the meeting, Sasson had not raised the burning issue of the moment in 1948: Israel's desire for the release of 700 prisoners-of-war. "Sasson, accompanied by the king, walked toward the door and when they had reached the door the king embraced him," Shlaim writes. "At this point Sasson slid his hand under the king's silk sash. Abdullah gasped because Bedouin tradition dictated that if a man placed his hand under the sash of a shaikh, the shaikh had to grant his wish. Sasson's victim raised both hands in a gesture of surrender and said: 'Elias, please ask what is possible.' Dayan looked on incredulously, wondering whether Sasson had taken leave of his senses.

"When Sasson pleaded for the release of the 700 prisoners-of-war, the king turned to Abdullah al-Tall (his adviser and later the supposed planner of his assassination) and asked for his opinion. Al-Tall replied that some of the prisoners were women and children and nothing but a burden for the Arab Legion. He also assured the king that the British would have no objection to the freeing of the prisoners. 'Good,' said Abdullah. 'Let them go and may they be blessed.'"

The next question was: could a permanent peace settlement between Arab and Jew be achieved? The Israelis wanted one; so did Abdullah. A ceasefire had been negotiated between al-Tall and Dayan on November 28th.[4] Fortunately for the king, negotiations on an armistice were initiated by Egypt; he would not be the first to hold official talks with the adversary. Negotiations dragged on, giving the Israelis time to advance south to the Gulf of Aqaba and take Eilat, under the command of a brilliant young colonel named Yitzhak Rabin.

Then Abdullah sat down with the Israelis: Walter Eytan, from the foreign ministry, Yigael Yadin, Dayan and Yehoshafat Harkabi. The Israelis presented him with an ultimatum: acceptance of an armistice line that had been redrawn to their advantage or face renewed fighting.

It looked unfair, and it was. Abdullah accepted the inevitable: several entirely Arab villages in the north and a large area of land became part of Israel and the number of refugees swelled. Hundreds of villagers were cut off from their lands. The Israelis gained much more than they had expected. However, the line was not in Transjordan but on the West Bank. It brought under Abdullah's wing a large part (though by no means all) of the Arab section of the most recent UN partition proposal, and it included Arab East Jerusalem.

An armistice agreement was signed on the Greek island of Rhodes on April 3rd 1949 under the aegis of the UN and its distinguished under-secretary-general, Ralph Bunche. There was a big and immediate reward for Abdullah apart from the formalization of his power over the West Bank: his representative signed the armistice agreement for the first time in the name of the new Hashemite kingdom of Jordan. The price he paid was high: after he approved the armistice, his popularity plummeted. An armistice was not a settlement, however. Abdullah's goal was to have partition accepted as permanent and his authority over the West Bank officially ratified. But the bitterness of hundreds of thousands of Palestinians, ousted from their homes, overflowed. Could any genuine Arab leader have willingly bowed his head and signed a permanent settlement accepting the humiliation of the Arabs by the Jews?

About 300,000 Palestinians had already left their homes by the time that Israel declared its independence. According to UN figures, the number of refugees had risen to 750,000 by the beginning of 1949 and 940,000 by June of that year.

Nobody could forget the massacre on April 9th 1948 at Deir Yassin, a Palestinian village 5 miles west of Jerusalem, where two Jewish extremist groups, the Irgun Zvai Leumi and the Stern Gang, led by Menachem Begin and Yitzak Shamir, killed 254 civilians, including about 100 women and children. Many bodies were mutilated and thrown into a well. The message to the Palestinians could not have been clearer. As if to make sure, however, members of the Jewish underground went through the Arab quarter of Jerusalem shouting, through loudspeakers: "The road to Jericho is still open.... Fly from Jerusalem before you are killed!"

The official Jewish leadership was also culpable. In July 1948, when Jewish units were attacking Lydda and Ramleh, two large towns outside the territory assigned to the Jews by the UN, Yigal Allon, the Jewish military commander, asked David Ben-Gurion what should be done about the two towns' population of about 70,000 Arabs. The historian Benny Morris writes that Ben-Gurion made a dismissive, energetic gesture with his hand and said: "Expel them!"[5]

This bitter experience remains engraved on the soul of the Palestinian people. The question which they had to answer was: should we fight on, using whatever means are at hand, until we drive Israel into the sea, or do we recognize reality and work out a way of living together? King Abdullah, and his grandson, King Hussein, along with many pragmatic Palestinian notables, took the latter view; so, decades later, did Yasser Arafat. The mufti chose confrontation.

It was not surprising, therefore, that the mufti's rejectionist followers hated King Abdullah as a traitor to the Palestinian cause. Had not his close adviser, Colonel Abdullah al-Tall, angered at being passed over for promotion to the rank of brigadier, moved to Cairo and in January 1950 published documents proving Abdullah's contacts with the Israelis? To the hardliners and their supporters in the streets, Abdullah symbolized betrayal.

There were UN-sponsored formal talks in Lausanne about a settlement. But Israel was lined up against an inevitably uncompromising joint delegation of Egypt, Jordan, Lebanon and Syria. All discussions were through UN mediators: none were face to face. Israel was unwilling to make concessions and certainly unwilling to take back any refugees. A talented young Israeli diplomat called Abba (previously Aubrey) Eban argued that the armistice was the only agreement on the cards.

Following the failure of the Lausanne conference, secret bilateral contacts between Israel and Abdullah resumed. Several encounters aimed at achieving a peace pact and lasting up to three days took place at the king's house at Shuneh, but to no avail. At the same time the mufti's men were on the warpath: several public figures received threats on their life if they backed a peace pact. A campaign was launched to oust Jordan from the Arab League. Next-door Syria threatened to close its border. Saudi Arabia threatened to isolate Jordan. The Arab world seemed united in opposition to a peace treaty between Israel and Abdullah.

Abdullah saw the terms of a deal. He would give up his goal of a permanent peace settlement between Israel and the Arab world and, as a *quid pro quo*, the Arabs would not oppose his annexation of the West Bank. In the first step, he voted at the Arab League for a resolution opposing any separate peace pacts with Israel. In the second step on April 11th, a general election was held for delegates representing not only Transjordan but also the West Bank. Most of those elected appeared to oppose a peace pact with Israel and to accept annexation of the West Bank. Thus on April 24th 1950 both houses of parliament approved a resolution supporting the "complete unity between the two sides of the Jordan and their union into one state, which is the Hashemite kingdom of Jordan".

Incredibly, Abdullah was not satisfied. On the next day he received Reuven Shiloah of the Israeli foreign ministry in great secrecy to tell him he was confident his people would accept peace with Israel. But sentiment in Jordan was strong against the idea, and the Israelis seemed unwilling to give up an inch of what they had gained in return for peace. Abdullah stood alone; his ministers had mostly become sceptics about the possibility of a give-and-take deal with Israel.

This did not worry men like Dayan, who seemed to assume that the Jews would always be hated and had to be unremittingly tough. But Abdullah's bold stance did worry the British. They feared that isolation would make the king vulnerable and they urged him to go slow.

Avi Shlaim, whose authoritative account of this period is based heavily on the testimony in reports of the Israeli leaders involved, is convinced that Israel's negotiators threw away an opportunity for a lasting peace. He quotes with evident approval from a cable from the ardently pro-Israeli British ambassador in Tel Aviv, Sir Knox Helm, containing a critique of Israel. "Her greatest disability," Helm wrote, "remains the most disagreeable features of the Jewish character, with an inability to realise that obtaining the last farthing does not necessarily mean the best bargain, that in an imperfect world unrelieved seriousness is not a virtue and, perhaps above all, that strength is not always displayed through force."[6]

Had Israel given Jordan guaranteed access to a Mediterranean port for its foreign trade, it might have been different, says Shlaim. It scarcely helped when, in January 1951, Moshe Sharett announced in Israel's parliament that only collective compensation would be paid to Palestinian refugees for the loss of their homes and land. And Israel did not win Palestinian friends by freezing Palestinian savings held in banks located in what had become Israeli territory. Israel's refusal to budge in a few remaining border disputes with Jordan and its apparent interference with the waters of the Jordan river were just another part of a dismal pattern. It was odd: Israel's interest, as a small power surrounded by adversaries, resided in establishing a friend on its borders, and Jordan's king was willing and able to fill the bill. Not only did Israel fail to win this friend over, it weakened him.

The king could not have been more explicit. "Why do you want peace with Israel?" asked Moshe Sasson, Elias's son. "I want peace," Abdullah replied, "not because I have become a Zionist or care for Israel's welfare, but because it is in the interest of my people. I am convinced that if we do not make peace with you, there will be another war, and another war, and another war, and we would lose. Hence it is in the supreme interest of the Arab nation to make peace with you."[7] Later, he told an American visitor: "Despite the Arab League, I could have the support of my own people and the tacit support at least of the British if I could justify a peace by pointing to concessions made by the Jews. But without any concessions from them I am beaten before I start."

This was a time to be tetchy. The inflow of refugees to Jordan coupled with Jordan's annexation of the West Bank altered the population balance. By 1951 Palestinians outnumbered Transjordanians by two to one, yet it was the Transjordanians led by their outsider king who held real power in the new country. There was a sort of parliament but the reality was that Abdullah did his level best to run an authoritarian government.

Many people, according to his grandson, were afraid of him. There were not enough jobs for the refugees. It was easy for Abdullah's enemies and their poorly educated followers to point to the "traitor" who was responsible for their plight. Some claimed that he was seeking peace at any price with the Jews. As the record shows, he was not.

His murder, on July 20th 1951, brought an era to an end. The chance of an early peace pact between Israel and Jordan dissolved. It would have to wait until 1995. But the king had established a policy of pragmatism and close contacts with the Israelis which his grandson adopted.

King Abdullah bequeathed a young and volatile kingdom that could be kept together only by a leader who was brave, astute, prudent — and ruthless when needed. Talal was robbed by schizophrenia of the opportunity to test his ability to survive in shark-filled seas. Hussein seized the opportunity. The sharks began to circle.

6 DEALING WITH POLITICIANS

On May 2nd 1953, his 18th birthday by the Muslim calendar, Hussein took the oath of office and became king in fact as well as in name. In a reaffirmation of the Hashemite dynasty's claim to be a guiding force in Arabia, Hussein's cousin, Feisal, became king of Iraq on the same day. Hussein's first appointment of importance was that of his friend Fawzi al-Mulqi as prime minister. This was the start of Hussein's long experience of dealing with politicians, many of whom he came to regard as "rapacious" and "opportunists", lustful for power.

Al-Mulqi set out to offer a new, more open style of politics with a constitutional monarchy. The new prime minister had befriended Hussein when he was the ambitious Jordanian ambassador in London and the young prince was at Harrow. His invitations to Hussein to come to London parties where he might meet girls went down well with Hussein but not with his teachers at Harrow.[1]

At the same time, Hussein gave a sign of what kind of king he would be – not like Talal or, indeed, his grandfather Abdullah. The king learnt to be a pilot. He was taught to fly by Wing Commander Jock Dalgleish, who had flown him from Jerusalem to Amman after his grandfather had been assassinated. Dalgleish was on secondment as chief of the tiny Jordanian air force, with the rank of colonel in the Arab Legion.

After he had decided to take lessons, the king recalled later, "I received almost daily deputations from political and other parties, from my family, from friends," pleading with him to desist. Dalgleish did his bit in the first lesson by looping the loop mercilessly and when it was over, the king was sick. However, asked when he wanted his next lesson, Hussein fixed an appointment for the following day.

Eventually the young king was ready to fly solo. But Dalgleish had been instructed by high court officials not to let him do so. Hussein recounted that one day he seized the opportunity when an aircraft had overshot the runway and all eyes were on it. He climbed aboard his De Havilland Dove and shouted to a worried engineer that he was picking up the co-pilot on the way to the runway. In a few moments he was airborne. The solo flight was a success.

Subsequently Hussein learned to fly jets, helicopters and his Lockheed Tristar. He took part in firing competitions, aerobatics and formation flying. It would have been surprising if some members of his family as well as high officials had not been worried. Although he was able to display his skill in the cockpit, a slight error, a technical fault or some poor maintenance could easily have been fatal.

Writing in 1962,[2] he recorded two incidents which must have been alarming. In the first, which happened while he was making a landing, the port wheel collapsed and the aircraft slid to a stop on a fuel tank – which did not explode. In the second, which also happened while preparing to land, he could not get the under-carriage down and solved the problem by using a compressed-air bottle to jolt the equipment out of its housing.

After the first of these mishaps, Hussein grumbled about the comments of a British officer, "a trifle patronising", who suggested that the aircraft touched down too far along the runway. Competitive as ever, he also reported that the same officer soon afterwards forgot to lower his under-carriage before landing.

(Later, Hussein was to terrify Henry and Nancy Kissinger by taking them on a hair-raising helicopter ride at tree-top level; when Mrs Kissinger said she did not realise that helicopters could fly so low, he finished the journey almost on the ground.[3] On other occasions, he enjoyed terrifying his passengers aboard a Hawk helicopter by making it fly so steeply that, according to one who experienced it, the royal chopper "nearly fell out of the sky".)

Flying solo gave the teenage king an enjoyable sense of peace and isolation from the hurly-burly of Jordanian politics and driving a fast car gave him a thrill. But after his aircraft was in the hangar, or his car was in its garage, he had to face the real world.

The start of a reign was a vital moment: it would reveal how power might be shared thereafter by the king, his advisers, the government and parliament. Would the king set his stamp on the government and rule much like his grandfather or would he allow himself to be dominated by his uncle, Sharif Nasser bin Jamil, much like his cousin Feisal in Iraq? Uncle Nasser was described by a European diplomat as "a bull of a man, who could kill a horse by repeated blows on its neck". How much power would he cede to his prime minister and parliament? How would he balance rivals for influence: the British, the East Bankers, the Palestinians and the Circassians?

It began to emerge that he would take orders from no one. Within reason, he did what he wanted. He enjoyed being a king. On one typical occasion, he and Dalgeish, while on a flight, decided they would dine in Nicosia – and did so. The royal entourage was appalled.

His prime minister, al-Mulqi, was a qualified vet who had never practised. He had served as a diplomat in Cairo, Paris and London and as foreign minister, and lacked a detailed grasp of Jordanian politics. He had no firm political base and therefore would not dominate Hussein (this would have pleased the queen mother, Zain). Not surprisingly, al-Mulqi picked a broad-based cabinet including many opposition figures. Press censorship was relaxed and newspapers promptly became intemperate. In the government's first six months, some political prisoners were released. Al-Mulqi acquired a reputation for being a liberal. The teenage king was still learning the ropes and did not intervene.

On his first test, al-Mulqi wobbled. Hussein had inherited a land whose population of 1.5m was made up of more Palestinians – residents or refugees – than East Bankers; many in the Palestinian majority accepted Hashemite authority reluctantly. Palestinian guerrillas wanted to attack the hated usurper, Israel, regardless of the consequences for Hussein, even after one Israeli retaliatory attack destroyed a Jordanian village. Fearing the worst, al-Mulqi asked for British troops to be stationed temporarily in the country to deter the Israelis, then changed his mind twice. When the British agreed, on October 14th, it was too late.

On the previous day, Palestinian guerrillas had set off a bomb in an Israeli village near Lydda, killing a woman and two children. Glubb said the Jordanians took "every possible measure to find the offenders".

They even allowed a team of Israeli tracker-dogs across the border to follow a scent (it faded away). They had been "straining every nerve to reduce infiltration, which in practice had become much less frequent".[4] The Arab Legion tried to stop infiltrators entering Israel and Israeli forces from retaliating successfully.

Nonetheless, the Israelis retaliated within 24 hours. Commandos led by a young officer named Ariel Sharon destroyed another Jordanian village, Qibya, killing 66 men, women and children. A large part of the village was reduced to rubble.

Al-Mulqi ordered the Arab Legion to police the frontier. When the Israeli army mobilized in response to his action, he made it clear that the Legion would shoot only in self-defence. Protests erupted in Jordan, led by leftists, against the inability of the British-officered Legion to punish Israel. There were calls for a court-martial of Glubb by people who claimed he was "in the pay of the Jews". Opposition politicians from Abul Huda down had a field day.

Glubb was convinced that at least some of the guerrillas were in the pay of Syria and Saudi Arabia which, for separate reasons, would be happy to see the young king undermined and possibly replaced. After carrying out their attack, they withdrew via Jordan, thereby "justifying" an Israeli retaliatory raid, out of all proportion, on a Jordanian village. In a similar but bizarre incident, a group of Palestinian guerrillas arrived by taxi from Damascus, crossed into Israel the same night, blew up a house, returned to Jordan and drove straight back over the border to Syria.[5]

Hussein, Glubb and al-Mulqi were trapped and outmanoeuvred. Israel invoked a clause in the General Armistice Agreement under which it could ask the UN secretary-general to convene a meeting with Jordan to discuss any changes to the agreement. The Israelis were aware that the nationalist fervour in Jordan was such that no Jordanian government would wish to be seen sitting down with representatives of the Arabs' oppressors. Jordan refused to take part – and the Israelis could claim to the world that their olive branch had been rejected.

In domestic policy, al-Mulqi remained liberal (or permissive, depending on the analyst). This meant that the press and parliament became more independent-minded. Glubb was increasingly criticized. The constitution was changed under pressure from the opposition. Parliament voted a resolution expressing gratitude to the Soviet Union for its votes in the UN Security Council in favour of the Arab cause. Al-Mulqi was under fire from royalists and leftists: the government was losing the initiative and power was slipping away. In May 1954, the 19-year-old monarch, disillusioned with Jordan's politicians, dismissed his prime minister. Nobody challenged his decision. Hussein had already begun to carve out a place for himself in Jordan's political establishment.

In al-Mulqi's place Hussein appointed the no-nonsense royalist and political manipulator *par excellence*, Tawfik Abul Huda, who as prime minister had steered Jordan skilfully through the transition crisis from King Talal to King Hussein. He had subsequently made way for al-Mulqi.

The new cabinet was 100 per cent loyalist and well balanced: every region was represented; half the ministers were from the East Bank and half from the West Bank; there were two Christians and one Circassian.

Abul Huda was a loyal monarchist and an unconvinced democrat. His task was to restore the authority of the establishment and to help the young king to consolidate his position. However, he indicated that he would carry on the main lines of al-Mulqi's policies. Sceptics hurried to form political parties before he changed his mind. Four had a chance of registration: the National Socialists (not, as the name implied, a fascist group but made up of leftish bourgeois Arab nationalists favouring closer ties with Syria and Egypt); the Nation (Umma) party, an establishment group led by a skilful former prime minister, Samir al-Rifai; the pro-Communist National Front; and the Baath party, linked to the Syrian party of the same name that promoted "Arab socialism".

By one account,[6] Abul Huda's plan was to win a parliamentary vote of confidence and register only the National Socialists and Umma. For all his skill, however, Abul Huda could not be confident of marshalling the votes that he needed. To avoid the embarrassment to the king and himself of a defeat, he asked the king to dissolve parliament and hold new elections. Hussein agreed. Before the election, and with little apparent justification, Abul Huda refused to register the National Front and the Baath party, and suspended four newspapers. The National Socialists and Umma appealed to the king to set up a broad-based government to supervise the forthcoming election. Hussein, worrying about political stability, wobbled. (Some critics said, in these early years, that the king changed his mind frequently and agreed with the last person who spoke to him.) At a tense moment, amid dire warnings of impending anarchy, Hussein took a holiday from July 11th to August 8th. It was a dangerous gamble. But he had left affairs of state in the willing hands of Abul Huda and Glubb, and the gamble paid off: order was maintained. When he returned, he decided that Abul Huda would administer the election, to be held on October 16th 1954.

In the campaign, the two loyal opposition parties could not agree on a common list of candidates and neither could the National Front and the Baath party. Abul Huda's policy of divide and rule, together with manipulation of the army vote, prevailed: the prime minister's candidates had an almost clean sweep. The Umma party and the National Socialists won two seats each; the National Front and the Baath party won only one seat each. The prime minister's followers won 28. The British ambassador reported that the vote-rigging had been carried out "very clumsily".[7] Street protests erupted.

Hussein risked being overly dependent on a prime minister who was unpopular but whom he could not abandon. He picked a logical solution: keep Abul Huda in power but at the head of a coalition. At the king's request, the prime minister managed to patch a coalition together and then made a bid to gain some street credibility: he called for the revision of the Anglo-Jordanian treaty. This apparently nationalist gesture won wide support. But when Abul Huda went to London to negotiate, it turned out that what he really wanted was to get his hands on the British government grant supporting the Arab Legion. This money went straight to Glubb Pasha. The British politely refused to change a method of payment that was "useful administratively". On returning home, Abul Huda lay low with a diplomatic illness.

7 DEALING WITH NASSER

In Egypt, a group of young officers had in 1952 overthrown the corrupt King Farouk and replaced him with General Muhammad Neguib as head of government. Two years later, Neguib was replaced by Colonel Gamal Abdel Nasser, a flamboyant nationalist who took the Arab world by storm. In 1954 he signed a heads of agreement ending 72 years of British dominance of Egypt. Nasser wanted to be the leader of the region. Looking back in 1962, Hussein said: "He was the first Arab statesman to throw off the shackles of the West. I must admit I sympathised with that view to a great extent."[1] Nonetheless, Hussein's throne was in peril.

The Arabs, demoralized by the disaster of 1948, dreamed of a leader who rebelled against Western dominance. Nasser did not hesitate to stick his finger in the eye of the "imperialists", and the crowds loved it.

The trouble started in 1955. In February, reacting against Nasser's brand of radical nationalism, Turkey and Iraq (under the Hashemite King Feisal and the wily Nuri es-Said) formed the Baghdad Pact, which was a mutual-defence treaty creating a northern tier of countries opposed to Nasser's ideas. Britain, the prime mover, joined later in 1995.

Jordan hesitated. The Arab nationalist media thought that Iraq's membership of what was obviously a British-engineered device only proved that King Feisal was still a British puppet. Jordan, the other puppet, was expected to join as well..

In the same month, Nasser was catapulted to fame by attending a conference in Bandung, Indonesia, of countries that were supposedly non-aligned in the cold war. He was photographed in the company of China's Zhou Enlai, Yugoslavia's Tito and India's Jawaharlal Nehru. He now played for much higher stakes.

Having failed during the summer to obtain Western weapons,

Nasser placed a large order from Soviet-bloc Czechoslovakia (in reality from the Soviet Union). The Arab masses were delighted with this assertion of independence from the West. Nasser signed defence pacts with Syria and Saudi Arabia. The British and American governments were thunderstruck.

What should the apprentice-king of Jordan do? By allying with Nasser he would risk being absorbed by Egypt. By joining the Baghdad Pact he would join his cousin Feisal and the British, his close associates, along with the friendly Turks, and be in congenial company – but he would be seen to be out of step with much of the Arab world.

Hussein thought he saw a compromise. But first he eased Abul Huda out of office in May 1955, partly because of his ambivalence to the treaty and his acute dislike of the Iraqi leader, Nuri es-Said, but also because he was hard to handle. Hussein replaced him with Said al-Mufti, a Circassian loyalist who was much more easy-going and manageable than Abul Huda. Al-Mufti had an open mind about the treaty. But he was a gregarious man who listened carefully and moved cautiously. By this appointment, the 20-year-old king again asserted his central role in Jordan's government.

To nudge Jordan into joining the Baghdad Pact, the British heavy-handedly sent the chief of the imperial general staff, General Sir Gerald Templer, victor of Britain's war against Communist rebels in Malaya, to Amman. Templer was peppery, highly strung and a chain-smoker who had the habit at receptions of putting out his cigarette in a subordinate's sherry-glass. In talks with the king, Templer shouted and punched the table, making the tea-cups and coffee-cups on it dance, when he wanted to emphasize a point. He promised extra battalions and tanks and the beginnings of an air force for the Arab Legion. Britain's subvention would rise from £10m a year to £12.5m. The Arab Legion's firepower would increase by 35 per cent. It was very tempting indeed.

The king gained enthusiasm for the pact and, when his cabinet was split on the issue, rashly offered to sign a letter of intent himself. He was dissuaded by cabinet ministers and probably also by the British. Such a gesture would have instantly made the king very vulnerable.

The mild-mannered al-Mufti became a key figure: at meetings with Templer, he could not be drawn into signing anything. The prime minister was aware of which way the wind was blowing in the Middle East: the 20-year-old king, already showing signs of impetuousness, was not.

While the meetings were being held, one of Nasser's astute assistants based himself in the Egyptian embassy in Amman to orchestrate popular opposition to any deal with Templer. His name: Anwar Sadat. Templer left without Hussein's agreement – and with a storm of adverse publicity in the Arab media whipped up by Sadat.

Hussein was still denounced by the Cairo radio station, the Voice of the Arabs, as a tool of Britain for maintaining the Anglo-Jordanian treaty, including a £12m subsidy from Britain, and because the Jordan Arab Legion (the armed forces) was commanded by a Briton, Glubb Pasha.

Hussein decided to try to get the best of both worlds. He would join the pact, thereby pleasing the British and his cousin in Iraq. He would be safe from attacks by Syria and Egypt. At the same time he would obtain more weapons from the British and obtain their agreement to end the Anglo-Jordanian treaty ahead of schedule, thereby speeding up the "Arabization" of the mainly British-officered Arab Legion and pleasing the Arab nationalists.

The young king thought Nasser would support him – and indeed the Egyptian leader made approving noises in private when he was briefed. But the fact remained that Hussein was proposing to join the British-led Baghdad Pact, which Nasser hated as an imperialist block to his pan-Arab dreams. It should have been clear to Hussein what would follow.

In December, to the king's surprise, anti-government rioting erupted in many parts of Jordan, encouraged by the Voice of the Arabs and, it was widely believed, by Saudi Arabia. (The Saudis had their eyes on Jordan's port of Aqaba, which they claimed as part of the old kingdom of the Hejaz.) The prime minister, Said al-Mufti, resigned. In another misjudgment, Hussein replaced him with his interior minister, Hazza al-Majali, who declared that he favoured joining the Baghdad Pact. Several ministers resigned. Rioting continued for five days. Offices were set on fire and the Philadelphia Hotel, full of tourists, was attacked. Crowds chanting anti-government slogans surged through the main streets. The Hashemite throne was in danger. Eventually the Arab Legion was called out and order was restored: the crowds were dispersed by tear-gas and the imposition of a curfew.

Al-Majali thought he could win approval for Baghdad Pact membership by putting the issue before the rubber-stamp parliament, most of whose members had been elected thanks to the manipulations of the loyalist former prime minister, Abul Huda. Al-Majali felt sure that these tame parliamentarians would support the king, regardless of strong feelings in the streets. But he did not have enough time to try. As the situation deteriorated, he resigned on December 20th.

Hussein found himself in a disagreeable hole which he had dug for himself. To get out of it, the king dissolved parliament, called for an early general election and appointed a trusted veteran royalist politician with a reputation for rectitude, Ibrahim Hashim, as caretaker prime minister. Hashim declared that his interim government had "no right to deal with any political questions or to commit itself in any undertakings or new pacts". That meant it would not sign the Baghdad Pact. Hashim instantly calmed things down. However, the king soon understood that his decision might be fatal: Nasserite radical nationalists might win the general election. Yet another crisis was looming.

Perhaps to head it off, in January 1956, the Supreme Council for the Interpretation of the Law was asked by some MPs who feared they would lose their seats to rule that the dissolution of parliament and the announcement of an election had been invalid. They said the documents were not signed by the interior minister as required (the minister had resigned). The council agreed that the procedure was invalid.

This set off more rioting, again "led by Communists" and encouraged by Nasser's Voice of the Arabs, according to the king. But the angry men demonstrating in the streets were the vox populi.

They were with Nasser, right or wrong. They disliked domination by the British and the Turks, however easy-going and benevolent their rule may have been. Many were aware that their king's great-grandfather, Amir Hussein, had obtained his job in the Hejaz thanks to the sultans of the Ottoman Empire when he and his family were living in Constantinople; that his grandfather, Abdullah, got his job in Transjordan thanks to Winston Churchill and that he took over the West Bank in 1948 thanks to Ernest Bevin and David Ben-Gurion. And what of the young king himself? Hussein, educated in Alexandria and at Harrow and Sandhurst, and protected by a British-officered army led by a British general, was by no stretch of the imagination a genuine Arab nationalist. Cairo Radio liked to call him the "Hashemite harlot", the "imperialist lackey" and the "treacherous dwarf".[2]

Unlike the Templer riots, however, the suspended election riots ended after the army was called out and the crowds dispersed. The king appointed as prime minister Samir al-Rifai, who declared that Jordan would not join "a new pact" (that is, the Baghdad Pact). Al-Rifai was another odd choice: as King Abdullah's personal secretary, he had been a secret emissary to the Israelis and was considered by critics to be pro-Zionist. But he was also prudent, astute and loyal, and the crisis was over — temporarily.

At this point, an entirely new threat to Hussein emerged from Saudi Arabia in January 1956. Saudi forces massed on the Jordanian border and seemed ready to advance. Hussein's army could not have stopped them. On January 12th, however, the British came to Hussein's rescue. The British envoy to Saudi Arabia warned the government that it would defend Jordan if it was attacked, The Saudis promptly retreated.

Having survived his first tests, the king knew he had to adapt quickly to the changing times or be destroyed by Nasser and the forces of Arab nationalism. He had to be able to defend himself against attack. Hussein knew exactly where he was most vulnerable: over the 1948 Anglo-Jordanian treaty (which made him seem to be a "puppet") and over the British officers who ran his army. Britain financed the Arab Legion with money paid to an account controlled by Glubb Pasha, not paid to the Jordanian government. This was no longer acceptable. Hussein concluded that the British would have to go.

"It was my express desire to have more Jordanians in high army posts, gradually to take over all commands," the king wrote later. "But this was against the prevailing policy of Britain, whose proposals were, to say the least of it, ridiculous."[3]

The king recognized Glubb's love of Jordan and his loyalty. Yet as an

Englishman his loyalty was inevitably split. As officer commanding the Arab Legion, this able realist with a disfigured chin was one of the most powerful figures in the country: he was almost a fixture, having served in Jordan since 1930.

However, under Glubb, the highest post to which a Jordanian officer could aspire was that of regimental commander. Staff jobs were reserved for better trained, experienced Britons, some of whom had commanded brigades in the second world war. As a concession to demands for Arabization of the Legion, the king said he was told in 1956 that the Royal Engineers would have an Arab commander by 1985. Such suggestions, reflecting a smug and mistaken British sense of superiority, made ambitious Jordanian officers restive and were a recipe for trouble. But was Glubb really going slow on Arabization? By his own account, he had worked on plans for the last British officer to leave in ten years and most to leave within three.

The young king and the middle-aged general also disagreed over strategy. Hussein wanted arms, ammunition and warplanes to retaliate against Israeli punitive attacks on the border (in response to raids by Jordan-based Palestinian guerrillas). The British, advised by the ever-cautious Glubb, declined to supply them. In the event of war, Hussein wanted better guarantees of supplies than the British would give – and freedom of action. The young king was also annoyed at Glubb's cold, dispassionate recommendation for handling the Israelis: they are stronger than your Arab Legion; do not fight them on the border; retreat and re-occupy your land later.

The trouble was that this sound military advice made no sense politically: in order to qualify to stand side by side with Nasser and to defend his throne against his critics, Hussein had to appear to be his own man, and to be ready to retaliate, albeit modestly, against Israeli reprisal raids. Only then could he hold up his head in the Arab world.

On one occasion, after Glubb had explained his policy at a meeting in the royal palace, the king took a piece of paper from his pocket and began to read nervously from it. "I do not agree with any of the plans we have heard," he said. "I will never surrender one hand's-breadth of my country. The army will defend the demarcation line. Then we shall attack. I will sanction no withdrawal."[4] He concluded by suggesting that Glubb take a holiday. It was a gesture of a young and inexperienced man.

A few days later, the king and the general met again in the royal palace. Glubb wanted to go over some points. The king's attitude was "transformed" and he was smiling and friendly, Glubb wrote later. The disagreements were, he added, small matters, of no importance. Glubb was left with the impression that "the king obviously listened to rumours or complaints made by junior officers. He assumed such stories to be true. But he never asked me for an explanation. I was therefore unaware of what he had heard."[5]

However, Hussein did give Glubb his undivided attention for three whole days to explain his defence strategy in the field at the demarcation line and elsewhere. "His Majesty admitted that he was convinced," Glubb wrote later.

According to Hussein, the crunch in his relationship with Glubb came for two specific reasons. His bid to transfer authority over the security service from the Arab Legion to the interior ministry was rebuffed (Glubb makes no mention in his autobiography of what was clearly a sensitive issue), and he was presented without prior consultation with a list of Arab Legion officers suspected of being subversives whom Glubb wanted to be dismissed. Glubb was extremely security-conscious; Hussein seems to have seen him as high-handed. The king had what he himself described as "a burst of rage". It was one of many.

It seems likely that Ali Abu Nuwar, then one of the king's aides-de-camp, played a key part in what happened. The first clue was a comment by the king to Glubb: "You know, Pasha, there are people in this country who are trying to make trouble between you and me." On the day before his dismissal, Glubb was phoned by Ali abu Nuwar and asked to confirm he would be in Amman on the following day. Looking back, Glubb wrote: "The key to the situation was the young king himself, and the problem was whether Ali could dominate him or convince him."[6]

The general, who presumably had access to security files, states flatly that Ali abu Nuwar was a member of Syria's radical leftist Baath party, which had long sought Glubb Pasha's dismissal. (Abu Nuwar subsequently became chief of staff of the armed forces.)

His mind made up, the king resolved to act quickly. He walked into a cabinet meeting and said Glubb was to be dismissed. "These are my orders," he said. "I want them executed at once." He would give no time to Glubb or the British government to put pressure on him. So it was that on March 1st 1956, at the age of 21, Hussein dismissed the 59-year-old Glubb and his two top aides: Colonel W.M. Hutton, his chief of staff, and Colonel Sir Patrick Coghill, director of intelligence. He also suspended eight British commanding officers. On the following day, Glubb was taken to Amman airport in the king's own car and bade farewell on the tarmac by the defence minister and the chief of the king's personal office.

Glubb was accompanied by his wife who, on hearing from her husband on the previous day that he had been sacked and was being expelled, made the classic comment: "We'll have some tea now, then I'll put the children to bed early and we'll pack all night."[7]

The British government was astonished even though reports from the British embassy in Amman often mentioned the king's private outbursts against his British mentor.[8] All other British officers were ordered to leave. The neurotic British prime minister, Anthony Eden, considered retaliation but wiser heads prevailed. Glubb, in a display of common sense, urged inaction. So did Sir Alec Kirkbride, not long retired as British minister in Jordan, who paid a secret visit to Amman and learnt that Hussein did not intend to abandon the Anglo-Jordanian treaty or its £12.5m. A tortuous attempt to amend it began.

The king had thus gained full control of his armed forces but still depended on the British to pay for them.

He had also made another gain: he became popular. Amman was described as being in a festive mood. The king was even praised in Cairo and Damascus. He appeared to be his own man. But he was not: tax revenues never seemed to cover expenditure and he would always depend on outside help. However, Hussein was to show how he could adapt to changing circumstances and find ways of covering his costs and keeping more of his independence.

The king lost much of the support that he had won in the Arab world only two weeks after sacking Glubb. At the suggestion of the misguided

British, he conferred with Iraq's King Feisal and his prime minister, Nuri es-Said, in Baghdad, who were widely viewed as "puppets of the imperialists".

Soon after the crisis over Glubb had passed, Hussein's throne was again at stake – and entirely without his knowledge. In 1956, the American secretary of state, John Foster Dulles, abruptly cancelled a plan for the construction of a large dam on the Nile at Aswan with aid from the United States. Nasser reacted by nationalizing the Suez Canal, hitherto run by a British-controlled company. To Eden, still an imperialist, this was intolerable.

So Britain, France and Israel launched what came to be called the Suez affair. The three countries perceived a common interest in ousting Nasser. The Israelis saw him as their prime enemy, somebody who would like to drive them into the sea. The French saw him as an incendiary who was setting French Algeria on fire. And Eden saw him as "another Mussolini" who directly threatened long-established British interests throughout the Middle East. Israel's David Ben-Gurion, France's Guy Mollet and Eden thought Nasser had to go.

The idea was for Israel, claiming a *casus belli*, to attack and seize Egypt's Sinai desert and for both Britain and France to send in troops as a sort of "peace force" that would occupy the Canal Zone pending a settlement. Nasser would be humiliated and fall from power. Top-secret agreement on the operation was agreed at a clandestine Anglo-French-Israeli meeting at Sèvres, in France.

The Suez affair was an unmitigated disaster for the three protagonists. Militarily, it was indecisive. The Arab world, almost in unison, turned against the three governments. President Eisenhower, the general who had commanded anti-German forces on D-Day 1944, was furious that he had not been informed in advance by America's two closest allies, Britain and France. Britain was split: the opposition Labour party under Hugh Gaitskell denounced the prime minister. The reputation of Eden, who as foreign secretary under Winston Churchill had been widely admired, was destroyed. He resigned. Under intense American pressure, British and French troops were withdrawn. Nasser survived. The Suez Canal was closed. The United States and the Soviet

Union moved into the power vacuum left by the British and French.

Jordan emerged unscathed, but no thanks to its headstrong young king. The Sèvres protocol took account of Jordan. Ben-Gurion had wanted the protocol to cancel, or override, the Anglo-Jordanian treaty. That might have given him a free hand to grab the West Bank. The final draft said Israel would not attack Jordan during the period of hostilities against Egypt. However, Britain would not help Jordan if it attacked Israel. That was exactly what Hussein wanted to do, with ground forces that were inferior to Israel's and virtually no air cover.

The king cannot have been told about the way his country was preserved at Sèvres. He also cannot have been aware of an equally secret démarche by President Eisenhower in the midst of his campaign for re-election. In a memorandum for the record of October 15th 1956, Eisenhower said: "It seems to be taken internationally as a foregone conclusion that Jordan is breaking up, and of course all the surrounding countries will be anxious to get their share of the wreckage, including Israel. In fact there is some suspicion that the recent savage blows of the Israel border armies against the strong points within Jordan territory are intended to hasten this process of dissolution...I have told the secretary of state that he should make very clear to the Israelis that they must stop these attacks on the borders of Jordan."

In an indirect allusion to the political power of America's Jewish community, Eisenhower also told Dulles to tell Ben-Gurion "not to make any grave mistake based on his belief that winning a domestic election is as important to us as preserving and protecting the peace". Israeli aggression could not "fail to bring catastrophe and such friends as he would have left in the world, no matter how powerful, could not do anything about it." The message could not have been clearer.[9]

Eisenhower knew the risk he was taking. He told his son that if America used force to stop an Israeli invasion of Jordan, "I'd lose the election. There would go New York, New Jersey, Pennsylvania and Connecticut at least." Nonetheless, his last words to Dulles were that he would not under any circumstances permit the forthcoming election to influence his judgment. "If any votes are lost as a result of this attitude," the president added, "that is a situation that we will have to confront, but any other attitude will not allow us to live with our conscience."[10] Hussein's survival was guaranteed.

As the Israeli armed forces advanced across the Negev desert to the Suez Canal, orders went out to mobilize Jordanian and Syrian troops, under the supreme command of General Abdel Hakim Amer of Egypt, for Operation Beisan. (Egypt, Syria and Jordan had signed a military pact in October 1956.) The idea was to cut Israel in two at its most vulnerable point: its "wasp-waist" from the West Bank to the Mediterranean. But there were no Egyptians available and the Syrians were shambolic; only the Arab Legion worked efficiently but it was too small, too poorly equipped and not up to the job.

Nonetheless, the king wanted to attack immediately. His chief of staff, General Ali Abu Nuwar, delayed matters. The general pleaded for more time to prepare an operation that was to not only cut Israel in two but also surround Jewish West Jerusalem. Hussein's newly appointed prime minister, Suleyman Nabulsi (of whom more later), was an Arab nationalist and a Nasserite but he did not want to attack Israel at all. He came to count it as his greatest achievement in office that he kept Jordan out of the war – and avoided defeat. The British ambassador, Sir Charles Duke, told Jordan's government leaders the vital point of the Sèvres protocol: if Jordan attacked Israel, the Anglo-Jordanian treaty would not apply and Jordan would be on its own. Finally, it was Nasser himself who sent a telegram to the king to say he wanted Jordan to keep out. And so Jordan did. There were no anti-government riots.[11]

The Suez crisis had coincided with drastic political change in Amman. The delayed general election was held on October 21st 1956 and was won by the combined opposition (the previous government having been made up of an assortment of notables in the broad category of king's friends). Under the 1952 constitution, every Jordanian man over the age of 20 could vote. Under a law of 1955, they could form political parties.

The opposition won 22 seats out of 40. Nabulsi's National Socialists, the biggest party, had 12 deputies. Second came the Muslim Brothers with four. Hussein asked Nabulsi, leader of the National Socialists, to form a government. Another crisis was approaching.

8   FIRST WIFE

It hardly seemed possible in such tormented, volatile times that the teenage king could have time to think of marriage and fatherhood. Nonetheless, in 1955, Hussein arrived in Cairo for a six-day visit with President Nasser. It was one of the few occasions when relations between the two men were cordial. At the end, the betrothal of the king to a distant cousin and Hashemite princess, Dina Abdel Hamid, was announced. They were married two months later.

The king and Princess Dina knew each other quite well due to their family links. Dina's great-grandfather had preceded Sharif Hussein as amir of the Hejaz. She was a great-grand-niece of Sharif Hussein. By one account, the proposal came "out of the blue" and Dina stalled, saying she wanted to be a teacher and writer. She was mature (aged 26), had graduated in English literature at Girton College, Cambridge, and gained a post-graduate diploma in social science at Bedford College for Women, a part of London University then situated in the middle of Regent's Park. On returning home, she began to teach English at Cairo University and to take an interest in social science in Cairo. She had been brought up strictly but was urbane and sophisticated. Dina wondered if such a marriage would be right not only for the young Hussein but also for her. Arrangements moved ahead quietly. Nonetheless, the announcement of the engagement took Dina and her father by surprise.

Dina may have blotted her copybook in Amman by her action on the occasion of the coronation of Hussein and his cousin, King Feisal of Iraq, on May 2nd 1953. Originally, the coronations were to be one month apart, allowing those concerned to attend both. However, the arrangement was changed, presumably for dramatic effect. This obliged family members to choose which coronation to attend. Dina was close to the Amman branch of the dynasty but she also adored Prince Feisal's mother and did not want to offend her. So she attended neither. This cannot have endeared her to Queen Zain. The queen mother had a strong influence on her son and may have opposed the marriage, which nonetheless took place on April 2nd 1955.

Dina displayed her independent mind and seems to have irritated the young king. After visiting Jerusalem she heard that the king had observed that she seemed to favour West Bankers over East Bankers; on another occasion, she heard that he suspected her of being associated with a plot.

Dina accompanied her husband on an official visit to London in June 1955. A senior British official who went to Northolt airbase, outside London, to meet them wrote in his diary afterwards: "The assembled cameramen were only interested in Queen Dina, who looked very nice but rather podgy in her Dior coat and skirt. Her king very young and solemn taking the salute of the RAF guard and shaking hands without a smile with the assembled Arab diplomats."[1] Five days later, after dining with the royal couple, the diarist pronounced the queen to be "attractive" (she was also pregnant). Dina bore Hussein a daughter, Alia, and he was "overjoyed".

Why did Hussein marry Dina? Perhaps his anxiety over the survival of the Hashemites, bearing in mind his grandfather's fate, prompted him to beget a successor as soon as possible. Hence his need for a wife with impeccable Hashemite credentials. If that was the case, he would have been disappointed by the birth of a girl.

Eighteen months after the wedding, Dina travelled to Cairo to see a relative who was seriously ill. Shortly thereafter, the Jordanian ambassador to Egypt came to her house with a thick letter. Dina wondered what it was and then, pleased, told the ambassador that it must contain photographs from Amman. The ambassador was embarrassed. For when Dina opened the envelope, she found that it contained a long letter from Hussein explaining why he felt the marriage was not working and, in effect, ending it. That was that. Dina would remain in Cairo; she would not return to Amman. Like the initiation of her marriage, the ending of it came "out of the blue".

How did it happen? Partly, perhaps, because Hussein was seven years younger; his education had ended with brief periods at Harrow and Sandhurst and he had no experience of university life; he had grown up in what sophisticated Cairenes regarded as a one-horse town, Amman. Partly, perhaps, because Dina was not about to kow-tow to His Majesty. Dina took a lively interest in Jordan's social problems, which were not high on Hussein's priorities (the first for the king was survival).

The king was not informative. He said in his book[2] that "I was married to" Dina (he did not say "I married" Dina), clearly implying it was arranged and devoid of the courtship leading to love that both might have dreamed of. (The couple did, however, enjoy dancing together.) His brief description of Dina stressed that she was "a highly intelligent woman with an MA degree from Cambridge and a few years my senior". Her personality, her looks, her family background were not mentioned.

At first, Hussein said, he hoped he could build a happy family life around the marriage. He hoped to experience the happiness in marriage of an ordinary man, but it was not to be – not then. The marriage was a failure, he said. It was just one of those things that did not work out, a sad and difficult period. There had been many criticisms about the divorce, he added. But it was better to meet such a crisis with "courage and frankness".

The king's version of the end of his marriage in his autobiography – "we separated and my ex-wife left for Cairo" – does not tally with other reports that she was in Cairo at the time.

Hussein did not mention that his daughter was three months old at the time and that he declined to allow Dina to see her for six years. Then, unexpectedly, Dina was in a London hospital when she received a visit from the king. He told her it was ridiculous that she had not seen her child, who was being brought up by Princess Muna (the king's English second wife), and that she could go to Amman. She did so, and in an emotional moment heard her seven-year-old daughter greet her: her first word was "mummy". There is no explanation for Hussein's original decision – by any standard a cruel one – or for his reversal of it. He later allowed mother and daughter to see much of each other and build up a mother-daughter relationship.

Hussein may have wished to protect the first-born of a king. Alia's fate in the hands of a divorced woman in the Arab world might be uncertain. Dina subsequently married a retired guerrilla officer who had served in Lebanon in Yasser Arafat's mainstream Fatah faction of the Palestine Liberation Organization.

9 CHALLENGE FROM THE LEFT

As Britain, France and Israel became more deeply mired in their operation in Egypt, Hussein continued a policy designed to off-set any criticism that he had not been firm. Had he not, at the start of the Suez operation, called for military action on Egypt's side? He followed this up by refusing Britain the use of its bases in Jordan to attack Egypt. These included a naval base at Aqaba, army bases at Aqaba and Ma'an and airbases at Amman and Mafraq. The British said they would not so use Mafraq. Hussein invited Iraq to send in troops to the East Bank, and it did. It was on this ambiguous basis, as an Arab nationalist in the pay of the British, that Hussein dealt with Suleyman Nabulsi.

The new prime minister was radical but also a pragmatist. His openly avowed long-term aim was some sort of merger of Jordan with the Arab nationalist regime in Syria. As such, he was Hussein's deadly enemy.

However, Nabulsi was a realist. Until this ideal state of affairs was agreed with Syria, the new prime minister favoured a constitutional monarchy: the government through parliament would exercise legislative and executive power. This was less bad for Hussein, but nonetheless unacceptable. The same applied to the volatile Nabulsi's slant on foreign policy: fervent "anti-imperialism", a desire to be on good terms with the Soviet Union and distaste for Hashemite Iraq.

As usual, Hussein stood for the preservation of his branch of the Hashemite dynasty, to be justified by improvements to the standard of living in Jordan, and his own version of Arab nationalism. He would welcome good relations with Egypt and Iraq, but certainly no merger, and close ties to Hashemite Iraq, but without Iraqi dominance. As for his new prime minister, the king kept silent.

Under Nabulsi, the first prop of Hussein's regime that the government intended to knock away was the Anglo-Jordanian treaty and its

£12m. The government won parliamentary approval by 39 votes out of 40 for a proposal to negotiate with Britain the abrogation of the treaty and its substitution of this sum by Arab money: 5m Egyptian pounds each from Egypt and Saudi Arabia and 2.5m Egyptian pounds from Syria. Hussein cannot have relished depending on these three unreliable and potentially hostile countries.

However, he was no fool. At the same time, the American State Department revealed that Jordan had informally asked for an increase of the equivalent of £12m in the foreign aid that it received. Such a request can have come only from Hussein, not Nabulsi.

President Eisenhower recognized that a sea-change had taken place. The Suez affair had robbed Britain and France of all standing in the Middle East, yet the region could not be left to Nasser and the Soviet Union. The president introduced the "Eisenhower doctrine" in a speech to a joint session of the American Congress in January 1957. The idea of the "doctrine" was to block any advance by "international Communism" in the region by fortifying anti-Communist governments with military and economic aid. Governments which supported the doctrine collected the cash.

However, such countries would become targets for "anti-imperialist" critics in the Arab world. So American contacts with Jordan would have to be clandestine. These were initiated by the American military attaché in Amman, Lieutenant-Colonel James Sweeney, and his ambassador, Lester DeWitt, in 1957. In American eyes, Hussein was clearly more sympathetic to the West than Nabulsi, with his friends in Syria and Egypt. The king must have seemed to be an ideal client for the "doctrine". The Americans obtained the agreement of the British, whose government was hard up and cutting its obligations overseas. America would take over: Jordan would move into the American sphere of influence.

In March, the Anglo-Jordanian treaty, with its £12m subsidy, was terminated by mutual consent. At roughly the same time, the American Central Intelligence Agency (CIA) began making payments of "millions of dollars" to Jordan.[1] If, as seems likely, this money went to Hussein rather than to Nabulsi's radical government, the king's position immediately became more secure. Nonetheless, the government remained opposed to him.

Reflecting both his own beliefs and those of his new paymaster, Hussein began to speak out against "Communist infiltration". He warned of a "new imperialism", spoke of Jordan's "right to exist" and reminded his listeners of his stand on the Suez affair and his dismissal of Glubb. One such blast coincided with the launching of Jordan's first Communist weekly newspaper. On February 2nd 1957, the king sent a message to Nabulsi which not only reaffirmed his anti-Communist line but also pressed his claim to exercise power independently of the government. His tone was striking. "We want this country to be inaccessible to Communist propaganda and Bolshevik theories," he wrote. At a cabinet meeting he issued instructions that the press should not criticize the "Eisenhower doctrine".

Parallel to these political ploys were conspiracies hatched principally by army officers. Hussein received a tip from a loyal officer in the first week of January 1957 about Jordanian army officers in Beirut and Damascus "spending fortunes in night clubs, money they couldn't possibly be earning. They always seem to be with Russians or the Egyptian clique."

The king launched a secret investigation but two army officers in civilian clothes, found taking down the number of a Jordanian car outside the St George hotel in Beirut, were detained and deported.

Next, Hussein used his contact with the director of security, Major-General Bahjat Tabara, to good effect. Tabara, who was loyal to the king, ignored the fact that he was supposed to report to the National Socialist interior minister. He seized the daily bulletin of the Soviet news agency Tass and closed its Amman office (its opening had been authorized by Nabulsi), and confiscated Soviet publications and films.

Nabulsi fired back. In March, parliament voted on a new government policy for a forthcoming meeting of Arab leaders in Cairo: support for neutralism and rejection of the Eisenhower doctrine. Hussein was bypassed. In the same month, however, he sent a personal envoy, Bahjat al-Talhuni, to Cairo, Damascus and Riyadh without telling the cabinet. His message: that Hussein would keep his word to them regardless of what government was in power in Jordan. The king worried about plots against him, financed by the Soviet Union. "The propaganda was terrific," he wrote. "Fortunes were being spent on bribery."

Again Nabulsi shot back. He sent proposals to the king for his approval which included the opening of diplomatic relations with China and the Soviet Union and the obligatory "retirement" of Tabara as security chief was announced. All these measures were unacceptable to the king.

For the first time, the 22-year-old monarch was in the midst of a political crisis. His adversaries seemed to hold the aces: they had a majority in parliament and they probably had the support of the man in the street for their demand for closer ties with Syria and Egypt.

At the same time, some senior officers in the "liberated" army turned against the king, perhaps hoping to copy Nasser's contribution to the removal of Egypt's King Farouk. Inexplicably, they showed their hand in Operation Hashim of April 8th. Troops from the first armoured-car regiment took control of Amman's four main crossroads ostensibly to take a census of cars entering and leaving the capital or, depending on the speaker, to check on the serviceability of the unit's vehicles. The real idea, by one account, was to intimidate the king's friends. The result was that the king immediately smelt a plot. He knew his back was against the wall. He felt "really alone" during Operation Hashim, which he blamed on Ali Abu Nuwar, his chief of staff. Daring moves were needed if he was to re-establish his authority.

Most depressing for Hussein was the report that Abu Nuwar was said to be in close and frequent touch with Cairo. Investigators also pointed to Abdullah Rimawi, minister of state at the foreign ministry and a veteran member of the leftist pro-Syrian Baath party, based in Damascus.

On April 10th Hussein fired Nabulsi. The prime minister stepped down at the "king's command", confident that the sovereign would find no alternative and would ask him to return. At first it seemed that Nabulsi was right: the royal nominee, 64-year-old Hussein Fakhri al-Khalidi, a former foreign minister, mayor of Jerusalem and a follower of the mufti until he switched sides and backed King Abdullah, failed to form a cabinet acceptable to the king and Nabulsi's group. Coalition leaders wanted the Baath party to be included in the cabinet; the king rejected the idea. Next, the king asked Abdel Halim al-Nimr, outgoing minister of defence and the interior, to try; he ran into the same snag.

On April 13th word leaked out that Hussein intended to ask Said al-Mufti, the Circassian royalist and former prime minister, to form a government. This meant open confrontation between the king and his adversaries, who controlled parliament. It seemed that the king was provoking Nabulsi and his allies. A lot was to happen on that day.

According to the king's account, Abu Nuwar summoned Said al-Mufti to an army camp outside Amman and gave him a blunt message: either the king agreed to the formation of a government acceptable to his adversaries or there would be "trouble". Already the situation was "explosive". The pressure on this young man of 22 was intense. He was told by his uncle, Sharif Nasser bin Jamil, that "everything seems to be lost". Sharif Nasser presented him on April 13th with the options of abdicating or fighting for survival. Writing later, Hussein recalled saying: "I have to stay. I am going to stand and fight, whatever the consequences." [2]

Abu Nuwar meant what he said when he threatened "trouble" on April 13th. It began when a group of loyal officers from Zerqa, Jordan's main military base, delivered a letter to the king in Amman warning him that trouble was afoot and that they expected to receive orders to surround the capital. Another officer told him "there are traitors everywhere" but the first armoured regiment was loyal. It is not certain that a coherent, secret, well-organized military coup was being launched; the situation at Zerqa appeared to be a muddle. There seems, however, to have been no doubt that much plotting was going on in an *ad hoc* sort of way. A loyal, predominantly Bedouin regiment was ordered out of camp on an exercise without weapons. The manoeuvrings, whatever they were, could have turned into a revolt if not nipped in the bud.

As Hussein told it, the same evening he demanded from Abu Nuwar, sitting in his office in Amman, an explanation for his behaviour. Abu Nuwar was interrupted by a telephone call from his cousin, Ma'an, commander of the Princess Alia Brigade. Ma'an reported to the chief of staff that the brigade's soldiers appeared to have mutinied against its treacherous officers and planned to advance on Amman to protect the king.

By his own account, Hussein responded with what amounted to a master-stroke. Abu Nuwar lacked the military support to seize power in a coup: he was in his king's office. The king took the initiative. He insisted on driving to Zerqa with Abu Nuwar and Sharif Nasser. On the way, the king recounts, he was met by loyal troops travelling to Amman to protect him. Abu Nuwar, hearing some of the men calling for his death, pleaded with the king to let him go home and protect his family. "Abu Nuwar was trembling with fright," the king wrote.

In Zerqa, Hussein was by his own report mobbed as a hero and restored order quickly. He was helped in particular by Bedouin officers and men, who proved their loyalty despite in many cases having been passed over for promotion by better educated non-Bedouins.

Then Hussein returned to Amman – and Abu Nuwar, his old friend with whom in happier days he had discussed plans for the future of their country and shared ideas and youthful enthusiasms. He said he found a whining man, tearful, incoherently mouthing lies. Hussein did not put him to death because he was "so tired, so sick with shame for my fellow human-beings, that I could not do it". Abu Nuwar went to Damascus. In the following days his alleged co-conspirators fled. Among them was the chief of military intelligence.

However, later events suggest that the original story might have been inflated – and displayed Hussein's gift for strategic generosity. Ma'an was subsequently acquitted of treason at a court-martial, rejoined the army, rose to the rank of general and became ambassador to Britain. Abu Nuwar was pardoned and became a businessman in Amman, protesting his innocence and claiming the car trip to Zerqa was his idea. He later became ambassador to France.

Hussein was to use this tactic on several occasions. It was reminiscent of the advice given by the American president Lyndon B. Johnson: it was better to have your adversary "inside the tent and pissing out than outside the tent and pissing in".

For the next few days, Hussein concentrated on restoring order, especially in the armed forces. It was difficult. The main transmitter in

Jerusalem was closed down by its staff when it was needed. His uncle, Sharif Nasser, formed an ultra-loyal unit of palace guards.

Crisis followed crisis. A Syrian armoured brigade commanded by an Egyptian general and based since the Suez affair in northern Jordan moved south and surrounded Irbid. However, a second brigade, from Saudi Arabia, that had been assigned to Jordan after Suez, was placed under Hussein's direct command by King Saud. Strengthened by this welcome gesture, Hussein countermanded the decision for the Syrians to move south. It was probably no coincidence that Abu Nuwar's successor as chief of staff of Jordan's armed forces, General Hiyyari, fled to Syria on April 20th.

Incredibly, in the midst of all these troubles, the king and the coalition of parties led by the National Socialists agreed on a new prime minister on April 15th. For a second time in the crisis, Hussein picked al-Khalidi; this time the former mayor of Jerusalem formed a cabinet. Curiously, his predecessor Nabulsi accepted a demotion to the post of foreign minister. The new government's line seemed unchanged from that of its predecessor.

After Zerqa, however, the king showed himself to be tougher as anti-government protests continued. On April 22nd a "Patriotic Congress" was convened in the West Bank town of Nablus. It was made up of members of parliament who supported Nabulsi and the National Socialist party and prominent doctors and lawyers. The congress issued a statement. It called for union with Syria and Egypt, a general strike on April 24th and a "purge of traitorous and corrupt elements" (translation: Hussein and the king's friends). Yet another crisis was building up.

Al-Khalidi, a man of modest pretensions, was in deep water. On April 24th he resigned. Hussein seized the moment. After a long emergency meeting with his inner circle of advisers on the same day, he formed a new government under Ibrahim Hashim as prime minister with a cabinet of loyal notables. Hashim was a dependable front man. The real power lay with the king, his deputy prime minister, Samir al-Rifai, his interior minister, Falah al-Madadaha, and his defence minister, Suleiman Toukan.

The United States government, urged on by President Camille Chamoun of Lebanon, moved units of the sixth fleet into the eastern Mediterranean and, "on Israel's promise to refrain from any attempt to take advantage of the situation", conveyed its "encouragement and political support" to the king; the White House spokesman said President Eisenhower regarded "the independence and integrity of Jordan as vital".[3]

Hussein moved with remarkable speed: at 1.30 am that night (April 25th), he imposed martial law and banned political parties. He placed five towns, Jerusalem, Amman, Irbid, Ramallah and Nablus, under curfew. He closed five weekly papers. Several hundred people were arrested, including Nabulsi (who remained under house arrest until 1961). He placed the purged army in overall charge of keeping order; the police and the security service were to report to the army.

The reaction from Jordan's neighbours was muted. Hussein did not try to pick a fight with Egypt or Syria and they reciprocated. But neither Egypt nor Syria contributed as they had promised to the Jordan aid fund that was to have substituted for the Anglo-Jordanian agreement. Saudi Arabia, on the other hand, kept its word.

Much more importantly, the United States contributed $10m. This was formalized in an exchange of notes on April 29th. "In response to a Jordanian request for economic and technical aid," the State Department's records say, the United States agreed to assure the "freedom" of Jordan and to maintain its "economic and political stability".[4]

Samir al-Rifai, foreign minister, referred in his note to the American ambassador to a previous offer of American help. "In view of current conditions," he added, "the Jordanian government will be grateful to your excellency and to the government of the United States for whatever additional assistance can be offered at the present time." (The "additional assistance" sought by al-Rifai implied that some money had already been sent to Jordan, possibly with the help of the CIA.) The ambassador responded with the $10m "to assure the freedom of your country and to maintain economic and political stability".[5]

The aid had been under unofficial consideration for some time. In a cable to the State Department on February 13th, the American ambassador reported that a political battle between Hussein and his adversaries was under way and recommended that American aid be granted if Hussein survived it.

Had the 22-year-old king been "really alone" as he claimed through the dramatic events of 1957? No. Queen Zain, wife of ex-King Talal and Hussein's mother, played a strong and discreet role in the background; her influence was to last for many years. A British ambassador once described her as "a woman of great intelligence and force of character". His uncle, Sharif Nasser bin Jamil, accompanied Hussein and Abu Nuwar to Zerqa and was at his side in other difficult moments. Nasser was Zain's brother. There were two personal aides who enjoyed Hussein's trust and on whom the king depended: Bahjat Tabara, who looked after internal security, and Bahjat al-Talhuni, chief of the royal court.

Hussein's handling of the Zerqa revolt, as he told it, marked an important new stage in his reign. The king showed he had guts and, by making Abu Nuwar travel with him on the road to Zerqa, the ability to make a quick decision and seize an advantage. He gave orders with authority and was usually obeyed. His success at Zerqa gave him the moral and political strength to impose his will. He told a news conference after it was all over that he had dismissed Nabulsi as prime minister because he had "disobeyed the king's instructions" – so much for a constitutional monarchy. But these were rough times: the source of political power in the Middle East was, all too often, the barrel of a gun. That lesson was soon to be hammered home to Hussein in Iraq. There was also another lesson that the young king learnt: apart from his close family and his veteran loyalist ministers, he should trust nobody.

10   CLIMAX IN 1958

Having emerged safely from an internal crisis, the king turned to regional strategy. In 1958, at the age of 23, he had to decide how to deal with an alliance of his two most feared adversaries: Egypt, under President Nasser, and Syria, its junior partner, in the newly formed United Arab Republic (UAR). The danger for Hussein was clear and immediate: Egypt and Syria did not share a land border which could be opened up; Jordan and Israel were in the way. If Jordan joined the UAR, and Hashemite Iraq followed, Egypt could link up to Syria in a four-nation federation. (The connection between Egypt and Jordan would have to be maritime, across the Gulf of Aqaba, bypassing the Israeli town of Eilat.)

Nasserism would be in the ascendant in the Arab world. Israel would be surrounded except for its access to the Mediterranean and to the Red Sea through Eilat. The Arabs might even dream again of "driving the Jews into the sea". Partly to counter the UAR, Jordan and Iraq formed the two-nation Arab Union in February 1958.

Both alliances were lopsided. Egypt and Iraq were bigger, more populous and more powerful than their partners Syria and Jordan respectively. However, Jordan and Iraq had an important advantage: there was a long Iraq-Jordan border, meaning the two countries could become united relatively easily, while Egypt and Syria were far apart. Both unions said they would share power, although such arrangements would obviously be full of difficulties.

Both were unions of Arab nationalists. But there were two kinds of nationalism. Nasser's was a radical version. As an "anti-imperialist", he had obliged the British and French to withdraw from Egypt. He had nationalized the Suez Canal. He had balanced his dependency on the West by making a strategic alliance with the Soviet Union, which would supply him with arms and trainers, and would build the Aswan High Dam on the Nile. Nasser also favoured socialist state intervention in the economy.

Hussein's Arab nationalism could scarcely have been more different. It was rooted in the destiny of one family, the house of Hashem, descended from the Prophet Muhammad himself. The patriarch of this rejuvenated family, Amir Hussein of the Hejaz, had "raised the banner of the Great Arab revolt against the Turks". It was the representatives in Jordan of this family – Abdullah, Talal and now Hussein – who had developed a Hashemite kingdom on a land that was little more than sand. True, the family depended on outsiders for its survival: but had not Glubb and his British officers been obliged to leave Jordan, having served their purpose? When the union of Iraq and Jordan was announced in 1958, the flag of the great Arab revolt was again unfurled as the emblem of the union. A passionate belief in the destiny of the Hashemites marked Hussein's reign.

As for democracy, Hussein astutely recognized the value of having a parliament where people could let off steam. Parliaments, if elected freely, had the added merit of telling the king which way the political winds were blowing. But parliament was not sovereign, as in Britain: the Hashemite king was sovereign. He might have to retreat strategically at times, and he might bob and duck and weave as he fought his adversaries at close quarters, but Hussein and his Hashemite family were in charge; it was he who had the final say.

And who in the Arab world had a right to criticize such a less than democratic stance? Virtually every Arab government at the time was in the hands of royal families or military dictators. Hussein did not promote a Nasser-like personality cult. Had a freely contested general election brought to office a political party intent on introducing a republican form of government in Jordan, Hussein would have been tempted to fold up his tents and leave. But more than likely he would have stood and fought such a government tooth and nail.

The idea of the Arab Union made sense: Hussein was well aware that his enemies in Egypt, Syria and Jordan itself would not rest until he was ousted. In May 1957, Syria agreed to Hussein's request that it withdraw the army battalion that had been stationed in northern Jordan since the Suez crisis: there was no alternative but war. But large contingents of the Syrian army waited, across the border, ready to pounce.

Jordan was small and vulnerable; allied to Iraq it was a tougher nut to crack. The Arab Union had another advantage: it was an alliance within the family. Hussein had a deep affection for his cousin Feisal and trusted him.

In an extraordinary act of self-abnegation and self-interest, Hussein placed himself under the authority of Feisal. Ibrahim Hashim of Jordan became deputy prime minister under the Iraqi Nuri es-Said; Suleyman Toukan of Jordan became the union's defence minister but the commander-in-chief of the union's armed forces was an Iraqi, General Rafiq Aref. The government and foreign embassies to the union were to be based in Baghdad, not Amman, where the embassies were downgraded to diplomatic missions.

The Arab Union was a direct challenge to Egypt and Syria. It was a rival power in the region: conflict seemed inevitable. But, Hussein might have argued, conflict between the two sets of allies was inevitable anyway. Hussein added fuel to the fire by answering anti-Hashemite propaganda on Cairo's Voice of the Arabs and elsewhere. Having survived Zerqa, he had gained confidence; his tone in dealing with Egypt was increasingly truculent.

At the same time, Hussein did his best not to be vulnerable to accusations of being a puppet of the imperialists. He had, with misgivings, declined to join the Baghdad Pact and he declined to endorse the Eisenhower Doctrine. However, this did not stop him accepting, in the spring of 1957, $30m and some arms from the United States.

Unfortunately for Hussein, the Arab Union had two weaknesses. The first was that his cousin Feisal lacked a political base. His unpopular uncle, Crown Prince Abdul Ilah, who had been regent, had a domineering personality. Feisal was weak: he allowed Abdul Ilah to break his spirit. Abdul Ilah would lose his temper with the king and treated him disdainfully in public. Hussein was furious with such marks of disrespect.

On one occasion while a teenager at Sandhurst, Hussein was present during an argument between Abdul Ilah and Feisal during a car journey in Feisal's car. He ordered the car to stop, got out and continued the journey in his own car, which had been following behind. On another occasion, Hussein observed that Feisal was driving in a motorcade in an obviously second-hand sports car while Abdul Ilah drove in a glistening new Rolls Royce. The next day, on an angry impulse, Hussein gave his prized Aston Martin to his cousin.

It was no good: Feisal could not stand up to Abdul Ilah or to the prime minister, Nuri es-Said. He was not allowed to travel around the country, meet clan leaders, show himself to the people and make speeches, as Hussein had done in Jordan. He was, therefore, in no position to deal with an Iraqi version of Hussein's troubles at Zerqa.

The second weakness of the Arab Union was the incompetence and smugness of the men who surrounded Feisal. They had not learnt the brutal axiom of Arab politics of that period: plots are inevitable and plotters kill. Hussein knew this from experience. He realized the inestimable value of intelligence and internal security. After Zerqa, he had formed a Bedouin Royal Guards regiment, later expanded to a battalion, comprising hand-picked loyalist soldiers and reporting to Sharif Nasser bin Jamil. The arrested plotters were not executed: following established policy, they were jailed. (Hussein saw no point in blood feuds if they could be avoided.)

Following the arrest of a Nasserite agent, a cadet in a tank regiment, Hussein obtained a tip-off that twin coups were planned in Jordan and Iraq in mid-July. The agent said the idea was for him to throw hand-grenades at the king and Sharif Nasser bin Jamil. Simultaneously, Hussein received a tip-off from the American mission about a Syrian-backed plot by army officers to kill Hussein and declare a republic in July. The plots may well have been linked.

Hussein increased the state of alert of his own security service and telephoned Feisal, asking him to send a top aide to obtain all the information available in Amman. The commander-in-chief of union forces, General Aref, was duly presented with "the damning details", Hussein wrote afterwards. He looked "politely bored". The Iraqi army was "built on tradition", the general replied, with a patronising smile. It was not like Jordan's army at all, he added.[1]

General Aref was ignorant of what was going on in his own backyard. King Feisal and Crown Prince Abdul Ilah as well as Nuri es-Said were deeply unpopular. Many Iraqis resented the fact that the obscure Hashemites, from the backward Hejaz, had been imposed on them by the British at the end of the first world war, substituting British imperialism for the Ottoman empire. Admiration for Nasser's brand of Arab nationalism was widespread, and the Baghdad Pact was seen as an anti-Nasser imperialist plot. Many politically active Iraqis were republicans, not monarchists.

On July 14th 1958, the republicans seized an opportunity that was virtually handed to them. A revolt erupted in Lebanon against President Camille Chamoun. There were fears that unrest would spill over to nearby Jordan and Hussein had not forgotten the tip-offs of a plot to overthrow himself and declare a republic. So he asked Iraq to send him a brigade to "show the flag". The Iraqis jumped at the opportunity to show Nasser that, where Jordan was concerned, it was Iraq that mattered.

A fateful decision was taken to send a brigade led by Colonel Abdul Salam Aref to Jordan. Disregarding the warnings from Jordan, the rulers of Iraq stupidly ordered the brigade to pass through Baghdad on its way to Amman. Making a slight detour, Aref entered and seized the radio station and personally broadcast an announcement that a revolution was taking place. He sent units to the royal palace. In such circumstances, an Iraqi Hussein plus uncle and advisers might well have prevailed against a single brigade. However, Abdul Ilah told the royal guard not to resist: they were surrounded. The next day, July 14th 1958, Abdul Ilah and the king tried to leave and were shot and killed. Nuri es-Said escaped by boat along the Tigris. He was subsequently discovered dressed as a veiled woman, shot on the spot and buried at night.

Aref urged the liquidation of traitors and mob rule took over. The body of Abdul Ilah was mutilated, dragged through the streets and hung naked from the gates of the defence ministry. Nuri es-Said's body was disinterred by the mob and dragged through the streets. King Feisal's body remained buried.[2] Two leading Jordanians were killed:

Ibrahim Hashim, the former prime minister who was deputy prime minister of the union, and Suleyman Toukan, its defence minister.

In Amman, Hussein was furious and frustrated. He took over the leadership of the Iraqi-Jordanian Arab Union, but it was a futile gesture. He sent some troops across the border into Iraq under the command of Sharif Nasser bin Jamil, hoping that an Iraqi regiment based in Jordan would join them.[3] But the Iraqis obeyed orders from Baghdad and went home, celebrating the coup. The Jordanian expeditionary force went home too. It was all over very quickly.

Could the Arab Union have succeeded? Probably not. If Colonel Aref's coup had failed, others would have followed and one would have succeeded due to the negligence of Abdul Ilah and Nuri es-Said and the weakness of King Feisal. Even if there had been no coups, it is hard to imagine this unique form of cohabitation working. Could Hussein have maintained a modest, subordinate position for long or would this strong-minded young man have grown restive, convinced that he could do a better job as chief of the union than his cousin?

But that is suppposing that Middle Eastern leaders in those days could think of the medium term or long term. They could not. For Hussein, survival was often a day-to-day affair. If a stratagem gave the beleaguered Hashemites a breathing space, it would be welcome. The Arab Union did. But the breathing space did not last long.

(Thirty years later, in 1988, the Iraqi dictator Saddam Hussein ordered that the graves of Feisal and his grandfather, King Feisal I, be refurbished. Hussein had long thought that the graves were a disgrace and he appreciated Saddam Hussein's gesture, however cynical it might have been. The king and the dictator visited the cemetery together, and Hussein became a closer ally of Iraq. In the mid-1990s, however, after the king turned against Saddam Hussein, there were signs that he was dreaming of a Hashemite restoration in Iraq.)[4]

All being lost in Iraq, King Hussein turned his attention to protecting himself. Yet another crisis loomed for the 23-year-old. The Western powers, especially the United States, reckoned he was finished. In a secret White House briefing on July 14th 1958, the CIA director, Allen Dulles, said that "if the Iraqi coup succeeds, it seems almost inevitable that it will set up a chain reaction which will doom the pro-Western governments of Lebanon, Jordan and Saudi Arabia and raise grave problems for Turkey and Iran".

It was not a wild exaggeration as far as Jordan was concerned. Egypt, Syria and Saudi Arabia were sharpening their knives. Three governments stood ready to defend Jordan, each in its own way: Britain, America and Israel. For Britain, Jordan was a foothold in a region it had once dominated; for America it might be a bastion against international Communism; and for Israel, the continuance of a moderate and pro-Western Jordan would mean the Jewish state was not entirely surrounded by hostile Arab powers.

Hussein needed guaranteed oil supplies and the symbolic presence of British or American troops to act as a deterrent. Oil was a worry: Syria had imposed a trade blockade against Jordan that included deliveries of oil from Syria by tanker lorry. So Jordan had begun to import from Iraq by road. That source also dried up, as a result of the coup. Next, the United States offered to airlift oil via Saudi Arabia. After a few deliveries, the airlift stopped because the Saudis refused to allow it. Hussein recalled telling King Saud, in a furious telephone conversation before slamming down the receiver: "To the end of my life I will never forget this action against my country in this hour of need."[5] The Saudi prime minister, Sharif Faisal, seems to have imposed the blockade because he thought Hussein was done for, and did not want to risk annoying Nasser. However, an Israeli historian says Hussein subsequently "dismissed the episode as an understandable piece of realpolitik".[5] In the end, the fuel came from Lebanon. But since Jordan and Lebanon have no common border, it was flown in, by agreement, across Israeli airspace.

The other worry was internal security. The ever-present Sharif Nasser bin Jamil conducted a purge of supposed radicals in the officer corps. But it was not enough: Hussein needed foreign military backing as well. Before asking Britain and America, Hussein discussed the crisis with the cabinet and parliament. They agreed with him that a request should be made. The king called in the envoys of the two powers, presented Jordan's request and said that he did not care which country sent the troops.

This was a watershed of sorts. In one sense it was humiliating for an Arab government to appeal to Britain and America for help in keeping its own people in order and fending off possible threats from fellow-Arabs. This was certainly not a request that an authentically nationalist government would have made, even if it was a matter of life and death for the ruler. Yet in another sense the notables agreed it would be better to support the headstrong 23-year-old king than to abandon him to a none too pleasant fate and submit themselves to a hard military dictatorship at the hands of Syria or Egypt. This feeling that they were better off as they were suggested a stirring of Jordanian nationalism intimately linked to the Hashemites. These were, however, the feelings of East Bankers: to many West Bankers, Hussein was still an autocratic outsider from the East Bank. Immediately after the decision to seek British or American aid was taken, the requests went to the envoys of the two countries (on July 16th 1958, two days after the assassination of King Feisal). They had been expected: both the British and the American high commands had been planning for such an eventuality. It had been agreed that the American marines would look after Lebanon and the British would return to Jordan.

Lebanon did not seem to be in peril. Earnest marines who stormed ashore in landing craft wearing full battle-gear were met by surprised bikini-clad girls on Beirut's sandy beaches. Hussein, however, claimed to have crushed the latest anti-government plot at the last minute. Hussein thought the government was "stretched to the limit" and Jordan's future was "hanging by a thread".

The British prime minister, Harold Macmillan, moved quickly. He convened an emergency evening meeting of his cabinet which approved a decision to send paratroops based in Cyprus to Jordan. Within hours, on July 17th, the aircraft were airborne. Again, Israel came to Jordan's rescue. The first three Beverley transports, carrying an advance party of about 100 men, were allowed by the Israeli government to fly across Israeli airspace straight to Amman, although they had inexplicably not obtained official clearance. Israeli warplanes buzzed them en route.

There was then a pause while the prime minister, David Ben-Gurion, considered what it would mean for Israeli sovereignty if he allowed the airlift to be completed (answer: it would have no effect at all). Some advisers apparently suggested that Hussein be left to his fate. But Ben-Gurion consulted Washington and his cabinet gave the go-ahead. On July 17th, two battalions of British paratroops took over Amman airport.

The presence of the British automatically gave Jordan a sense of national stability. The paratroops stood ready to fly anywhere in the kingdom to make an invading force retreat behind its borders. The British force also constituted a sort of trip wire which, if crossed by an adversary, would automatically bring the British into the fray in large numbers.

However, the British force was running short of fuel in Jordan and encountering difficulties in arranging flights across Israel. Macmillan sought President Eisenhower's help. The president replied that "we would have to seek and find some accommodation with Israel" and that John Foster Dulles "has already talked with their embassy here about this matter". There was an accommodation and American Globemasters flew in the needed supplies.

So the military threat to the young king receded. Propaganda went on, however. Hussein recalled turning on his radio one day and hearing the Voice of the Arabs (Cairo Radio) say: "We shall fight until we exterminate the criminal king of Jordan."

And there were plots. Hussein recorded one attempt by the Egyptian embassy to bribe a Jordanian official to kill him, and another by Egyptian army officers to "take over Jordan and eliminate me".

Most bizarre was an incident on November 10th when Syrian jets buzzed the king's aircraft as he piloted it from Amman to Cyprus for a stopover en route to Geneva for a family holiday. The flight was to cross Syrian and Lebanese airspace. Hussein said the Syrians knew all about his flight and that it had been preceded by a speech at a goodbye ceremony at Amman airport. However, an Israeli historian says that Jordan subsequently admitted that, due to an "administrative slip", the government had not formally asked Syria for clearance for the flight.

From Hussein's account, the control tower at Damascus airport told him that he did not have clearance and should land at the nearest Syrian airport or landing strip. Hussein was well aware that if he did so, the

Syrians would be highly unlikely ever to let him return home. He and his uncle, Sharif Nasser, who was one of his passengers, would face an uncertain future, to say the least.

So his pilot, Jock Dalgleish, took their old propeller-driven De Havilland Dove (which had also been used by King Abdullah) into a dive and scooted back towards Amman at close to ground level. As Hussein described it, two Syrian MiG-17 interceptors flew at the Dove at high speed apparently from Jordanian airspace. There followed a terrifying air chase in which the MiG pilots seemed to Hussein to want to cause the Dove to crash. Eventually the old plane crossed into Jordanian airspace and the MiGs flew off. As the Dove flew to Amman, those aboard celebrated their survival with a cup of tea from a thermos and a Lucky Strike cigarette.[6] The king returned to Amman to a warm welcome.

Was it really a brush with death? Had the Syrian nationalist regime wanted to kill the king, the MiGs could have been ordered to shoot at him: his ancient Dove was a sitting duck. But they did not fire. It is possible that the MiG pilots were told to give the king and his uncle the fright of their lives; if so, they succeeded. Syrian air force generals monitoring the operation may well have had a good belly-laugh as they ordered the MiG pilots to fly at the old Dove from opposite directions simultaneously, and scream past it.

It is, however, more or less certain that the Syrians wanted to force the king to land in their territory so that they could both end the Hashemite monarchy by detaining Hussein and his uncle and, with Nasser's Egypt, surround Israel. As evidence for this theory, Dalgleish said later he had learnt that the Syrian regime had brought some 200 Jordanian opponents of Hussein to the Damascus airfield as a welcoming committee to greet the captive king. Amid the speculation, however, a fact stands out: knowing they had nothing to lose, the king and Dalgleish risked their lives by disobeying Damascus and refusing to land when outmanoeuvred by the MiGs, and they survived. Hussein said he subsequently "forgave" Syria. But he did not forget.

11 A NEW STAGE

Having tried by diverse means to destroy Hussein and his regime, and failed, the king's adversaries spent a quieter 1959. This was a time for the UN. Its secretary-general, Dag Hammarskjold, had toured the Middle East and done his best to reduce tensions in the region. A special UN mission, under Pier Spinelli, settled into Amman. The presence of Spinelli, a senior UN official, at the head of a small team gave Jordan more international credibility and deterred adversaries. On November 2nd 1958 British troops had completed their withdrawal from Jordan and the Americans had withdrawn from Lebanon; the Israeli border was incident-free; and, on December 1st, both houses of parliament approved the king's plan to end martial law, which had been in effect for 19 months. Nasser seemed subdued. Nothing happened.

There was even time to think about the economy. An Israeli historian, Uriel Dann, reckons Jordan was receiving $50m a year from the United States.[1] Remittances from Palestinians working in the Gulf states provided a constant source of hard currency. Investments appeared to be increasing. An oil refinery was built at Zerqa. Production of cement and phosphates was growing; so were small industries.

The University of Jordan had been opened and expanded so that in 1966 it had 2,500 students, of whom 650 were young women. Small Palestinian businesses began to prosper and their owners built themselves bigger houses. There was a little boom in the housing industry. A start was made on the East Ghor canal, designed to irrigate 30,000 acres of farmland. The Bedouins did well. By 1964 Jordan had 800,000 sheep, 650,000 goats, 65,000 cattle and 19,000 camels.

The first priority was to build a basic infrastructure for an unnatural economy. The Mediterranean was blocked off by Syria, through which supplies had to pass on their way to and from Beirut, and by Israel. The road from Amman to Aqaba, Jordan's undeveloped harbour at the head of the Gulf of Aqaba in the Red Sea, was paved. The docks were slowly improved. By 1967 Aqaba would be handing 1m tonnes of cargo a year. The road to the Syrian frontier was also paved. Attempts were made to promote tourism to East Jerusalem and Bethlehem, on the West Bank, and the magnificent hidden city of Petra on the East Bank.

The second priority was social services, which were in short supply in such a poor country. Hussein seems to have put much of his American money to good use. He could boast in 1962 of having increased his education budget from the princely sum of £41,749 in 1950–51 to £2,857,000 in 1960–61. He claims that spending on public health quadrupled in the same period. As the king and his regime survived test after test, business people gained confidence and began to invest.

In March 1959, Hussein felt strong enough to embark on a seven-week world tour. The first stop was Taiwan, where he presumably obtained economic aid. Next came Washington, where he talked to President Eisenhower in the White House and was given nothing more: the aid programme was well under way. But the intangible boost to his personal prestige and to the credibility of Jordan as a state was priceless; the White House visit was an American signal to Jordan's Arab and Israeli neighbours that the United States did not want to see the Hashemites unseated. It confirmed Jordan's status as an American rather than a British client. (Britain paid Hussein a modest £2.5m in 1959.) The Washington visit also confirmed the Eisenhower administration's statement on April 24th 1957 that the independence and integrity of Jordan were vital to the security of the United States. For the American fiscal year 1960, the administration proposed over $50m in aid to Jordan of which $40.5m was in direct budget support.

However, a secret American national intelligence estimate made before the king's visit to Washington and dated March 10th 1959, coordinated by the CIA, said that "over the long run we have little confidence in Hussein's ability to hold his throne or indeed in the viability of Jordan as a state. In the short run, however, his own position and Jordan's existence are bolstered by an uneasy equilibrium of external forces which maintains Jordan as a buffer and preserves the region in default of a generally acceptable alternative. Israel prefers Hussein to a pro-Nasser successor. Nasser wants to avoid a showdown with the West and Israel over Jordan's future."

The Americans were under no illusions about the means used by Hussein to stay in power. "For almost two years," the intelligence estimate said, "Hussein has kept his domestic opponents off balance by repression and intimidation, including the use of martial law, the jailing of numerous opposition figures and rigid controls over the parliament." Some opposition figures had fled to Syria and other countries where they plotted against Hussein's regime and "the effectiveness of those who remain has been circumscribed by the regime's security measures". However, as the intelligence estimate added, "the king has shown striking personal courage in the face of dangers and provocations".

Danger was always close. Hussein was informed of yet another plot involving a senior army officer, Major-General Sadiq Shara, the chief of his general staff. Perhaps recalling his method with the suspect Abu Nuwar at Zerqa, Hussein took Shara with him on his world trip and let him sweat it out. After his return the general and his brother were tried, convicted and sentenced to death – but reprieved.

This canny strategy of pardoning plotters worked well, and displayed the king's native intelligence at its most effective. It was not on display, however, in his choice of prime minister. Why did he pick his ultra-loyal "court minister", Hazza al-Majali, to succeed the 60-year-old Samir al-Rifai as prime minister in May 1959? Al-Rifai had been a scornful critic of the Nasser-controlled Arab League; al-Majali, in a previous stint as prime minister, had tried energetically to do his master's bidding and push Jordan into membership of the Baghdad Pact, thereby provoking riots. To Arab nationalists and Palestinian radicals in Jordan it must have seemed like the replacement by a hated monarch of a hated prime minister with a politician even more hated. It was asking for trouble from violent extremists.

On August 29th 1960 two bombs were planted in the prime minister's desk. One exploded, killing al-Majali. In his memoirs the king said he drove immediately towards the prime minister's office but was stopped by the army commander and the defence minister. They "refused point-blank to let me pass".[2] Forty minutes after the first blast came a second: it killed many rescue workers and bystanders and, writes the king, might have killed him if he had not been restrained. Shortly afterwards two employees of the prime minister's office were said to have crossed into Syria.

Why al-Majali? The king, still only 25 years old, had been through a lot in his choices of head of government. At the outset of his reign he had tried a local version of a constitutional monarchy with his friend Fawzi al-Mulqi as prime minister. But his adversaries mistook tolerance and openness for weakness; the experiment collapsed. He had later tried cohabitation with a prime minister of whom he strongly disapproved, Suleyman Nabulsi. That experiment collapsed too.

In between, he had relied on loyal servants of the Hashemites to keep good order and military discipline, men such as al-Rifai. They were able to balance cabinets shrewdly so that each region of the country, and Circassians as well as Arabs, were represented. By appointing newcomers to ministerial posts, they created more loyalists who were pleased that their worth had been recognized. There may well have been financial advantages to be gained by these loyalists from holding ministerial posts.

The king had, by now, become accustomed to facing down his adversaries and stood ready to face them down again. He liked "Hazza Pasha". But this was surely the time for a technocrat or a loyalist untainted by bitter memories.

After al-Majali came another ultra-loyalist who had served for six years as head of the king's private court office (*diwan*), Bahjat al-Talhuni. Such was the young king's influence that he told his outgoing cabinet: "I have decided that my chief of *diwan* will be prime minister."[3] Most ministers nodded their approval; a few resigned. There was no doubt who was in charge. However, there was some doubt whether the choice of a royal mouthpiece as prime minister was the right one.

In 1960 there were more attempted assassinations but no attempted coups or mass demonstrations. In addition to the murder of al-Majali, the authorities claimed to have uncovered two plots to kill Hussein's uncle, Sharif Nasser bin Jamil, and two most bizarre bids to kill the king. One royal assassination was to have been carried out by a palace cook in the pay of Syria. He had poisoned several palace cats to test the effectiveness of his brew, Hussein said, and was caught before slipping it into the king's food. On another occasion, the king recounted, a powerful acid was substituted for the anti-asthma fluid in a nasal spray which he used. A few drops were found to have peeled off the chromium around the plug-hole of a bathroom wash-basin.

Plots did not prevent the king from sounding increasingly pugnacious, however. At the UN General Assembly, he accused Nasser of trying to dominate the Middle East. In the following year Hussein boldly tried a new approach to his nemesis on the Nile: in 1961 he began a correspondence. In two letters each, the two leaders agreed to disagree over strategy for the co-ordination of the Arab world. Hussein, who had most to lose, argued for "Arab solidarity" in which Arab states remained sovereign, tolerated each other and worked together. Nasser, whose popularity was still high and who had most to gain, favoured a much closer "Arab unity". It was not difficult to imagine who Nasser thought should be the great unifier.

Hussein may have thought that publication of this curious exchange would add to his credibility in radical Arab nationalist circles: the former British puppet would be seen to be corresponding with the hero of the Arab nationalists on the basis of one Arab head of state to another. Inevitably, this aroused the man in the street and several demonstrations were held in which photographs of Nasser and Hussein were held high. The king realized the potential for trouble and the demonstration organizers were told firmly that enough was enough.

12 SECOND AND THIRD WIVES

In 1961, what kind of man was the 26-year-old king? His teachers at Harrow had not been far off the mark: he had proved to be vigorous, headstrong and determined. Unlike the sad, wistful Feisal of Iraq, dominated by his uncle, Hussein was his own man. So far, the young king had asserted his power and not made a serious mistake. When about to take a rash action, his advisers had intervened and he had listened to them.

This was the case during the Suez crisis, when he was anxious (or said he was) to go to the assistance of the man he most feared, distrusted and hated, Nasser, by attacking Israel. He had been restrained from such a suicide mission. His prime minister, Nabulsi, urged him to hold back; eventually, Nasser himself had given the same advice.

Hussein was also restrained immediately after the bomb blast which killed another prime minister, al-Majali; he was stopped from visiting the destroyed prime ministerial office by his defence minister and army commander.

It is a measure of Hussein's vigour and growing political skill that some suggested that he slyly proposed rash and brave acts in the knowledge that he would be restrained. This is, however, out of character. The consensus of those observing him was that, regardless of whether his decisions had been right or wrong, this was a brave man.

Even in his early 20s, Hussein managed to command respect. His loved and respected uncle and close adviser, Sharif Nasser bin Jamil, called him: "Sir". (He delighted his visitors by appearing to reciprocate: later, Henry Kissinger's outsize ego swelled when he recounted that he was, as President Nixon's national security adviser, called "Sir" by "an hereditary monarch".)[1]

Perhaps this monarch exuded authority in part to compensate for his stature. A photograph of him at Sandhurst shows a handsome young man in army uniform standing ramrod-straight, chest out, shoulders back, arms straight down and with a very determined expression on his face.

It must have mattered to him that President Nasser was about one foot taller than him. It must have annoyed him that the Israelis referred to him dismissively as the "plucky little king" or "PLK". But it did not show.

The king was also aware that he was no intellectual, and had had an inadequate education for which his grandfather and father were to blame. The fact that his first wife was an articulate Cambridge graduate can have done little for his self-esteem. His brother, Hassan, was the intellectual of the family, educated at Harrow and Christ Church, Oxford.

Hussein compensated. He had a hot temper. He managed to exude a regal presence. He got his own way: a good many governments had risen and fallen on his say-so. He became a highly competent pilot and driver of fast cars.

There was, however, another side to him. Before Harrow, as a small boy, Hussein must have passed through a particularly difficult period. He came to realise that his grandfather the king, whom he revered, thought that his father, whom he loved, was worthless. Hussein thought through what he felt about his father. His memoirs treat Talal with sadness and filial respect. He faithfully records what he sees as his father's achievements and laments that he was not given the opportunity to fulfil his promise.

He must have worried that his father's schizophrenia was hereditary. (The British Foreign Office certainly did: the head of its Eastern Department asked Hussein's house-master at Harrow if he had spotted any unstable behaviour. He replied that he had not.)[2]

Such an intense family experience is not one to share with friends, and Hussein must have called up all of his emotional reserves to deal with it. At that time, he seems to have established his rapport with his uncle, Sharif Nasser bin Jamil. It was to serve him well.

At the same time, it would be surprising if Hussein felt no resentment towards his father for failing the family, as it must have appeared to a schoolboy. Conversely, Hussein may well have felt, like many children in such situations, that in some unfathomable way he bore the responsibility for his family's troubles. After all, did not his grandfather love him and hate his father? It was a background tailor-made for emotional insecurity. Perhaps his saving grace was his mother, Zain, through whom he could learn to have a stable relationship with a woman.

However, after the failure of his first marriage to Dina, he led a solitary emotional life, caught up with politics, flying and fast cars. He described himself as "nervous, irritable and bad-tempered" and fed up with the official appearances at which he forced himself to smile. But at the age of 26 he was too young to be a recluse. He wanted to marry, but not to have another arranged marriage. He wanted somebody who would make a home and family for him but not be a permanent intellectual challenge. He wanted a woman with whom he could relax and feel comfortable and switch off.

Hussein found the woman he was seeking. She was the 19-year-old Antoinette (Toni) Gardiner, daughter of Lieutenant-Colonel Walker Gardiner of the Royal Engineers, who was advising the government on ways of conserving water during the drought. Her innate shyness did not stop her from observing, when introduced to Hussein dressed as a pirate during a fancy-dress party in 1961: "You look pretty scruffy, your majesty!"

Toni was a vivacious outdoors girl with simple tastes and no intellectual pretensions. She was pretty, charming and the same height as the king. Like Hussein, she enjoyed riding, swimming, dancing and parties. The king began to invite her to film showings in his palace. She could not drive, and Hussein took delight in teaching her. They went Go-Karting together. They had tea with Lieutenant-Colonel and Mrs Gardiner. "For the first time in my life," he wrote, "here was a girl who took an interest in me as a human being and not as a king." Toni's first question after Hussein proposed marriage was: "Do you really want to marry me?" He did.

The British Foreign Office and its representatives in Amman were worried. They feared an anti-British reaction on the streets. But

Hussein had taken precautions: Toni became a Muslim (under the instructions of the venerable Sheikh Muhammad al-Shankiti) and a Jordanian citizen and took the name of Muna al Hussein (Hussein's delight).

Hussein's political advisers were just as worried as the British. "He took a hard road," said one of them. "There was a lot of opposition in the country and among his officials to the marriage. But he decided."

There was also a political angle. "He had to make a pre-emptive move towards Nasser at that time because we were on bad terms and there were lots of accusations over the radio and it was Ramadan," this adviser added. The king suddenly decided to go to Cairo and to reconcile with Nasser. People were really puzzled why the king did this. A few months later, he married Muna." There was a connection. Fearing bad publicity in the Arab world, the king was carefully neutralizing Nasser and Cairo Radio's anti-Jordan Voice of the Arabs.

The king announced, cautiously, that he had married "a Muslim, not an Arab". Muna became a princess and not a queen. The Jordanian on the street did not react, as feared, with anger at the traitorous British puppet emerging in his true colours. On the contrary, Jordanians seemed to be genuinely pleased that Hussein, after a very rough ride as king, had found some happiness as a man. The streets were crowded with well-wishers.

After Muna gave birth to her first son, Abdullah, on January 30th 1962, her title was upgraded to the equivalent of "her royal highness". Abdullah became crown prince. Muna concentrated on making a home and a family for Hussein at their country house at Hummar, called the House of Goodness and Happiness, about 10 miles from Amman. It had two living-rooms and four bedrooms. Later, they built a larger and more convenient home nearby, with a swimming-pool. Muna brought Alia, Hussein's daughter by his first wife, Dina, into the family which, in addition to Crown Prince Abdullah (named after Hussein's grandfather), comprised Feisal (named after his assassinated cousin) and twin girls, Zain (named after his mother) and Aisha.

"We live a very quiet life in our little farmhouse," the king wrote. Really? His life might have been quiet at Hummar but it was certainly not quiet in Amman. It looked as though the king was using his country home as an escape from his other life, which seemed to be full of politicians, poisoners, plotters and petitioners.

At the start, his second marriage worked. The king's autobiography, *Uneasy Lies the Head*, ends with his marriage on a note of euphoria. Unlike Dina, his first wife, Muna posed no intellectual challenge to the king, who was not known for reading books. However, a stable marriage may depend on both partners developing at the same speed; otherwise one partner might become bored. Hussein was maturing fast: as crisis followed crisis he gained self-confidence and became increasingly adept at exercising authority and what British army officers refer to as man-management. Muna, on the other hand, kept out of the hurly-burly of Jordanian politics; during the 1967 war, she stayed (wisely) at home. Insiders said that the couple were moving apart, having separate programmes even when they were in Amman. "Muna had her group of English and liberal Jordanians while the king had his group," says one insider. "They were not going out together." The insiders knew that "something was wrong" but "it was not well-known".

One problem, says a well-placed Western diplomat, was that the king was strongly attracted to women and rumours about his proclivities were whispered in the "hothouse atmosphere of the royal court". As an ex-minister put it: "The king is a macho." These rumours must have reached Muna's ears.

As yet, however, no serious threat to Muna's marriage was visible. But there was always the possibility that Hussein might meet, and fall for, an attractive Jordanian woman with international connections with whom he could not only have children and a happy home life but also share his intense political life.

This happened in 1972 when the king met Alia Toukan, a member of a prominent family with deep roots in the West Bank town of Nablus and a branch in the East Bank town of Salt for 150-odd years. She received her early education in Amman but later accompanied her father, a senior ambassador, and her mother on overseas assignments. In the early 1960s she completed her education at the St Ignatius Loyola University (a branch of a Chicago-based institution) in Rome, where her father was ambassador, and later at Hunter College in New York, when her father represented Jordan at the UN.

Her first job was in the public-relations department of Royal Jordanian Airlines, in which capacity she met the king. It would have been hard to miss her: Alia was attractive with angular good looks, flashing eyes, long hair and a big smile. Her personality was, says her brother, "bubbly" and "extremely sensitive to other people's needs and emotions". The family used to joke that home had become a mental hospital because Alia would often bring friends with emotional problems to stay. "She attracted that kind of friendship," says her brother. She had friends in Amman, Rome and New York.

Alia met the king in 1972 when she was working on a trip that the king was making on Royal Jordanian. At this time, by one account, the king and Muna were estranged and living apart. By another account, their divorce had been decided, a surprise that was not sought or wanted by Muna. Her version of events is not available: as part of the divorce settlement, she undertook not to make it public.

Hussein's courtship of Alia was quick: two months at most. The king approached Alia's father and told him he was serious. It was not an arranged marriage. "She told me she genuinely felt strongly for him as a person," says her brother. It was a quiet wedding without a large public ceremony in the Toukans' home. Why? "I think he just didn't want to make a big issue of the fact that he was marrying again," says her brother. Also, it was a time of tension after Black September and before the Yom Kippur war, no time for festivities. Nonetheless, Alia was proclaimed as queen, not as a princess like Muna. It came as a surprise to most Jordanians.

Haya was born ten months after the marriage and Ali a year and a half afterwards. (In 1998 Haya, an accomplished horse rider, was hoping to represent Jordan in the Olympic Games; Ali had become a courtier, sowing his wild oats). Hussein and Alia also adopted a young Russian who had escaped death in an airliner crash at Amman airport.

Hussein appears to have loved Alia deeply. Her brother recalls that she coaxed him out of a social shell. "We were struck by how outgoing the king had become," he says. "He was more ready to go to people's houses on a 'let's go and visit so-and-so and have dinner' sort of thing."

"He's already a down-to-earth person but he did more visits, going to weddings, and so on. I saw them as a close couple, a happy couple." Perhaps one of the essential lubricants to the relationship was the fact that, as an Arab, Alia spoke Arabic and the king had no social worries on that score; Muna's Arabic (like Noor's later) was limited.

Alia was happy with the king and he was with her. She fulfilled herself as a wife and a mother and in social welfare projects that she pursued with such energy that a Queen Alia Foundation was set up. On the day of her death, Alia had read in a newspaper a letter from an inhabitant of a southern town complaining about bad medical services. She ordered up a helicopter to fly her there to make a surprise visit, accompanied by the minister of health, disregarding warnings of bad weather, in particular of low clouds, high winds and rain. The queen and the minister inspected the medical services, left on their return flight for Amman and crashed into a hillside. Alia was widely mourned, and Hussein was stricken. He built a beautiful mosque in her memory and named Amman's international airport after her. The foundation continued its work after her death.

13 DEALING WITH THE PLO

 News on September 28th 1961 of a military coup in Syria led by men opposed to the union of their country with Egypt might have been expected to cause rejoicing in the house of Hashem. However, voicing serious concern about the situation in Syria, Hussein mobilized the Jordanian armed forces and seriously considered a military intervention. (Was he, perhaps, thinking rashly of fulfilling his grandfather Abdullah's dream of a united kingdom of Syria and Jordan? If he was, the dream came to an abrupt end after conversations with the American and British ambassadors.) Tension gave way to euphoria. The armed forces were stood down, and Hussein enjoyed the discomfiture of his old adversary. Syria's new rulers seceded from the United Arab Republic. Nasser had not only been humiliated, he had shown himself to be vulnerable. Hussein lectured him for having arrogated to himself the leadership of the Arabs, of trying to impose Egyptian rule on Syria and of fostering disunity.

This event gave Hussein more confidence. A general election was held on October 19th. This time there was no actual vote-rigging: instead, the regime's formidable powers of persuasion were deployed to good effect. Potential trouble-makers were firmly told by their local authorities that it would be unwise to stand or, if they had already registered as candidates, to withdraw. Those who did not listen were not given the police certificate of good behaviour that all candidates were required to obtain and display. This was the "consensus election": of the 60 seats in the lower house, 47 were uncontested.

Next, Hussein installed as prime minister a man who was to become a forceful and controversial figure in Jordanian politics until his assassination in 1972: 42-year-old Wasfi al-Tall. A half-Kurdish farmer-businessman from one of the best families of Irbid, he had been

educated at the American University in Beirut and had acquired a reputation for being hard-working, efficient, honest – and blunt. He had
been Hussein's representative in Baghdad. Al-Tall was to become Hussein's "hard man": when a tough job needed doing, such as the elimination of the *fedayeen* from Jordan, Hussein called on him. When the king
needed to respond to criticism from Cairo and give as good as he got,
al-Tall was his master propagandist.

Al-Tall also felt free to express unpopular ideas to the king. He was
one of those who tried to dissuade Hussein from marrying his English
second wife, Toni Gardiner. He was one of the very few who urged the
king to keep out of war in 1967. Al-Tall realized that if Jordan were to
keep out of the war. it would be discredited for some time, but he
thought it could nonetheless brazen it out. He had the very un-Arab
habit of chain-smoking his pipe. The king gave al-Tall the job of shaking up the slow-moving and, at times, corrupt bureaucracy, and he made
a start.[1]

Al-Tall apparently persuaded the king that since the September elections were rigged, the chamber of deputies lacked credibility. Accordingly, new elections were held, freely, on November 25th 1962. This
time the 60 seats were contested by 166 candidates and there was a single candidate for only three seats. About 70 per cent of the voters went
to the polls. The result spelt trouble for the king and al-Tall.

It showed that many Jordanians actively disliked the Hashemite
regime. On the vote of confidence in al-Tall's government, 18 MPs, 12
of them from the West Bank, voted against. Hussein would have difficulty keeping such a parliament under control.

Seemingly unperturbed, the king carried on confidently. In a clear if
indirect insult to Nasser, Hussein agreed with the spendthrift King
Saud of Saudi Arabia in August 1962 to form a "total military union"
complete with joint military command. (It was a paper agreement: genuine co-operation including joint exercises was not really seriously
considered.)

Next, Hussein caused trouble for Nasser in Yemen after the Egyptian president plunged into that country's civil war. It started in September after the death of the dominant imam (who was described by

some as medieval). His successor, Imam Muhammad al-Badr, disappeared into the mountains after a military coup overthrew the regime. Nasser supported the new military ruler, Abdullah al-Sallal; Hussein and Saud backed the new imam. Nasser sent in thousands of soldiers, some of them in his best regiments, to help the revolutionary cause. They became bogged down, with fatal consequences in 1967. Hussein sent some warplanes to Saudi Arabia to help the imam across the border, but the pilots of two of them flew to Cairo instead.

Hussein had no time to relax. A coup in Iraq on February 8th 1963 ousted the military ruler, Abdel Karim Qassem, and a coup on March 8th in Syria removed the separatists opposed to union with Egypt. Now Syria, Iraq and Egypt favoured a new union, and signed an agreement on April 17th. The house of Hashem seemed once again to be in mortal peril. It had to adapt to the new situation. (Hussein was not to know, although he might have guessed, that the union would quickly collapse.)

The king moved swiftly. On March 27th, he asked al-Tall, an outspoken critic of the earlier United Arab Republic and cheer-leader when it failed, to resign as prime minister and replaced him with the familiar and capable Samir al-Rifai, who formed his sixth and last cabinet. It contained the usual mix of loyal notables. Hussein himself adopted a much milder and more respectful tone towards Egypt and Syria.

It was not enough. Demonstrations in favour of Arab unity erupted in half a dozen towns including Jerusalem. At Amman University, angry students burnt the Jordanian flag. Elsewhere, demonstrators turned on Hussein. Once again, voices were heard predicting the imminent downfall of the Hashemites. However, although he was only 27 years old, Hussein had faced trouble on the streets before and knew what to do: he called out the troops and the demonstrations stopped.

Next, he had to deal with his uppity new parliament. In the debate on a vote of confidence, a majority denounced his new prime minister, Samir al-Rifai. The call was for "another type of government, with another mentality, to enter into immediate negotiations with Cairo, Damascus and Baghdad, to join the new Union". The old pro did not wait for the final vote. He resigned, and Hussein defiantly replaced him with a family member: Sharif Hussein bin Nasser, his great-uncle. Sharif Hussein would not win a vote of confidence but he could clear the way for a new election, which was held on July 6th. It was unlike al-Tall's free election and more akin to the previous one, where the local authorities did the necessary arm-twisting. The result: a tame assembly.

Israel was pleased. Like Hussein, its rulers worried about being surrounded by united Arabs. If Jordan descended into chaos and seemed ready to join the new union, the Israelis had their contingency plan ready to occupy the West Bank. It was called Plan Granite.[2] Some parts of this plan were to be used in 1967.

Later in 1963, Hussein adopted his grandfather's policy. Like King Abdullah, Hussein kept channels open with Israel through secret meetings. One was opened in London in September, when Hussein talked with Yacov Herzog, a specialist on the Middle East in the office of the prime minister, Levi Eshkol. The distinguished Israeli historian Uriel Dann reports that this meeting was followed by one with Golda Meir, then foreign minister.[3] (Mrs Meir was one of the first Israelis to secretly meet King Abdullah before 1948.) In his clandestine contacts, Hussein did not start to negotiate the big issues, such as a final settlement of frontiers or the fate of the Palestinian refugees. But he did make at least two secret agreements: on use of the waters of the Jordan and Yarmuk rivers (in 1965); and on limiting the deployment of recently acquired American Patton tanks to the East Bank, as a confidence-building measure.

There followed a quiet period. Jordan's neighbours were more interested in their own affairs than in Jordan's. Nasser was busy in Yemen and in organizing an Arab summit, supposedly to take action against Israel's diversions of part of the flow of the Jordan and Yarmuk rivers. This was held in Cairo on January 13th 1964, and achieved little. The Arabs sought unity and again it proved elusive. A "unified command" was created and an Egyptian general was put in charge, but it was all on paper; nothing practical was done to implement it. Only in 1973 would the Arabs have a coherent fighting force. The summit also established the Arab Jordan Diversion Authority, a meaningless agency since the Arabs had no official contact with the country diverting the water.

Its third decision was thoroughly dangerous for Jordan and Hussein in the medium term. The summit approved the organization of the Palestinians so that they could "play a role in liberating their country and deciding its future". The fact that the Palestinians already had a government and a voice – in Jordan – was ignored: Arab leaders had always considered Jordan to lack legitimacy and tried to ignore it wherever possible. The summit members allowed a Palestinian leader, Ahmed Shukairy, to take part in the proceedings. The seeds of a long struggle for power in Palestine were sown. This was a historic blunder by the Arabs, born of their suspicion of the Hashemites.

Aware of his low standing, Hussein resolved to establish a better relationship with Nasser, who was still the dominant figure in the Arab world. In return for Egypt re-opening diplomatic relations with Jordan, the king released several political prisoners such as ex-General Abu Nuwar, who had opposed him in the incident at Zarqa, and Abdullah al-Tall, who had betrayed King Abdullah's contacts with Israel and was said to have conspired to kill him. Jordan switched allies in Yemen and backed the Nasserite regime. (The king also added some sheen to his reputation by being received in 1964 by the American and French presidents, Lyndon B. Johnson and Charles de Gaulle.)

Nasser may have gained some lustre from these Jordanian concessions and Hussein may have gained status in Arab eyes, but a much bigger issue had been posed: who would represent the Palestinians? Would it be Ahmed Shukairy, a voluble, volatile and abrasive figure, who was leader of the Palestine Liberation Organization (PLO), then a modest, embryonic group. He attended the summit as the Palestinian representative on the Arab League's council. Shukairy was in the habit of delivering long-winded off-the-cuff and inflammatory speeches.

The Cairo summit having given him the green light, Shukairy set about organizing the PLO with vigour. Since this was the wish of the summit, albeit an interference in the internal affairs of Jordan, there was not much that Hussein could do about it. He accepted the decision, but he was certainly not about to promote an alternative source of power in his own country.

Shukairy did his best to reassure him. "The emanation of the Palestinian entity in Jerusalem does not aim at carving the West Bank from the Hashemite kingdom of Jordan," he said when the PLO was founded in 1964 at a congress in Jerusalem. "We are in no way touching on the Jordan entity." Hussein was unlikely to swallow that. However, he welcomed the PLO in a personal appearance at the congress. He would not lay himself open to criticism for failing to help the Palestinians. He could afford to make a generous gesture: after all, he held power. Nonetheless, a fatal split was being created. It would only benefit the Israelis.

After the summit, Hussein veered away from Nasser again, perhaps under the influence of Wasfi al-Tall, whom he had again appointed as prime minister in February 1965. Moving closer to Saudi Arabia, he signed a border agreement in which the Saudis formally agreed for the first time that Jordan had a right to a strip of coastline at the head of the Gulf of Aqaba. A grateful Hussein promptly called for the convening of an Islamic summit in Mecca (and not Cairo). When Tunisia's president, Habib Bourguiba, called on Arab states to recognize Israel on the understanding that the Palestinian refugees would be allowed to return home, Nasser led the ostracism of the Arab world. Hussein, who had greeted Bourguiba on a visit to Amman just before his declaration, avoided the issue. When West Germany recognised Israel and Arab states withdrew their ambassadors from Bonn, however, Hussein felt impelled to do likewise, albeit reluctantly.

At this point in his reign, in the mid-1960s, where did Hussein stand? First, he had become a past master in the art of survival with the help of the armed forces, the security service and notables who took pride in holding high office. Second, he well understood his weakness as the head of state of a small and poor land whose legitimacy was widely doubted. He realized that, at times, he had to change tack abruptly. Third, although he presented himself, probably genuinely, as a fervent anti-Communist and democrat, he was disillusioned by democracy. The two free elections that he had tolerated had brought hostile majorities to the lower house of parliament and eventually he had dismissed them. The other elections were firmly controlled.

What drove the young king? Sheer will-power and a sense of authority made him determined not to be ousted, or even bested, by Nasser or his cohorts in Syria. Stronger even than this was a determination to consolidate the house of Hashem so that its sons did not suffer the fate of his great-grandfather, King Hussein of the Hejaz, who was ousted from his throne, or his grandfather, King Abdullah of Jordan, and his cousin, King Feisal of Iraq, both assassinated; he wanted them to have worthy successors.

For the Hashemites to survive, the successor to Hussein would have to be not only a canny operator but also a man with a will of steel and a deep understanding of Arab history and politics. In 1965, Hussein's half-British first son, Crown Prince Abdullah, was three years old. If Hussein was assassinated, there would inevitably be a long transition that the Hashemites might not survive. At the same time there was one member of the family who was highly intelligent, strong-willed, all-Arab and 18 years old: Hussein's brother Hassan. On April 1st Hussein appointed Hassan as crown prince and his successor in the place of his own son. It was a possibly unique act by a ruler who put his dynasty before his immediate family. It was, in effect, an insurance policy. It also had an unexpected outcome: by 1996, the brothers had formed a well-established team and worked on the Jordan-Israel peace treaty together.

During this period a new threat to the Hashemites loomed. The PLO was growing. Other Arab states supported it, firstly out of genuine feelings of solidarity but secondly because it might serve as a Trojan horse in Amman. Arab leaders in Egypt, Syria, Saudi Arabia and Iraq would rejoice to see Hussein brought down.

The king might have been able to keep the residents of the West Bank and East Jerusalem under control but he could not control the flamboyant Shukairy. So he simply withheld co-operation wherever possible. Thus when Shukairy thanked governments which had allowed units of the Palestine Liberation Army to train on its territory, he pointedly failed to mention Jordan. It would have been foolhardy for the king to allow PLO units to train in Jordan. They would be out of control and their raids on Israel could cause endless trouble along what was mostly a quiet Israel-Jordan border.

The king needed a firmer hand at the tiller than that of his prime minister, Bahjat al-Talhuni, and he brought back Wasfi al-Tall in

February 1965. The firmer hand was evident when Hussein spelled out his position in October. The PLO was welcome in Jordan provided that it submitted to Jordanian authority. PLO leaders were welcome, but in top positions in the Jordanian government or army. "No organization should act outside the framework of the United Arab Command," the king said. (The PLO was not a member; Jordan was.)

At the same time, Hussein and al-Tall were being conciliatory to non-PLO people. In March 1965 the government said it had burnt 2,000 general intelligence dossiers (having presumably made copies of them beforehand). In April it announced an amnesty.

As Hussein's relations with the PLO worsened, Shukairy's demands grew. He insisted on the right to recruit fighters freely in Jordan and said the Jordanian government should deduct 6 per cent of Palestinians' salaries and hand the money to him. An agreement of sorts was cobbled together in Cairo in March 1966: PLO volunteers could train at Jordanian army summer camps and a tax levy of up to two per cent would be raised on Palestinians; Amman Radio would dedicate one hour a day to the PLO. Result: the king kept control but the PLO expanded in Jordan. This was, however, just a stage in a process. The PLO would come back, asking for more.

To Hussein, it had become the enemy. So he dropped his policy of guarded willingness to co-operate in favour of confrontation. "Be the hand cut off that menaces the integrity of Jordan," he declared on June 14th 1966. As for co-operation with the PLO, "all hopes have vanished". The description of this speech by the British ambassador, reporting back to London, shows how far Hussein had developed. "I cannot recall any Arab spokesman having delivered such courageous and outspoken sentiments and lived," he wrote. "By any standard it was a remarkable performance. The king scarcely drew a breath for nearly an hour, and never once hesitated or lost his way."[4] To this speech Shukairy responded that Jordan had no right to exist and Jordanians should revolt against their rulers.

The government banned the holding of elections to the PLO's national council, which clearly had the potential of becoming a popular state within a state in Jordan. The upshot of these moves was that

Hussein still held the upper hand and the PLO was in retreat. When Shukairy rashly called on Palestinian members of Hussein's cabinet to resign, none did. Negotiations between al-Tall and Shukairy over the PLO's hopes for an independent set-up in Jordan went on for months to no avail: al-Tall made no major concessions although an "agreement" was approved. The PLO was to be given air-time on Jordan Radio.

Earlier, another related crisis had loomed. On November 11th 1965 guerrillas of the Syria-based Fatah faction of the PLO, encouraged by the radical government in Syria, crossed the Israeli border and planted a mine, killing three Israeli soldiers. In their customary response, the Israeli armed forces demolished a Jordanian village, Samu, and killed 21 people. Many Palestinians, egged on by Egyptian diplomats and by Cairo Radio, blamed Hussein for failing to retaliate and preserve Arab honour.

What was Israel up to? Certainly it was applying its rule of revenge after being attacked: ten eyes for an eye. Hussein thought there was more. "There is a feeling in Jordan that what Israel wants is war and expansion," he said. "My own feeling is that Israel wants the collapse of this country because the people who would benefit would be the left-wing elements. This is what Israel is after. If this did happen, the Palestine problem would no longer be a dispute between the Arabs and Jews but between the western and eastern blocs."

Bravely and sensibly, the king recognized the limits of his armed forces and refused to order a retaliation which he knew would only escalate the conflict disastrously. Unfortunately, this policy played straight into the hands of the radicals.

The Americans were worried. "The sizeable infrastructure which the United Arab Republic [Egypt and Syria] has built up in Jordan is beginning to swing into action now," the CIA station chief in Amman reported back to Langley, Virginia. "The UAR will probably seek to pull down Hussein in spite of the possible repercussions in Israel."[5]

The king was quoted as saying that morale in the army was "frankly bad". The commander of an armoured brigade told the visiting American senator, Edward Kennedy, that the army was sick of being called upon to put down demonstrations. A British Foreign Office mandarin, in a secret minute, wrote: "King Hussein and his government are fighting for survival more seriously now than at any time since 1958."[6] Talking to Amman-based correspondents, the king described the PLO as "an instrument being used to destroy us".

Demonstrations were held in Nablus, Jenin, Qalqilya, Ramallah and in the capital. They were put down by the army and police. In Nablus, demonstrations began on the morning of November 21st. Thousands of students and workers marched through the main streets, shouting in favour of Nasser and Shukairy, trampling underfoot pictures of King Hussein and calling for a republic. The demonstrators blocked many streets with old tyres and barrels and even had a mock funeral of the king. Although the main police station was surrounded by demonstrators, some of whom were armed, the police stood fast and obeyed orders not to fire.

By 10 am, according to the British ambassador, "the situation seemed to be getting rapidly out of control". The demonstrators began firing at random; three civilians were killed by ricocheting bullets. Then the demonstrators began looting shops, including one belonging to the mayor and one selling arms and ammunition. Then troops arrived, a 24-hour curfew was imposed – and obeyed – and the ringleaders were arrested. Al-Tall said, with a touch of arrogance, he had "dealt with Nablus for the next ten years".[7]

On November 23rd, demonstrators in Jerusalem threw stones at the police, who responded with tear-gas. "Old hands, British and Arab, say the situation on the West Bank is the worst they have known since the establishment of Israel," the British consul in Jerusalem told the Foreign Office. "The lid is off pent-up emotions. The king is in a corner and the broadcasts from other Arab states calling for his elimination are having an effect." The consul was wrong: the demonstrations were put down successfully. Once again, Hussein had survived. However, the British ambassador in Amman was right when discussing the root of the problem: "What we are witnessing seems to be the result of a signal failure over years by the Amman government to understand the West Bank's special requirements and also the rise of the second generation of refugees, more indoctrinated than their fathers."

It had helped that the deputy commander of the army was none other than Sharif Nasser bin Jamil, although he had recently been in hot water with his nephew. A report in Amman said the king was "thoroughly fed up with Sharif Nasser's arms and drugs smuggling activities and is determined to put a stop to them once and for all. The king has said that if Sharif Nasser fails to toe the line, he will have to go."[8] He toed the line, and was present at headquarters the following year when Egyptian generals led Jordan to disaster in the six-day war.

(Sharif Nasser was also in hot water at that time with Queen Zain, the queen mother. He married a Miss Hind Mango, a member of a well-known merchant family, some of whose members had been in political trouble. The king gave a reception in their honour at the Royal Guest Palace but the strong-minded Zain was furious at the marriage and refused to see Sharif Nasser or have any part in the ceremonies. Sharif Nasser shrugged his shoulders and took his bride on honeymoon to the Dorchester Hotel in London.)

The big issue being debated in Jordan was whether or not Israel should come under attack from Jordan-based guerrillas. To no avail, al-Tall argued that the United Arab Command, of which Jordan was a member, opposed acts of infiltration that might drag the Arabs into a premature war with Israel with disastrous results. Hussein urged that the authorization for a guerrilla attack in Israel should come from the United Arab Command and not from the guerrillas. If adopted, that idea would oblige all the Arabs to take part in a decision that would cause death and destruction in Jordan and possibly premature war.

Al-Tall asked which Arab "ally" had come to Jordan's aid when under Israeli attack and, in particular, why Egypt's air force had failed to provide air cover. Nasser answered that Hussein was "ready to sell the Arab nation".

Hussein answered his critics with an attack on Egypt that hit home. He pointed out that Egypt's frontier with Israel was unlike Jordan's. Since the Suez crisis, it had been patrolled by the UN, based on the Egyptian side. By this arrangement, sneered Amman Radio, the president of Egypt was contributing to Israeli border security while at the same time sheltering the Egyptian armed forces under the UN umbrella.

Even worse, Nasser had deprived Egypt of the opportunity to close the Gulf of Aqaba, and the Israeli port of Eilat, to Israel-bound shipping by allowing the UN to occupy a post overlooking the Strait of Tiran at the opening of the gulf.

The insult hurt because it was true. The fact that Egypt and the UN were sensibly co-operating to preserve a tenuous peace was disregarded. The king and his propagandists on Amman Radio had hit a raw nerve: Nasser was exposed as a hypocrite. These taunts were to contribute to Egypt's rash decision that led the Arabs to disaster in 1967.

Life was not all hard work and worry, however. At a party given by his brother, Prince Muhammad, in July, King Hussein was "entirely relaxed, in excellent humour, and stayed as is his custom until after 4 am".[9]

There were many sides to this royal personality. In a cable to London reporting on speculation about the possible appointment of a new prime minister, the British ambassador observed that "with someone as fickle as King Hussein, the tenure of any prime minister is bound to be precarious".

(The "fickle" aspect of Hussein had long been recognized by the notables. One of them, Samir al-Rifai, trying to cheer up Glubb Pasha after dismissing him in the name of the king, had told him: "I dare say it's only a temporary pause. Perhaps in a few days we'll be welcoming you back. I've been prime minister several times, then I have been dismissed, and now I'm back again!")[10]

By 1967 the king had survived his domestic troubles but was well aware that he was surrounded by enemies at home and in Egypt and Syria. He was vulnerable. If he gave the false impression that he was soft on Israel or a traitor to Arab nationalism he would be in deep trouble. On the other hand, if he was hard on Israel he would be the target of a massive Israeli retaliation. Logic suggested that he should cultivate allies among the conservative rulers of the Gulf states to offset the power of Nasser and Syria, and he toured the area. But *force majeure* intervened and the king suddenly became an ally of his old adversaries.

14 ON THE WAY TO WAR

The troubles rumbled on into 1967. In January the United States delivered arms and ammunition to Hussein by air, in what seems to have been a signal to the Israelis to lay off Jordan in any conflict that was to come. Angry with Nasser, Hussein in February withdrew his support for the republican government in Yemen which Nasser was supporting. A landmine killed an Israeli soldier. There were clashes on the Israeli-Syrian border. On April 7th Israeli jets shot down six Syrian MiGs over Mount Hermon. "Where were the Egyptians?" asked Amman Radio.

Israeli rhetoric sounded increasingly belligerent. The mild-mannered prime minister, Levi Eshkol, who wanted to prove he could be tough, threatened: "We shall hit them when, where and how we choose." The Israeli chief of staff, General Yitzhak Rabin, was reported in Cairo as having said on May 12th: "We will carry out a lightning attack on Syria, occupy Damascus, overthrow the regime there, and come back."[1] The slide to war had begun.

Egyptian and Syrian leaders became convinced that Israel was about to attack Syria. They were told by Soviet diplomats on May 8th of an Israeli build-up. An Egyptian parliamentary delegation in Moscow, led by Anwar Sadat, was given the same information. Nasser did not wish to be vulnerable to criticism that he was hiding behind the UN Expeditionary Force (UNEF): he promised that Egypt would come to Syria's aid if attacked. On May 14th, not to be outdone by Syria for pan-Arab militancy, Nasser mobilised the Egyptian armed forces. Five days later, mischievous Jordanian propagandists on Amman Radio suggested that if the hypocritical Nasser was serious about being tough with the Israelis, as he was saying Jordan should be, then he should close the Strait of Tiran at the opening of the Gulf of Aqaba. It was not serious: just part of the knockabout war of words between Amman and Cairo.

What followed was bizarre almost beyond belief. According to the account of the Egyptian foreign minister at the time, Mahmoud Riad, the first disastrous move was made by Field Marshal Abdel Hakim Amer, a vain and foolish man who was commander-general of the Egyptian armed forces. Amer seems to have had considerable freedom of action and was not entirely subordinate to Nasser.

On May 16th 1967 Amer, seeking to counteract Israeli pressure on Syria, "undertook an indiscreet and uncalculated measure", Riad wrote afterwards, with massive understatement.[2]

Amer instructed General Muhammad Fawzi, the chief of staff, to write to General Indar Jit Rikhye, the capable Indian commander of UNEF, at his headquarters in Gaza. By an Egyptian account, his message said: "Egyptian armed forces have been alerted for any action against Israel the moment it undertakes any hostile action against any Arab country.... . Our forces are massing in Sinai and along the eastern borders. To ensure the safety of the international force...I request that you give them orders to pull them back from these positions." A former senior UN official, Sir Brian Urquhart, gives another version. He says Fawzi wrote that "for the sake of complete security of UN troops which install observation posts along our borders" Rikhye should "issue your orders to withdraw all these troops immediately".

UNEF was established in 1956 after the disastrous Anglo-French-Israeli adventure at Suez. It had provided ten years of peace by keeping an eye on an agreed buffer-zone between the Egyptian and Israeli armies. But it consisted only of 1,400 lightly armed soldiers on a 300-mile front. Nonetheless, its permanence was taken for granted by the Western powers.

Riad in his memoirs wrote that he immediately saw the danger that a withdrawal of UNEF from Sharm el-Sheikh, at the entrance to the Gulf of Aqaba, would leave it in Egyptian hands and Egypt would feel free to close the gulf to Israeli shipping. It would be a *casus belli* for Israel. Fawzi claims that he himself wrote to the UN secretary-general, U Thant, specifying that UNEF should withdraw only from international borders and not from Sharm el-Sheikh, and that U Thant would not countenance a partial withdrawal. Urquhart's version is that Riad's request was for a withdrawal from Sinai in 24 hours and from Sharm el-Sheikh in 48 hours.

Riad claims that he was not consulted on so grave a decision and learnt about it only from a tip by General Fawzi. He does not say in what way Nasser became directly involved. It is hard to believe, however, that Amer did not consult Nasser before making his move.

Nasser became caught up in a war that he never intended to wage. Asked if he would leave Israel alone if not attacked, Nasser replied on June 2nd: "Yes, we will leave them alone. We have no intention of attacking Israel."[3] Hussein, writing two years later, said: "I don't think the Egyptian president wanted it to come to actual war. I even suspect that he didn't really believe war would break out. In my view it was inescapable."[4]

In any event, the crisis developed. Under intense international pressure, Nasser refused to back down (and lose face). He was possibly acting on Riad's bad advice (which the foreign minister later admitted) that there would be no conflict with Israel. On May 17th Egyptian troops occupied the buffer-zone between Egyptian and Israeli forces and entered Sharm el-Sheikh. U Thant left for Cairo on May 22nd, hoping to persuade Nasser to withdraw the letter.

On a stopover in Paris he was told that Egypt had closed the Strait of Tiran to Israeli shipping. In meetings with U Thant, Nasser would not withdraw his decisions but he insisted that Egypt would not fire the first shot against Israel. U Thant warned him of the potentially disastrous consequences of his action. Nasser would not listen. UNEF went home.

War was inevitable. The General Assembly, which had set up UNEF, had a pro-Nasser majority yet was not convened in a special session; the Security Council was deadlocked. U Thant suggested the installation of a UN force on Israel's side of the border; Israel turned the offer down.

Nasser was told by the UN there were no signs of a military buildup on the Syrian border. On May 19th UN observers along the Israeli-Syrian border reported on the "absence of troop concentrations and significant troop movements on both sides of the line". Israel invited anybody, including the Soviet ambassador, to inspect the area where the build-up was supposed to have been taking place (the ambassador refused). Nasser took the word of the KGB.

One explanation for Nasser's blunder was that Egyptian intelligence was incompetent. It failed to advise him of the striking power of Israel's armed forces. (Nasser was convinced that his Soviet MiGs and Sukhois would be the equal of Israel's aircraft and might even get the better of them.) It also failed to advise him that the Israelis were not massing for an attack on Syria. In a typical example of his rhetoric at the time, Nasser told a press conference on May 28th: "If the Israelis want war, then I say: go to it! We are ready!"

Another explanation, a Machiavellian one, is that Nasser may have fallen into a Soviet-Syrian trap. Both governments wanted Nasser to get a bloody nose: the Soviet Union hoped to make Nasser an ever more dependent client and Syria's leaders wanted to take Nasser down a peg or two. Neither expected Egypt to suffer anything worse than a bloody nose with the fight being stopped by the referee (the Security Council) in an early round – and certainly not by a knock-out.

A third explanation is that Nasser believed the propaganda of Field Marshal Amer and his publicists, who said war with Israel would be a walkover since the Egyptian armed forces were far superior to Israel's. Israel knew better. Its foreign minister, Abba Eban, promised that "Nasser would have the beating of his life". President Johnson, briefed by the CIA, thought Israel had nothing to fear.)

Jordan was caught in the maelstrom. By May 24th, when war seemed inevitable, Hussein took steps to participate in the general Arab mobilization and gave permission for Saudi and Iraqi troops to enter Jordanian territory. He had been given the same Soviet intelligence. Although war seemed imminent, the protagonists on the Arab side, Nasser and the Syrians apart, were not talking to each other.

Hussein's need for an understanding with Nasser as war approached did not prevent him from voicing some blunt views. "I am worried, really concerned," he said at a press conference on May 28th, "that Nasser and his command are extremely confident, happy with their preparations, and that if war did occur [they thought] there was nothing to worry about."[5]

Hussein took a disastrous initiative and asked Nasser if he could go to Cairo to see him. "Come as soon as you can," came the reply. On May 30th, a day after receiving the message, Hussein flew to Cairo accompanied by his prime minister, Sa'ad Jumaa, Major-General Amer Khammash, his deputy chief of staff, and Saleh Kurdi, his air force commander. Wasfi al-Tall and Sharif Nasser bin Jamil, hard-headed voices of common sense to whom the king would have listened, were not on board.

For most of the journey to Cairo, Hussein piloted the Caravelle airliner himself. He would have done better to have reflected quietly on what he intended to do. Reason took second place to *machismo*.

At the airfield, contrasting attitudes to the imminence of war were obvious. Hussein wore his military uniform showing his self-appointed rank of field marshal. He had an American 357 Beretta revolver with six automatic barrels in a canvas holster fixed to his belt on the left hip. Nasser was wearing a well-cut civilian suit.

The Egyptian president asked Hussein if he wanted his arrival to be photographed or kept secret. The king replied that the secret would soon become public knowledge. The two adversaries thereupon gave each other a bear-hug for the waiting photographers.

"I see you are armed and in uniform," Nasser observed.

"We have been dressing this way for more than a week," Hussein replied.

"Since your visit is a secret, what would happen if we arrested you?" asked Nasser, seemingly in jest.

"The possibility never entered my mind," the king responded.

For six hours the two delegations conferred. Nasser told Hussein that the United Arab Command was dead and he was dealing with Syria, the other directly interested party, under the terms of a bilateral treaty. Hussein proposed that this treaty be used as a model for an Egyptian-Jordanian pact: "Jordan" could be substituted for "Syria" throughout the text. Nasser agreed, functionaries were set to work, and the two men signed the agreement. Then Hussein, evidently under Nasser's charismatic influence, did a most extraordinary thing: he agreed to place the

Jordanian armed forces under the command of an Egyptian general, Abdel Monem Riad, deputy chief of staff of the defunct United Arab Command. Nasser and Hussein spoke to Iraq's strongman, General Abdel Rahman Aref, by telephone and he promised to send help, including tanks, to Jordan. Hussein was, by these acts, accepted back in the Arab fold. But the welcome was temporary and the price was astronomical.

While discussions were proceeding, Nasser unexpectedly produced an oddly dishevelled Ahmed Shukairy from a back room. The PLO leader, who had been spewing poison about Hussein and had been expelled from Jordan to the Gaza strip, greeted the king in a servile, gushing manner. Nasser promptly announced that Hussein would be taking Shukairy back to Amman with him and could throw him into jail if he felt so inclined. Hussein unhappily concurred. The king returned to Amman the same day, and Shukairy was seen leaving the Caravelle and smiling happily. Some observers said this was the price Nasser had exacted for the treaty. Hussein released PLO and Fatah detainees and allowed Shukairy to reopen his office in Jerusalem.

What were Hussein's motives? The king took the view that if war broke out, the Israelis would try to grab the West Bank whether or not Jordan fought with Egypt and Syria. It made sense, therefore, to hope that three armed forces – Egyptian, Syrian and Jordanian – fighting on three fronts would somehow hold off one force on its own. But Jordan's land forces were modest: the army had only two tank brigades with some 170 tanks and only six infantry brigades with some 20,000 men.

Second, Hussein thought an alliance with Egypt should have provided crucial Egyptian air cover to supplement Jordan's tiny air force, comprising 22 Hawker Hunters (Israel had roughly 200 warplanes).

Third, Hussein thought he could not stay out of a war waged by the Arabs against the Jews. Had he done so and survived, while Egypt and Syria were defeated, he would have been branded as a traitor to the Arab cause. He would have been boycotted by many Arab leaders, and denounced by the Palestinians (whom he would have saved from Israeli occupation). Many Arabs would have drawn comparisons with his grandfather, King Abdullah, who had been criticized for seeking self-aggrandisement in 1948 in league with the Jews by taking control of the West Bank. Hussein listened to the street and knew pro-war feeling was running high. Ordinary Jordanians felt they had been humiliated enough by Israel, their ruthless and better armed neighbour. If Hussein stayed out of the war, by invitation of Israel, the anger of the street would be turned on him.

However, if the Arabs were defeated, as Hussein expected, and the Jordanian front was seen to have been commanded by an Egyptian general (not a Hashemite one) in an alliance with Nasser, the threat to the royal family's survival would be much diminished.

Fourth, the former Harrow schoolboy and Sandhurst cadet with his English wife was a true believer *in extremis* in Arab unity and felt in his heart that the Hashemites had to support and defend it.

Hussein seems to have adopted a fatalistic approach. When UNEF withdrew from Gaza, he said: "To me it was obvious: war with Israel was inevitable." But what kind of war? "We Jordanians tried to pull our weight as a diversion, thus minimizing the damage when war came," Hussein said later. "We had no hope of winning."[6]

What kind of diversion? The idea, as agreed with Egypt, was that, at the outset of war, Jordan would adopt a defensive posture, keeping a good part of the Israeli army in place and unable to go to Egyptian and Syrian fronts. Its posture was to change only after the arrival of reinforcements – troops, tanks and aircraft – from Saudi Arabia, Iraq and Syria and positive information that the Egyptian forces were advancing as planned. Thereafter, Jordan would go on the offensive. That meant at first little more than a joint artillery and air operation to put Israeli airfields out of action plus a few operations behind Israeli lines.[7]

If the war developed, the Jordanians were to occupy Mount Scopus, in the Israeli-held part of Jerusalem, and to try to cut off Jerusalem from the rest of Israel. But the king must have hoped that the war would not reach such a point before the Security Council intervened and ordered a ceasefire. He knew better than anyone what Israeli revenge meant. But Jordan's war turned out to be no diversion.

Dean Rusk, then American secretary of state, wrote: "We tried hard to persuade Hussein not to become embroiled in the fighting, but he said: 'I am an Arab and I have to take part.' As an Arab he felt honour-bound to assist Egypt, especially since Israel struck first. I think we could have got the Israelis to stay their hand. But Hussein insisted on getting into it. It was one of the saddest moments of this crisis."[8] Israel's prime minister, Levi Eshkol, "urged King Hussein to stay out, but to no avail", the former prime minister, Shimon Peres, wrote.[9]

At home, many voices urged Hussein to hold back and observe events. His uncle, Sharif Nasser bin Jamil, deputy commander-in-chief, appealed to him to stay his hand. Wasfi al-Tall, still an influential figure although out of office, urged the king to wait and see what happened to air cover. Al-Tall believed an alliance with Egypt and Syria would lead to disaster. He knew the Jordanian armed forces were in a defensive posture and not geared up to attack Israel. If they had been, they would still have been too small and would have anyway lacked air cover from Jordan's tiny air force. Al-Tall was one of the few outspoken Jordanian leaders not to be taken in by the boasts of Field Marshal Amer about his arms, aircraft, tanks, artillery and (non-functioning) missiles. He had not forgotten that Egypt's best-trained army and air force units were far away in Yemen.

There were other negative signals. The United Arab Command was dead. Egypt, Syria and Jordan had never worked together. Communications were negligible. There were no arrangements for re-supply. There were no contingency plans. The king knew this from his capable army chief of staff, Major-General Khammash, who had visited Cairo.

But the trend was to side with Nasser and Syria, regardless of their vicious attacks on Hussein. Jordan had broken diplomatic relations with Syria after a lorry packed with dynamite exploded at a Jordanian border post on May 21st, killing 21 people.

Zeid al-Rifai, who later became prime minister of Jordan, caught the mood: "There was a war fever prevalent in Jordan and throughout the Arab world…a mass euphoria about the possibility of war and that this was something we had been waiting for for a long time," he said later. "We were going to defeat Israel once and for all."

It is possible that Hussein's agreement with Nasser may have helped the Israeli cabinet, after several votes and anxious debates, to decide to go to war. On May 27th the vote was 9-9. A new, harder-line national government, including Menachem Begin and Moshe Dayan, was formed on June 1st: the new majority favoured war. On the same day in Jordan, the Egyptian General Riad arrived from Cairo to take up command of an armed force and a terrain with which he was entirely unfamiliar, on the brink of war. It was madness.

On June 5th Israel attacked, ferociously and effectively. "Fighting broke out in Jerusalem where Jordanian forces moved forward despite our efforts to persuade Jordan, in its own interests, to stay out of the battle," Urquhart writes. "The Israelis had authorised our [UN] military representatives in Jerusalem to assure Jordan that there would be no fighting in Jerusalem if Jordan did not attack." By answering Nasser's call to join the battle, "Jordan lost, almost at one stroke, Arab Jerusalem and the West Bank, thus creating a problem which the world has been grappling with ever since."[10]

15   DISASTER

Blunders committed by Egyptian generals during the six-day war were of such a magnitude that they are hard to believe. It was not surprising that Field Marshal Amer, the man principally responsible for the disaster apart from Nasser, was reported to have committed suicide afterwards.

On June 3rd Hussein was advised by the Turkish ambassador that Israel would start the war with an attack on Egyptian air bases on June 5th or 6th. The Iraqi ambassador gave Hussein similar information. This tallied with his own intelligence reports. All the information was sent to Cairo. "We expect such an attack and are ready," came the reply.[1]

On June 5th, Amer inexplicably withdrew air cover over military airfields, flew to a base in Sinai on a routine inspection tour and, to ensure that his aircraft was not shot down by his own side, ordered the air force not to engage in action. The air defence system was shut down. Army field commanders were called to the base to meet the field marshal.

Amazingly, Egyptian military codes were changed on June 5th and two urgent messages, one of them from General Riad in Amman, informing Cairo that attacks had started and the Israeli air force was on its way to Egyptian airbases, went unheeded firstly because they took time to decode and secondly because there was nobody in headquarters to act on them.[2]

At about 7 am on June 5th, the Israeli air force swung into the Mediterranean and moved in on its Egyptian targets from the west, flying low to avoid detection by radar. The operation was a total success: Egypt's air force was destroyed and Israeli warplanes proceeded to cripple the Egyptian army and put it to flight.

Egypt treated Jordan abominably. At about 9–10 am, Field Marshal Amer told Amman that Egyptian jets had downed 75 per cent of the Israeli air force and the Egyptian army was advancing into Israel. Amer ordered General Riad to launch offensive operations from Jordan forthwith. By the time that Hussein arrived at his headquarters, the Egyptian general had ordered Jordanian artillery to start firing at Israeli airfields, itself a *casus belli*. At midday, Nasser repeated Amer's lies and urged Hussein to seize as much Israeli land as he could before the Security Council brought fighting to a halt on the night of June 5th, as he expected it would.[3]

Did Nasser know Egypt was finished on the morning of June 5th and want to bring down Jordan as well, by pressing Hussein to provoke Israel into seizing the West Bank? Anwar Sadat said Nasser knew the scale of the disaster on the morning of June 5th because he saw him at GHQ with a dazed and despairing Amer.

Hussein believed what he was told about the Egyptian air force's success because his radar showed many aircraft flying from Egypt to Israel. The king assumed they were Egyptian aircraft on bombing missions in Israel; in fact they were Israeli jets, returning home after completing their missions successfully. To all intents and purposes, the war was over. But the king of Jordan did not know it.

Jordan's war on the ground started at about 9 am when Riad sent out orders to field commanders to go on the offensive and, in some cases, to leave entrenched positions to co-ordinate Jordan's movements with supposed movements by the Egyptian army. Jordanian generals at headquarters, including Sharif Nasser bin Jamil, and field commanders were appalled. For years they had planned their strategy on the assumption that their tiny army and air force, no match for Israel's, would be used only for defence except for Operation Tariq. Hussein described Jordan's concept of its role as a diversion to hold down some Israeli forces while the main event, war between Egypt and Israel, unfolded.

The idea of Operation Tariq was for Jordan to seize Mount Scopus, a vulnerable piece of Israeli territory jutting into Arab East Jerusalem, and to use it as a base for a lunge around Jewish West Jerusalem, cutting it off from the rest of Israel. If Jordanian forces could hold their defensive positions and carry out Operation Tariq, they would have done their duty by the Arabs and been in a good bargaining position during the inevitable negotiations following a ceasefire that would be ordered by the Security Council. Even if Operation Tariq failed, they would stand a good chance of holding on to their defensive positions (assuming that Egypt provided its promised air cover).

But it was not to be. Riad's troop movements meant it would be impossible to carry out Operation Tariq, which needed a concentration of forces near Jerusalem, or its long planned defence.

At GHQ, arguments raged and insults flew thick and fast, but General Riad, with his five-day experience of Jordan, felt sure that he knew best. So he used his senior rank as commander of the eastern front and prevailed over his Jordanian hosts. Riad appeared to take orders only from Cairo and advice only from the five Egyptian staff officers who had accompanied him from Cairo. He communicated with Cairo by radio-telephone or by telegrams sent by public telegraph. Both were, of course, monitored by Israel.

At about 11.30 am, General Uzi Narkiss, commander of Israel's eastern front, asked permission to attack Jordan. He was refused. He asked again at 11.50 am and 12.10 pm but it was only after his fourth request, at 12.30 pm, that his civilian masters authorized air attacks on Jordanian targets. At about 11.50 am, 16 Jordanian Hawker Hunters bombed three military airfields but found hardly any planes on the ground to destroy (they were busy bombing Egypt). Why only 16 Hunters when 22 were available? Because Jordan had only 16 pilots capable of flying Hunters available in Amman: there were more, it was said, on courses abroad. It was a pathetic excuse given the time that Jordan had had to prepare itself for war.

At about the same time as Israel's army and air force were smashing Egypt's in the Sinai desert, Levi Eshkol, Israel's prime minister, handed a message for King Hussein to the UN intermediary, General Odd Bull. "We shall not initiate any action whatsoever against Jordan," Eshkol wrote. "However, should Jordan open hostilities, we shall resist with all our might and King Hussein will have to bear the consequences." Hussein, swept up in the Arab euphoria, replied: "They started the battle, and now they are receiving our reply by air."[4]

Brave rhetoric, but the fact was that Hussein's air force had been delayed in leaving on its mission of bombing Israeli airfields by the failure of the Syrian and Iraqi air forces to join it on time. It could have taken off earlier and hit Israeli aircraft on the ground preparing for take-off. As it was, the Hunters completed an unsuccessful mission and returned to base for refuelling just as the Israeli air force, having finished off the Egyptian air force, was ready to do the same to the Jordanian one. By 2.30 pm, the Israelis had completed the job, also managing to destroy Syrian and Iraqi jets at the base known as H3. Two Israeli Mystères, their job done, peeled off and bombed Hussein's palace.

Thus far, it was an unequal tit-for-tat: each side had bombed the other's airfield and the Israelis had made a better job of it. The earlier shelling ordered by General Riad had little effect. Up to 2.30 pm, General Narkiss had not been given the go-ahead for a general offensive against Jordan – just an attack on its air force. It still seemed possible to avoid utter disaster.

But by 1.30 pm, on the orders of General Riad and to the despair of Jordanian staff officers, Jordanian soldiers in Jerusalem took control of Government House, in the Israeli part of the city. The Jordanians were immediately outnumbered and forced out by the Israelis, suffering heavy casualties.

It seems to have been another *casus belli*. By this time the Israelis thought they had been sufficiently patient with the king. At 2.30 pm on June 5th, General Narkiss was authorized to begin a general offensive. Helped by air supremacy, Israel's army, better equipped and trained than Jordan's and easily outnumbering it, swept to victory. By the evening of June 7th, Israel controlled the West Bank.

Where was the 32-year-old king during the fighting? Only at times was he in his GHQ. He was not in command: he had delegated control over Jordan's destiny to an ill-informed and amazingly laid-back Egyptian general. Hussein may have felt he lacked the necessary experience or wanted to avoid the blame for failure. By one account, he paid many visits to troops in the field and did not sleep during the conflict. He was described as haggard and red-eyed.[5] Maybe. But should he not have been permanently at his command post, and should he not have countermanded General Riad's disastrous orders on the advice of his own commanders?

Hussein said afterwards that he would never forget the "hallucinating sight" of defeat: roads clogged with trucks, jeeps and all kinds of vehicles, twisted, dented, disembowelled, some still smoking. "I came out of it all desperately tired and discouraged," he said afterwards. "It was all too hard, to painful."[6]

He came close to death on one occasion when standing near a road bridge when an Israeli jet swooped to demolish it. He kept in touch with his wife, Muna, by telephone. She did her duty by looking after the family at home and asking her husband for nothing.

When the time came to admit defeat, the king made a point of deferring to Nasser and Field Marshal Amer. In a telephone call on the morning of June 6th, the king obtained the advice of Nasser. The Egyptian leader suggested asking General Riad to report on Jordan's dire position to the field marshal and to seek his advice. Hussein did this; he also sent a telegram to Nasser asking for his advice as well. Both Amer and Nasser replied in the evening of June 6th, recommending withdrawal.

"Our front is crumbling too," said Nasser. "I think that our only chance now is to evacuate the West Bank of the Jordan tonight and hope that the Security Council will order a ceasefire....Your courage and tenacity will be remembered.... . The heroic Jordanian people went into battle without hesitation... . We appreciate your heroic behaviour."

The king was covered. It was a disaster, but Hussein was not officially responsible. He could point the finger at Nasser. For the survival of the Hashemites, this was the least bad solution.

On June 7th, Israel's defence minister, Moshe Dayan, replied with contempt to Jordan's request for a ceasefire. "We have been offering the king an opportunity to cut his losses since Monday morning," Dayan said. "Now we have 500 dead and injured in Jerusalem. So tell him that from now on, I'll talk to him only with the gunsight of our tanks."

Looking back, Hussein could draw conclusions from his failure. First, do not trust your supposed allies. Syria, which helped to foment the war, Iraq and Saudi Arabia contributed next to nothing: all three may well have been pleased to see Hussein humiliated. Second, do nothing without air power. Third, do not put a foreigner in charge of your troops. Fourth, assign a trusted staff officer to your ally's HQ to report on it (nobody in Amman knew what was going on in Cairo). And fifth, employ a UN ambassador who obeys orders (Jordan's ambassador refused to press the Security Council urgently for a ceasefire, as requested by Amman: he believed Egypt's propaganda about victory and thought he knew better than his own government).

Then there was the question: why does a country risk everything and fight a war it knows it cannot win? In this case it was for political reasons and because of the king's own personal convictions.

Hussein felt he had to be fighting for the Arabs – but how hard? Enough to convince the Arabs, and especially his Palestinian adversaries, that here was a fighter for the cause. But did he have to fight so hard as to provoke the Israelis into a general offensive? It might have been enough for him to fire some artillery shells in the direction of some Israeli airfields and cause some trouble on the border, perhaps even launch Operation Tariq – and wait.

Had he waited a day, he would at least have picked up hints of the destruction of Egypt's air force and the failure of its land offensive and realised what a deceitful game his supposed allies, Nasser and the Syrians, were playing. He would have realized he had little or no air cover or ground support and so had a good case for inaction to put to public opinion.

Assuming that an able Jordanian general was in charge, would the outcome have been different? Probably. A general who knew the terrain and the Jordanian armed forces might have kept to the well-established defence plans and might even have carried off Operation Tariq successfully. Assuming Israeli air superiority, the Jordanian army would eventually have had to withdraw, but not in the rout ordered by General Riad. Much would have depended on when Israel would have felt obliged to heed a Security Council order for a ceasefire. For the Jordanians, the longer they hung on, the better the terms of the ceasefire would have been.

Perhaps the best judgment is that of history. The one certainty is that the Hashemites survived the setback. When this book was being written 30 years later, Hussein was still king. In a speech in 1997, Hussein said:

> *Thirty years ago I lived through the most difficult days of my life. All the Arab countries' preparations for war at the time were mere propaganda, mere talk over the radio and in the press, not based on facts in any way. On that day, I had to choose, and to show Jordan's commitment to defending the nation in the face of danger. It was clear that we all had to rise in the face of danger, defend our nation, carry out our duty and honour our pledges. There was a struggle over taking a decision on this matter because had we decided to avoid entering the battle, the country would have faced an explosion at the internal level at the hands of the old school of out-bidding, of bragging about imaginary acts of heroism and bravery. Such elements, some of whom are perhaps still lurking amongst us, tend to disappear once they are called on to do service to their country at the time of need.[7]*

As the dust settled, the losses were counted. Seven hundred Jordanian soldiers had been killed and 6,000 were wounded or missing. There was an influx of Palestinian refugees from the West Bank to what was left of Jordan on the East Bank. They were eventually put in 11 camps where they nurtured their hatred of Israel and of their host, King Hussein. Few army units were functioning. More than 170 tanks were lost. The air force was annihilated: all 22 Hawker Hunters were gone. The economy, which had been doing very nicely thanks to the entrepreneurial spirit of the West Bankers, was crippled. Income from tourism to the Holy Land was halted. The supply of the West Bank's farm produce was cut off. Tax revenues were probably halved. (Israel's losses were officially put at 679 dead and 2,563 wounded.)

Jordan and Egypt also suffered an intangible loss: that of the sympathy of the non-Communist world. In the eyes of Westerners, the Arabs were in the wrong. They had refused Israeli offers of negotiation, threatened Israel repeatedly, provoked the war by closing the Gulf of Tiran, formed a military pact to drive Israel into the sea, and were perceived to deserve their punishment. Israel had a glowing reputation, especially among Westerners who felt a collective guilt for Nazi Germany's gas-chambers. This reputation was enhanced by the brilliant performance of Israel's armed forces, commanded by General Yitzhak Rabin. Subsequently, however, that changed as Israel's occupation of the West Bank placed it in the role of colonial master, with dire consequences.)

Hussein and Nasser added to the ignominy by accusing the United States and Britain of having taken part in the Israeli air attack on Egyptian airbases. The two men discussed what they would say in public during a radio-telephone conversation that was monitored by the Israelis and published.

For Nasser there was no defence: he had reports from his own airbases and knew the allegation was a lie. Hussein, on the other hand, relied on Nasser's word and his own imperfect radar. If, as Nasser and Field Marshal Amer had assured him, Egypt had put 75 per cent of the Israeli air force out of action, what were those blips doing coming in from the sea and seeming to stop in Israel? They must have come from American and British aircraft carriers anchored in the vicinity. They were, of course, Israeli jets returning home, taking a roundabout route via the Mediterranean. The king was not aware that British Hunters and Israel's French-built Mystère jets had similar radar signatures.

Hussein seems to have been duped. He called in the American and British ambassadors and accused their governments of helping Israel, sweeping aside their denials in a display of seemingly sincere anger. However, he should have known better than to have swallowed Nasser's story without any apparent reservations. Wasfi al-Tall was not so easily fooled.

"We have fought with heroism and honour," the king said, in a nationwide address. "Our soldiers have defended every inch of our earth with their precious blood...They were not afraid, in the face of the total superiority of the enemy's air power, which surprised and paralysed the Egyptian air force (on which we counted)." He did not shrink from admitting that "our calamity is greater than anyone could have imagined". But it could have been avoided, and the king must bear much of the blame for it.

Hussein found himself in a dismal but not impossible situation. He would have to rebuild his country on the East Bank alone. He would have to raise money urgently to help pay the government's operating expenses and its bills for food imports (Saudi Arabia, Kuwait and Libya promptly offered a joint $40m a year; help came later from America and Britain).

He would have to re-equip the shattered armed forces (he received 20 Hunters and some Centurion tanks from Britain and 18 Starfighters from America after having threatened to turn to the Soviet Union).

He would have to launch a diplomatic offensive to regain the West Bank. There, his hands were tied: at an Arab summit in Khartoum from August 29th to September 1st, the participants vowed "no peace with Israel, no recognition of Israel, and insistence on the rights of the Palestinian people in their own country".

The best they could manage was the famous resolution 242 of the UN Security Council, drafted by Britain's Lord Caradon and approved on November 22nd 1967. It contained three key points.

The first was that the Council was "emphasizing the inadmissibility of the acquisition of territory by war and the need to work for a just and lasting peace in which every state in the area can live in peace and security".

Second, in order to establish a "just and lasting peace", it called for the "withdrawal of Israeli armed forces from territories occupied in the recent conflict".

Third, it called for the "termination of all claims or states of belligerency, and respect for and acknowledgement of the sovereignty and territorial integrity and political independence of every state in the area and their right to live in peace within secure and recognized boundaries free from threats or acts of force".

The radical Syrian regime rejected it. So did the Palestinian refugees, because there was no mention of their right of return to their homes. Jordan and Egypt accepted it. So did Israel, not as the recipe for a prompt withdrawal from the West Bank, East Jerusalem and the Golan Heights but as the basis for a long-drawn-out negotiation if the Arabs would ever come to the negotiating table.

There was much debate over the key word "territories" which should be returned to their rightful owners. This left it vague whether "all" captured territories should be returned or even if "the" captured territories should be handed over by Israel. Mahmoud Riad, the Egyptian foreign minister, who played an active part, took solace in the French and Spanish translations, which referred to "the" territories.

Gunnar Jarring, a distinguished Swedish diplomat, was given the fruitless task of trying to bring the adversaries together. Many Palestinians simply could not stomach the idea of sitting down with an enemy who had not only humiliated them on the field of battle but had also taken their land and homes. About 150,000 Palestinians were said to have fled across the Jordan river to the East Bank; 90,000 of them were in refugee camps. Many Arab nationalists sympathized with the Palestinians.

Nonetheless, while King Hussein might have been impulsive and headstrong at times, he was a cautious pragmatist where his all-powerful neighbour, Israel, was concerned. He knew Israel was in the Middle East to stay. It was therefore important to have a line of communication open.

Abba Eban, the Israeli foreign minister, began his direct personal contacts with Hussein in 1968. Apparently Eban made the first approach. By Eban's account, the two men met clandestinely in the home of a British friend of the king's, in north-west London; aboard a motor-launch in the Red Sea off the Jordanian-Israeli coast; or on a coral island near Eilat. They are also said to have met at the Dorchester Hotel in London. On one occasion in London the British prime minister, Harold Wilson, said to Eban: "There are rumours that you saw King Hussein today. Absurd, isn't it!" Eban recounts: "Wilson then winked at me with prodigious emphasis in a gesture of conspiratorial reassurance."

The eloquent and articulate Eban's assessment of Hussein was that he "never failed to communicate a passionately Arab national pride, but he respected the allegiances of his Israeli interlocutors".[8] "Meetings with him, and a study of his Arabic rhetoric, which was classically perfect in diction and range of expression, were for me an antidote to

[Moshe] Dayan's bleak theory that struggle had been eternally 'decreed' as the law of Arab-Israeli relations."

In Eban's eyes, Hussein and not Sadat was the pioneer of realism in the Arab perception of Israel. But his power base was always inadequate to bring his innovations "to effective expression within the larger Arab context". He gave his Israeli interlocutors "maximum courtesy and minimal commitment". He seemed embarrassed that the Israelis were asking him to "take the burden" of the first Arab-Israeli breakthrough.

Eban well understood Hussein's paradoxical position. He thought that Hussein, as an Arab leader, would have preferred it if Israel did not exist; as a king, on the other hand, he depended on Israel at times for his survival. "Nothing preserved Jordan's survival more than Israel's interest in preserving it," Eban wrote. "It was known that any conquest of Jordan – either by Iraq or by Syria – would risk Israeli intervention."

In addition to his meetings with Eban, Hussein is said to have held seven in the Negev desert with another political leader, Yigal Allon, as well as two sessions with Dayan in London in 1977. There is also a story, probably apocryphal, that Hussein was once taken for a drive by Yitzhak Rabin down Dizengoff Street, the main street of Tel Aviv. (Much later, the king held unpublicized meetings with Shimon Peres, Yitzhak Shamir and probably other Israeli leaders.)

Eban rightly saw Hussein in his Middle Eastern context and regarded the "Jordan option", the idea of a peace settlement with Jordan as the central partner, as a non-starter: before doing anything, the king would have to obtain at least the tacit support of the PLO, Egypt, Syria and Saudi Arabia.

There was a chance that the king might have signed a peace with Israel if he had regained all of East Jerusalem and the West Bank from the Israelis. But that was a non-starter too. The Israelis tried hard to persuade the king to take the plunge. They failed. Nonetheless, the "Jordan option" took a long time to die.

It was in Hussein's interest for Jordan's new border with Israel to be quiet. He needed time to repair the country and to persuade the world to put pressure on Israel to return the Occupied Territories to their owners. The last thing he needed was guerrilla attacks on Israel from the Jordanian side of the border: he knew all about Israel's excessive, brutal reprisals. He knew that the world would tolerate them. Such an approach suited Israel nicely.

But the Palestinian refugees, seething with anger and anguish, wanted only to punish their oppressors. And the Arab world was waiting for a leader who would restore their lost pride by attacking the Israelis without being crushed. Such a leader emerged: a short, plump, unshaven and unheroic engineer named Yasser Arafat. It was he who would present Hussein with his next challenge.

16 CIVIL WAR

Muhammad Abdel-Rauf Arafat al-Kudwa al-Husseini, known to the world as Yasser Arafat, was born in Cairo (according to his university records) on August 4th 1929, the sixth child of a Palestinian couple who moved from Jerusalem to the Egyptian capital in 1927. His mother, Zahwa, died when he was four and the young Arafat and his brother, Fathi, were sent to Jerusalem to live with their uncle, Selim Abu Saoud, whose house adjoined the Wailing Wall.

After his father's remarriage to an Egyptian woman in 1937, Arafat returned to Cairo, where in 1956 he graduated as an engineer after seven years at Cairo University. He became a Palestinian militant at the university and began to hone the skill which was to stand him in good stead in later years: as an organizer with a photographic memory for names and faces. He could also disappear from view when convenient and had seemingly endless reserves of energy. In 1956 he travelled to Prague with two companions to attend a students' congress and donned a *keffiyeh*, or head-dress. He immediately attracted attention, and his two comrades followed suit. "I have my style," he says, with quiet satisfaction.

Arafat qualified as a reserve officer in the Egyptian army and during the Suez campaign of 1956 he was called up to serve as a bomb disposal expert. He claims to have worked in the headquarters of the then General Abdel Hakim Amer.[1]

His first post-graduation job was with the Egyptian Cement Company. It was dull. Nasser was spreading his ideas of pan-Arabism, which did not fit in with the young Arafat's Palestinian nationalism. So he obtained work in Kuwait and began also to plot, helped by his close friend Khalil al-Wazir (later known as Abu Jihad).

The decision of the 1964 Arab summit, dominated by Nasser, to authorize Ahmed Shukairy to set up the Palestine Liberation Organization (PLO), was seen by the little group in Kuwait as a setback: the members thought the PLO would be official, dominated by Nasser and cautious. Arafat was talking increasingly of the armed struggle and not a diplomatic solution to the plight of the Palestinian refugees.

In 1959 Fatah was founded. In 1965 Arafat gave a display of what Israelis would call *chutzpah*. With a grand total of 26 badly armed fighters, his movement announced: "Let the imperialists and Zionists know that the people of Palestine are still in the field of battle and shall never be swept away." It was signed by Al-Assifa (The Storm), the name under which Fatah at first conducted its military operations. More such statements were to flow from Khalil al-Wazir's typewriter.

Money began to arrive. Sheikh Ahmed Zaki Yamani, Saudi Arabia's oil minister, contributed. Later, the Saudis supplied arms and ammunition clandestinely. Al-Assifa conducted occasional pinprick raids on Israel. For Arafat everything changed after the 1967 war: Shukairy, exposed as a failure, was forced to retire as PLO leader. Many Palestinians, stunned by defeat, felt impotent: Israel seemed invincible. But the ambitious Arafat saw his opportunity. Like Shukairy, Nasser had failed the Palestinians; a new leader was needed.

In 1968 the number of raids increased. After an Israeli school bus was blown up by a mine laid in the road, killing a doctor and a schoolboy and injuring 29 children, Arafat knew his opportunity had come. The Palestinian infiltrators had crossed into Israel near the Jordanian village of Karameh. Israel's vengeance was imminent. A Jordanian general advised Arafat to withdraw his men from the border area. He refused. Men from an allied guerrilla group, George Habash's Popular Front for the Liberation of Palestine (PFLP), withdrew into the hills.

Israel's onslaught began on March 21st. A raid by commandos to open up the way for an Israeli advance was met by guerrillas in hand-to-hand fighting. Jordanian army units, disobeying orders from Amman to keep out of the fight, aimed artillery and tank fire at the main advancing force. By the end of the day the Israelis had failed to destroy the guerrilla base and, amazingly, Israel had suffered 28 dead and 69 injured. Thirty-four tanks had been hit, some by 17 of Arafat's *fedayeen* (guerrillas) who fired at point-blank range from trenches near the Jordan's bank which they had suicidally built for themselves. (The 17 martyrs were subsequently remembered in Fatah: Arafat named his security service "Force 17". In fact, one survived.) Much of the damage was inflicted by the Jordanian army's units under General Mashour Haditha.

By the end of the day, a quarter of the 400-odd fighters lay dead and Karameh was destroyed by the Israeli army. Arafat, who claimed he took part in the fighting, displayed his talent for being elusive: he disappeared and survived to tell the tale of *fedayeen* heroics. To the Arab world it did not matter that the guerrillas had lost or that the Jordanian army played a key role: the romantic rebels had not run away but had fought the Israelis, caused casualties and emerged with honour. Even Israel's General Aharon Yariv was impressed. "After Karameh, we understood that we had on our hands a serious movement," he said.

Arafat's publicity machine went into top gear: within days thousands of young men had applied to join up. By the end of 1968, Fatah had some 2,000 fighters under arms. Some were trained at Nanking, in China, and in Egypt. Money came from Saudi Arabia, which deducted a 7 per cent tax from the wages of Palestinians working for the government and sent it to Arafat. On February 3rd 1969 the Palestine National Council, an *ad hoc*, appointed but broadly representative body, met in Cairo firmly under *fedayeen* influence and elected Arafat as chairman of the PLO's executive committee.[2]

For King Hussein this development spelt trouble. There was no comparison between Arafat's and Shukairy's PLO. Shukairy was an embarrassing windbag. True, he had challenged Hussein's claim to the West Bank and the leadership of the Palestinians. But his challenge was mainly rhetorical. Arafat's challenge was military.

The PLO needed a base. Nasser would not give it one in Egypt, which in any case was far away on the other side of the Suez Canal. Syria permitted the guerrillas to have bases on its territory but forbade attacks on Israel from Syria. The most convenient base for supplies and operations was the East Bank of the Jordan. King Hussein was perceived as weak after the 1967 war. Furthermore, embryonic PLO bases already existed in Jordan: the teeming refugee camps. The border with

Israel was porous. The population was sympathetic.

By 1968 the *fedayeen* had begun to flex their muscles. They began to form a state within Hussein's state. They were the heroes of Palestine and the Arab world. They were also armed and powerful. How could Hussein oppose them? There was nothing he could do except bargain – and wait.

In October 1968 thousands of *fedayeen* marched through Amman for the first time, ostensibly in a funeral procession but also to give a political and military demonstration of power ; some marchers fired their rifles in the air and shouted slogans against Hussein's government. In November *fedayeen* invaded the American embassy.

Hussein reacted by setting up roadblocks to check on *fedayeen* movements, seizing arms caches and shelling troublesome camps. Arafat asked for a meeting with the king, at which the two men agreed that the *fedayeen* would not carry arms or wear uniforms in Jordanian towns and would not fire at Israel from Jordanian territory.

"I try to exert control," Hussein said. "But it is difficult to tell who is a *fedayeen* and who is not. Besides, what do you expect me to do? What should I do to a people who have lost everything, who were driven out of their country? Shoot them? I think we have come to a point where we are all *fedayeen*." [3]

It was rhetoric. The fighters had made themselves thoroughly unpopular in Amman. They were out of control. By one reckoning there were more than 50 factions, mostly reporting to nobody but themselves. Many financed themselves by holding up shopkeepers, demanding contributions to the cause. One group broadcast Marxist slogans from a minaret to mark Lenin's birthday. Arafat lacked both the military means and the political will to bring the groups under his control.

Pressures on the king to crack down on the *fedayeen* came increasingly from Bedouin army officers and from his closest advisers, such as Sharif Nasser bin Jamil and Wasfi al-Tall, the former prime minister. All were baffled by his reluctance to act.

The pressure increased after July 23rd 1968, when the PFLP launched a new form of guerrilla warfare by hijacking to Algiers an Israeli El Al airliner while it was flying from Rome to Tel Aviv. The passengers and aircraft were released in exchange for the liberation of 16 *fedayeen*. It was to be the first of several such challenges to Israel and, indirectly, to Jordan.

Troubles rumbled on in Amman between the authorities and the *fedayeen* until Hussein made a move on February 10th 1970. In the eyes of the rest of the world, for which they may have been intended, Hussein's measures seemed perfectly reasonable: the guerrillas would have to carry identity cards; they had to license their cars like everybody else; they could not carry guns or stockpile ammunition. This was unacceptable to the guerrillas, who fought with Jordanian police for three days; the government shut off water and electricity to the camps. Having made his point, Hussein showed the world how reasonable he was by quickly rescinding the measures and accepting the resignation of the interior minister who implemented them, Rasul Kilani.

But it was not the end of the story, as Hussein knew. Ultimately it was a question of "us or them". Two political leaders heading military forces with opposite strategies could not coexist peacefully in the same small country.

In June 1970 the *fedayeen* kidnapped an American diplomat and tried to kill Hussein. The diplomat was released after the government intervened. The attempt on Hussein's life came when he had been informed that the *fedayeen* were firing on the government's intelligence headquarters, and insisted on seeing for himself. He drove from his country residence in a convoy with Zeid al-Rifai and Sharif Nasser bin Jamil. At a crossroads they stopped at a barrier, where they came under fire from unknown attackers. Their escort returned the fire. Sharif Nasser, so the story goes, jumped out and urged the king to do likewise, fast. He did so but, it is said, almost as if in a dream. Once out of the car, he made for the ditch and Zeid al-Rifai and the escort commander fell on top of him. They may or may not have saved Hussein's life but they certainly strained his back: he had to spend the next three days in bed.[4]

In the same month Hussein and Arafat negotiated another ceasefire that was promptly rejected by Palestinian radicals. Again the king ate humble pie. The PFLP held 68 people hostage in two Amman hotels. Subsequently, Hussein replaced his uncle and cousin, Sharif Nasser bin

Jamil and Zeid bin Shaker, in key army posts. Next, by Arafat's account, the king allowed him to nominate ministers for a new government and even invited him to form it (he says he refused).

There are two interpretations of these moves by Hussein. One is that they were indeed what they appeared to be: obligatory retreats in the face of pressure from his adversary. The other is that they were tactical. By seeming to give way time and time again, the king was building up an unimpeachable record for patience and reasonableness. When the time was ripe to oust the *fedayeen*, the king could tell his critics: "I tried the peaceful approach, and here is the evidence." This would be a case of *reculer pour mieux sauter*.

The United States was already worried about the accession to power of radicals with sympathies for and links with the Soviet Union. Henry Kissinger, President Nixon's national security adviser, had privately urged the king to crack down on the *fedayeen*.

In August, Zeid bin Shaker, who had been recalled as deputy chief of staff for operations, began drafting a plan to kick the *fedayeen* out of Jordan. Arafat and the other PLO leaders unexpectedly helped.

First they alienated Nasser. The Egyptian president had accepted the terms of an American proposal for a Middle East settlement. The PLO was virulently opposed and denounced Nasser by name. He was furious. Nasser knew that if the Palestinians ousted Hussein, the Israelis would be tempted to fill the void, and nobody could stop them. It would be yet another humiliation for the Arabs. So Nasser's angry message to the Palestinians was: "Leave Hussein alone." They did not do so: on September 1st, while driving to Amman airport to greet his daughter, Alia, his motorcade came under rifle fire in an incompetent ambush.

Second, the guerrillas overplayed their hand with a spate of dramatic hijackings. On September 6th 1970 members of the PFLP hijacked a Swissair DC-8 and a Trans World Airlines Boeing 707 to a remote Jordanian airstrip called Dawson's Field, near Zerqa. Six days later they added a British Overseas Airways Corporation VC-10. Eventually the passengers were released and the airliners were blown up. Hussein's army surrounded Dawson's Field, but did next to nothing. Richard

Nixon, the American president, and Henry Kissinger, who feared that the Middle East would be "revolutionized" if the guerrillas ousted the king, looked on anxiously and impotently from Washington. Nonetheless, the episode gave Hussein an even stronger case for reasserting his authority.

Arab leaders did not like this turn of events and advised the Palestinians to reach a settlement with Hussein. It was too late. The king had given them enough rope to hang themselves and they had obliged him. He could also say that he was under intense pressure from his loyal Bedouin officers and men in the army, now almost mutinous, to take action. The Western world, concerned about the hijacking of airliners, would not object if the guerrillas were kicked out. And many of his closest advisers urged a crackdown. Among them were Wasfi al-Tall and Zaid al-Rifai, both former prime ministers, Sharif Nasser bin Jamil and his brothers Hassan and Muhammad.

The American sixth fleet, led by the aircraft carrier *USS Independence*, dropped anchor in the eastern Mediterranean on a high alert, ready to come to Hussein's rescue if the operation failed. Six American C-130 Hercules transports were sent to Incirlik air force base in Turkey and their crews were told to stand by. American airborne units in West Germany were placed on semi-alert. US policy was for an evacuation of Americans, if necessary, to be carried out by American forces. As for who would react to a *fedayeen* victory, the consensus was to leave it to the Israelis (who would not permit the establishment of a PLO state east of the Jordan). Kissinger and Nixon seem not to have discussed what the Israelis might or might not do with Jordan: if they restored Hussein to his throne his position would have become untenable. Nixon was, however, strongly opposed to the Israeli option at this stage.[5]

Finally, on September 15th, Hussein acted. Typically, he kept his head beneath the parapet. Out of the blue, he summoned an obscure but capable brigadier named Muhammad Daoud, ordered him to form a military government and handed him a list of ministers. Daoud obeyed. Why pick an infantry brigadier? Daoud had three qualities: he seemed loyal; he was himself a Palestinian; and he had deplored the Palestinians' excesses.

His orders were clear. If by 8 am on September 16th the *fedayeen* were not fulfilling the terms of the latest agreement, between Arafat and Hussein's previous prime minister, Abdel Monem Rifai, under which they would move out of Jordanian towns, the brigadier was to order the armed forces to attack them. True to form, the guerrillas did not keep their word and the order to attack was given. Hussein said in a radio broadcast that he had acted because "a situation of uncertainty, chaos and insecurity prevails in our dear country and the danger that threatened Jordan has increased" and he wanted to "restore law and order and preserve the life of every citizen".

Nixon and Kissinger had ordered two more aircraft carriers, the *USS Saratoga* and the *USS John F. Kennedy*, accompanied by the helicopter carrier *USS Guam*, a cruiser and 12 destroyers, into the eastern Mediterranean. The president said in an interview with senior editors of the *Chicago Sun-Times* that if Iraq or Syria intervened, only America or Israel could stop them. The signal flashed to the Middle East and the Soviet Union. It said: keep out.

The armed forces had to be quick and decisive. The *fedayeen* were still, for all their faults, the darlings of the Arab world and their appeals for help would inevitably meet with a sympathetic response: the calls from Arab governments for yet another ceasefire might be overwhelming.

It was by far the biggest crisis in the long history of threats to the survival in power of the house of the Hashemites. The royal family was out of Amman: at Hummar, their country home outside the capital, at Aqaba or, in the case of Muna, Hussein's English wife, in England. Having handed over to the army, Hussein kept his head down at Hammar.

Infantrymen and tanks entered Amman at 5 am on September 17th. Fighting spread to the main towns and the *fedayeen* proved hard to dislodge. The assault lasted longer than had been expected (Hussein had hoped it would all be over in 48 hours) because the army had not been trained in street-fighting. Nonetheless, many were killed.

By September 20th, the *fedayeen* were holding on but worse was to come: the Syrian army invaded from the north at Ramtha to support them. Iraqi army units which had been stationed in the north of Jordan since the 1967 war (and had refused a request in August by Hussein to return home) moved out of their way and gave the Syrians a secret signal to advance.

Hussein's first appeal for American help was not specific. This was followed by a request for satellite photographs showing where the Syrian tanks were. These appear to have been supplied. In the evening of September 20th, Hussein telephoned Sir Denis Greenhill, permanent under-secretary at the Foreign Office, asking for American and British air strikes; Greenhill endorsed the idea of letting the Israelis handle it. (The king could not communicate directly with Washington because the circuits were out of action.) The American secretary of state, William Rogers, issued a statement demanding a Syrian withdrawal and sent a firm private message to the Kremlin demanding that the Soviet Union, Syria's friend, put pressure on the Damascus government to withdraw. But the idea of air strikes was set aside: America lacked targets to hit.

Kissinger contacted the Israeli ambassador to Washington, Yitzhak Rabin, and asked for his latest intelligence. This was that 200-odd Syrian tanks had reached the north Jordanian town of Irbid. Kissinger asked Rabin, who had been the Israeli chief of staff in the 1967 war, if the Israeli air force could take some reconnaissance photographs of the Syrian advance. Rabin asked if the Nixon administration would look with favour on an Israeli air strike if the Syrians were advancing south rapidly. Kissinger replied that he wanted to see the photographs first. Then Hussein phoned to report the fall of Irbid and to make another request for air strikes.

With the approval of the president, Kissinger telephoned Rabin again to say that the situation had deteriorated and the United States "would look favourably" on an Israeli air attack.[6] At 11.20 pm on September 20th, the Israeli prime minister, Golda Meir, replied that reconnaissance flights would take off at first light and she would consult with the White House when the results were known. But early the next morning Rabin phoned to say that although no reconnaissance photos were yet available, Israel thought a ground attack might be needed in addition to air strikes.

Nixon approved the idea in principle, subject to the king's agreement and a final decision in Washington. Hussein's response, according to Kissinger, was ambiguous on Israeli air strikes and negative on a ground attack. Meanwhile, Israel quietly mobilized, especially on the Golan Heights (within heavy artillery range of Damascus, Syria's capital).

Christopher Dobson of the London *Daily Telegraph* wrote that he had accidentally come across an Israeli tank task force heading towards Jordan just south of the Sea of Galilee. He added: "I learnt later that if Hussein had not managed to deal with the Syrian tanks, the Israeli forces would have gone into Jordan and would have had the support of the United States if it had been militarily necessary."[7]

The situation on the ground changed dramatically. On September 20th the Jordanian army appeared to have blocked the advancing Syrian armour by firing at it from well-chosen vantage points. Nonetheless, by September 21st the Jordanians looked outnumbered and outgunned and the Syrians began to move south towards Amman. The next day, however, the Jordanians took the initiative: artillery, tanks and air force Hunters slammed the Syrian forces which, amazingly, lacked air cover. Why they did not do so earlier is a mystery. What was Hussein waiting for?

The Syrian air force commander, General Hafez Assad, may have feared that an intervention by his MiGs would bring in the next-door Israelis in defence of Jordan and his air force might be wiped out, like Egypt's in 1967. On the night of September 22nd, the Syrian ground forces retreated, leaving the charred hulks of tanks and armoured personnel carriers behind them. The Syrians withdrew for three reasons, according to Asher Susser, an Israeli specialist. Firstly, the Jordanian armed forces fought better; secondly, there was an "Israeli show of force in the area facing the concentrations of Syrian forces in north Jordan"; and thirdly, there were "Israeli air force overflights of the Syrian invasion force".[8]

Assad, who cannot have wanted to risk the survival of his air force and who had received warnings from the Soviet Union and America as well as Israel, kept his air force on the ground. Commenting on the crisis afterwards, the Syrian military commander, General Mustafa Tlas, did not mention the air force and claimed that "Arafat and his clan ran away to Syria, so we withdrew the two battalions".[9] (The air force's inaction did Assad no harm: he later became president of Syria.)

Hussein's throne had been preserved, the Syrians had been turned back, and a Middle East conflagration had been avoided by pressure on the Damascus government from the United States and a threat from Israel, by the skill of the Jordanian air force and above all by the bravery of Jordanian soldiers led by Colonel Atallah Ghasib, who had been injured badly at the outset and had nonetheless kept firm control and shown an example to his men.

The Syrian withdrawal was a setback not only for the radical regime in Damascus but also for the PLO. Nonetheless, the *fedayeen* remained a state within a state in Jordan. Yet the Arabs did not spring to Arafat's defence as they might have if Hussein had launched the assault earlier. Instead, they held a summit in Cairo on September 22nd, attended by Arafat and Hussein, and appointed a committee under Sudan's bluff military strongman, General Jaafar Nimeiri, to try to mediate. The outcome, after an initial failure by Nimeiri, was a chilly meeting between Hussein and Arafat in Cairo on September 27th, and yet another ceasefire and troop withdrawal agreement which neither side seemed inclined to keep. A commission to supervise the truce was set up under the Tunisian prime minister, Bahi Ladgham. (The effort was too much for Nasser, who was already a sick man. He collapsed and died of a heart attack.)

The crisis dragged on, with Arafat being challenged by the Marxist radical George Habash's Palestinian faction whenever he reached an understanding with Hussein. The king was given a two-stage plan of action by Zaid al-Rifai. First, the *fedayeen* would be cleared out of Amman and the main towns in the period between November 1970 and April 1971; second, the remainder would be surrounded in the hills between Ajlun and Jerash and expelled from Jordan by July.

Somebody would have to lead the charge and incur the everlasting wrath and desire for vengeance of Arafat and the *fedayeen*. It would not be Hussein himself but somebody who could be blamed and discarded if the plan failed. The king picked Wasfi al-Tall, loyalist, hardliner, decisive and dynamic, as his prime minister in October 1970. Again, the die was cast. Nixon and Kissinger egged the king on and airlifted arms and ammunition discreetly to the abandoned Dawson's Field. British arms also arrived. It cannot be ruled out that Israel too again provided help.

In any event, the king issued an order that the guerrillas still in Amman should leave the capital, assemble in Ajlun and Jerash, and take their fight against Israel inside the Occupied Territories. Outnumbered by the army, the guerrillas obeyed. Most travelled in buses which the government had helpfully provided.

The murder of a farmer in Jerash by the guerrillas on June 1st 1971 gave Hussein a *casus belli* and on the following day he ordered al-Tall to take action. "If there is on our soil today a handful of people who make plotting their profession and treachery their vocation...then we wish our opposition to them to be firm, decisive and valiant, allowing no room for hesitation, tolerance or compromise."[10]

The mainly Bedouin troops had been patiently awaiting this order and they obeyed it ruthlessly, hunting down the guerrillas as they hid in caves and fled across hills and through ravines. Some even fled into Israel. Many were killed, especially during the *fedayeen's* last stand against Hussein's Bedouin at Jerash. Nobody knows how many: some say 4,000. One of the myths peddled by the PLO was that the Bedouin tortured and killed a charismatic guerrilla leader, Abu Ali Iyad, and dragged his body through neighbouring villages tied to a rope at the back of a tank. In mid-July the guerrillas had gone, and the king and his friends rejoiced. On July 16th the king claimed that Jordan was "completely quiet".

Hussein could claim he had done everything possible to work out a *modus vivendi* with the guerrillas, but they were undisciplined and split into factions and they had been directly challenging the government; Arafat commanded the loyalty of only some of the groups. Even assuming they could all work together under a disciplined, unified command, they were utterly incapable of taking on the armed might of Israel. They did not care that their raids provoked automatic Israeli reprisals which usually killed innocent civilians. They treated ordinary Jordanians with careless arrogance.

Nonetheless, the *fedayeen* remained the darlings of sentimentalists in the Arab world, and Hussein remained in the dog-house. And the Palestinians would never forget the month in 1970 when Hussein began his assault on their state within a state. They called it Black September.

17 ASSASSINATION OF A FRIEND

Wasfi al-Tall, the Jordanian prime minister who had supervised the final operations to expel the Palestinian guerrillas, was in Cairo for a meeting on November 28th 1971 at the Sheraton Hotel near the Nile. As he entered the hotel through its swinging door, accompanied by Egyptian bodyguards, four young men who had inexplicably been allowed to hang about the area came forward and one of them shot him. Al-Tall tried in vain to draw his own revolver but the shots had been fatal and he fell to the ground in a pool of blood. In an act of gross obscenity, one of the four men is reported to have crouched and lapped up some of al-Tall's blood. As they were bundled into a police van, they shouted: "We are Black September!"

Later it emerged that the gang had three names on its death-list: King Hussein, al-Tall and Zeid al-Rifai. Hussein's security was too tough to penetrate. So was al-Tall's in Jordan. Egypt's laxness was inexcusable.

The PLO guerrillas sought revenge on al-Tall for forcing them to leave Jordan for inhospitable Syria, where the government, fearful of Israeli reprisals, allowed them to live but not to use the country as a base from which to attack Israel. Previously, the *fedayeen* had based themselves in Syria but raided Israel across the Jordanian border (and Jordan had borne the brunt of Israel's excessive retaliation). That route was now cut off.

"We have taken our revenge on a traitor," said the alleged blood-drinker, Monsa Khalifa. The gunman, Essat Rabah, said: "We wanted to have him for breakfast but we had him for lunch." Al-Tall's wife, who had been waiting for her husband in the hall, screamed: "Are you happy, Arabs? What a loss you have caused! Arabs are sons of bitches!"

Later, King Hussein, burying his friend in the royal cemetery in Amman, sobbed as he gave the eulogy. "The tragedy is not death," he said, "but the degree to which cowards and sub-humans will stoop."[1]

To Egypt's lasting shame, the four men did not go on trial. On the contrary, many treated them as heroes; the radical Libyan leader, Colonel Muammar Qaddafi, offered unlimited funds for their legal defence. After a year, two of the four were allowed to move to Beirut; the alleged killer and blood-drinker remained in Cairo. In Beirut in April 1973, a Datsun similar to the one used by one of the two released men, Ziad Helou, and parked nearby, was blown up by a bomb. Without any evidence, agents of Hussein were blamed for seeking the king's revenge.

Al-Tall's visit to Cairo was ill-advised. In Egyptian eyes, he was the destroyer of the *fedayeen*, with heavy loss of life, and the master propagandist of Amman Radio who knew how to cut Egypt down to size. Jordan's ambassador to Egypt had advised him not to go to Cairo. If anyone was *persona non grata* in Cairo, it was al-Tall. This of course does not absolve the Egyptian security service.

How influential was al-Tall, and what were his relations with Hussein? Al-Tall was the most forceful Jordanian politician of his day. He did not hesitate to express his opinion even if he knew the king would disagree. Hussein, used to supine courtiers, found this refreshing: al-Tall was by one account the only non-Hashemite admitted to some of the ruling family's inner councils. Like Hussein he was no great democrat. This was not surprising in the volatile Middle East. He spoke his mind bluntly: after the 1967 six-day war, al-Tall said the Arabs suffered from serious weaknesses of national character and intellect which had prevented them from developing the required collective motivation to fight. He was contemptuous of the penchant of some Arab leaders for the politics of the rabble.

Although he was strong-willed and uncompromising, there was no evidence of al-Tall wanting more power than that of prime minister or of suffering any temptation to be disloyal after the disaster in 1967, for example. He was a quintessential member of the loyal East Bank elite. Hussein had no intention of letting him become anything more. In a clash of wills, as in 1967 or when the king delayed action against the *fedayeen*, it was Hussein's that prevailed.

Al-Tall's assassination was the start for Black September. Less than three weeks later, a young Arab was spotted loitering on a traffic island in an upper-class part of Kensington, in London. As a Daimler approached, he pulled out a Sten-gun from under his overcoat and began firing. The passenger shouted to the chauffeur to drive on. The car stalled, then moved away quickly; blood poured from a cut on the passenger's wrist, but that was all. Miraculously, the third man on Black September's list, Zeid al-Rifai, had survived.[2]

Who controlled Black September? Arafat strove to set a distance between himself and the terrorists but a captured leader, Abu Daoud, alleged to his Jordanian interrogators that the mission to kill al-Tall was organized by a senior PLO figure responsible for relations with Lebanon. Also involved was another PLO figure: Abu Youssef, who was killed by an Israeli death squad in Beirut in 1973. However, there was no direct link between these men and Arafat or his mainstream faction of the PLO, Fatah. Nonetheless, after Abu Youssef's murder in 1973, the leading figure behind the scenes in Fatah was Arafat's old friend Khalil al-Wazir (Abu Jihad). (Much later, another Israeli death squad assassinated him in his home in a Tunis suburb.)

There may well have been a loose tie-in between Fatah and Black September for which there was one very good reason: as leader of Black September, Arafat would not be acceptable elsewhere in the world as an official guest and a spokesman for the Palestinian cause (except in Libya); as leader of Fatah and chairman of the PLO, he could even address the UN General Assembly.

The new terrorists must have taken a strategic decision in or around 1971, for their operations changed. They seem to have concluded that border raids against Israel, or murders of Jordanian ministers, aroused little international interest: what riveted the world's media was a hijacking, a kidnap or an assassination involving Americans or Europeans. The guerrillas knew this from their experience at Dawson's Field, but that episode took place when the *fedayeen* were still trampling over Jordan. In 1971, having been expelled from Jordan, they were building bases in Lebanon but were still essentially homeless. Jordan, rearmed by the Americans and British, looked impregnable to attack by their much reduced forces.

There was only one viable option for a fractured grouping of defeated but angry men determined that the world should take note of the injustice of Israel's seizure of their homes and land. That option was terrorism. But not terrorism against insignificant Jordan, which was dropped as a prime target.

The first of a new round of hijackings started in February 1972 when two Palestinian men and two women hijacked a Belgian Sabena airliner to Tel Aviv's Lod Airport but were outmanoeuvred by the Israelis (who killed the two men). This was followed in May by a massacre of passengers in Lod airport by Japanese terrorists and, later, by the massacre of Israeli team members at the Olympic Games in Munich. This in turn set off a wave of revenge killings by Israeli death squads, ordered by the angry prime minister, Golda Meir. The Israelis went about their work with grim determination.

The next of the more atrocious acts of terrorism took place in the Saudi Arabian embassy in Khartoum, capital of Sudan, on March 1st 1973. Terrorists apparently directed by Black September interrupted a reception and shot and killed the American ambassador, his deputy and the Belgian chargé d'affaires after their demands were rejected. There were a dozen terrorist acts of lesser importance.

In one of many cases of state counter-terrorism in April, Israel sent a group of daring seaborne assassins into Beirut, where its members killed Abu Youssef, Black September's operations chief, Kamal Adwan, in charge of operations in the occupied territories, and Kamal Nasir, the PLO spokesman (and a noted poet). The Israelis escaped after grabbing scores of secret documents. In July, agents of the secret service, Mossad, killed the wrong man, an innocent waiter, in Lillehammer, Norway. In August, Israel's air force hijacked an Iraqi Caravelle airliner on its way from Beirut to Baghdad because spies had reported that George Habash was on board (he was not, having changed his mind at the last minute).

By October 1973 the guerrilla war appeared to be over for three reasons. First, the Israelis had been acutely embarrassed by the Lillehammer murder and decided to stop such operations. Second, the Israeli raid on Beirut was a stunning setback for the Palestinians.

Third, and most important, on October 6th Egyptian troops swarmed across the Suez Canal and pierced Israel's defences at the start of the Yom Kippur war. A war between two armies was much more impressive than the dirty war of terror and counter-terror.

Nonetheless, in what looked like a final convulsion, the terrorists protested against the decision by Egypt's president, Anwar Sadat, to negotiate, with the help of Henry Kissinger, with the hated Israelis. In December, discovered at Rome airport customs to be carrying guns, five terrorists ran on to the tarmac and threw two phosphorus bombs into a Pan American airliner, killing 31 people.

To King Hussein's relief, in no case was Jordan involved. After a period of relative calm, however, the king found himself once again in danger of being drawn into a war that was not of his making.

18 WAR AGAIN

Ever since the disastrous six-day war of 1967, in which Israeli forces
virtually annihilated the combined forces of Egypt, Syria and Jordan, Nasser had dreamed of a war of revenge that would restore Arab
honour and pride as well as recapture lost Arab land. For years, Egyptian generals, humiliated in 1967, applied their lessons in meticulously
planned exercises of their troops. Nasser and his aides thought that the
only way of extracting concessions from Israel was through negotiation
after a conflict which Israel did not win. The Egyptians' main supplier
of arms and trainers for this endeavour was the Soviet Union.

While there might have been some genuinely fraternal feeling
between the Egyptian and Soviet leaders, the relationship was driven
by mutual interest. Having concluded that America was hopelessly a
supporter of Israel, Egypt turned to the second superpower, the Soviet
Union, for its armaments and the Soviets acquired, in Egypt, a powerful and influential cold-war client state.

All went well as long as the conflict was limited to Nasser's post-
1968 war of attrition against Israel. This amounted to Egyptian
artillery and warplanes shelling Israeli positions east of the Suez Canal
and Israeli reprisal raids in which Egypt's Soviet missiles began to
shoot down the incoming Israeli invaders.

Eventually, the penny dropped in Moscow: the Arabs were serious
about another war with Israel. In 1972 President Brezhnev became
alarmed at the prospect that the Soviet Union might be drawn into a
Middle East war which it might be unable to control. If America sided
with Israel with troops on the ground, a much wider war might explode.
The Kremlin slowed down its supplies and counselled delay.

Nasser's successor in 1970 was his little-known vice-president,
Anwar Sadat, who turned out to be a strategic thinker and lover of the

grand gesture. Like Nasser, Sadat realized that the situation on the ground in the Middle East would be changed to Egypt's advantage, in possibly recovering the lost Sinai desert, only if it had a solid negotiating position. This would require an invasion of Sinai, the seizure of some of the lost land, a UN-brokered ceasefire and negotiations with Israel about a withdrawal. Sadat also realized that the Arabs' only hope of achieving an honourable settlement with Israel lay with the United States, the only country with any leverage over it, rather than with the Soviet Union, which had no status in Israel at all. Syria's president, Hafez Assad, was less far-sighted, but he realized that he too needed to regain at least part of the Golan Heights in order to be taken seriously by Israel as a negotiating partner. Like Egypt, Syria had been heavily armed by the Soviet Union. Unlike Egypt's Sadat, however, Assad was rigid, inflexible and lacking in pragmatism.

Jordan had no enthusiasm for war, fearing a repeat of the Six-Day War, which in Jordan had lasted for only two wretched days. The king wanted peace. In 1972 he launched a proposal for a united kingdom of Jordan including the West Bank and Gaza Strip after they were liberated. Such an arrangement implied a bilateral peace deal between Jordan and Israel and was rejected by the PLO and most Arab countries. It was a logical idea but one whose time had not come. The propaganda mills in Cairo and Damascus worked overtime against it. Egypt suspended diplomatic relations with Jordan, which reverted, temporarily, to the status of a pariah.

The essentially first step in the Middle East war of October 1973 (also known as the Yom Kippur war, because it started on the Day of Atonement, the holiest day in the Jewish calendar) had been taken by Sadat in July of the previous year. He summoned the Soviet ambassador and told him of his decision to terminate the work of Soviet experts and to put Soviet military units under the command of the Egyptian army; if this was not acceptable to the Soviet Union, they could leave Egypt before July 17th. They did, all 20,000 of them.[1]

The second step was to ensure Egypt had air cover to match the Israeli air force. Egypt received offers of squadrons of warplanes from Saudi Arabia, Libya, Iraq, Algeria, Morocco and the United Arab

Emirates. Egypt and Syria acquired ground-to-air and surface missiles.

Next came an attempt to woo King Hussein. Mahmoud Riad, then secretary-general of the Arab League, flew to Amman to try to persuade the king to take part. "The memories of 1967 were still with him," Riad recalled later. "When I explained to him the drastic changes that had taken place since then, he expressed his complete willingness to participate in the battle which should, however, be preceded by a meeting of the heads of state of the three countries."[2]

To participate did not, however, mean to invade Israeli-held territory, as Egypt and Syria planned. That would spell disaster for lightly armed Jordan. So Riad made a limited request. "I mentioned that I did not know the specific date of the battle but, whenever it did start, there was a danger that the Israeli forces might encircle the southern Syrian front by moving across Jordanian territories. In this case, could the Jordanian forces be deployed in a manner that would prevent such a possibility? King Hussein readily agreed....When the war broke out, he accomplished this promptly."

On September 10th 1973, the presidents of Egypt and Syria and the king of Jordan held a meeting in Cairo at which diplomatic relations between Egypt and Jordan were restored and Jordan agreed to help its arch-enemy, Syria, after the war started. In a display of contempt for the Jordanian monarch, the two presidents did not reveal to him the date of D-day. When the war started without any advance warning from Cairo, Hussein felt that Egypt had let him down again, as it did in 1967.

Sadat did not hold Hussein in high esteem. As a young army officer based in the Egyptian embassy in Amman, he had tried to foment public opposition to the Hashemites with some success. To this republican and Arab nationalist, Hussein's ties to Britain, the United States and Israel, like those of King Abdullah, were unacceptable. In May 1973, writes Henry Kissinger, Hussein tipped off the Nixon administration that Syrian and Egyptian military preparations were too realistic to be considered manoeuvres.[3]

The time and date of D-day (2.05 pm on October 6th) were secrets to be closely guarded. Sadat had chosen Yom Kippur, when many Israeli soldiers would be on home leave, to launch his attack; the Israelis, although they knew something was afoot, were nonetheless in a low state of alert. Even Egyptian army commanders of frontline invading forces knew the war was starting only when they were ordered to advance. Israeli intelligence was convinced an attack would come only after 6 pm.

At the start of the war, the Soviet Union urged Hussein to join in on the side of the Egyptians and Syrians, promising full support; Hussein declined. King Feisal of Saudi Arabia asked Hussein for permission to move a Saudi brigade based in Jordan into Syria; Hussein refused. Hussein was, however, ready to send a tank brigade to Syria (albeit as far from the front line as possible) if he was certain that Israel would not use this as an excuse for an invasion of the East Bank.[4]

An indirect request for such an Israeli guarantee came from the British prime minister, Edward Heath. Kissinger handed the request to the Israeli ambassador to Washington, Simcha Dinitz, who later responded with a mild refusal, containing no threats.

It did him no good in the eyes of his "allies", but Hussein kept his word. As he had promised, the Israeli army could not enter Jordan as part of a stratagem to cut off Syria's southern front. And Jordanian tanks went to rescue Syrian tank forces *in extremis* on the Golan Heights. There was a bitter irony in Hussein's choice of his 40th armoured brigade to help the Syrians: it was this brigade which had bravely blocked the southward advance into Jordan of Syrian tanks during the civil war in Jordan in 1970.

James Lunt, Hussein's 1989 biographer and a retired British major-general, writes that the Israelis were impressed by the professionalism of the Jordanian tank crews. But the Jordanians' intervention did not appear to have been marked by any particularly notable exploits.

The 40th armoured brigade crossed into Syria on October 13th. Three days later, it was attacking an Israeli unit. According to the retired Major-General Chaim Herzog (who subsequently served as president of Israel), the Israelis hit 28 tanks and the Jordanians withdrew.[5] In a second encounter with the Israelis, alongside an Iraqi tank unit, the Jordanians moved too slowly, writes Herzog. The Jordanians' slowness enabled the Israelis first to pick off the Iraqis and then the Jordanians.

Herzog claims that by the time that Syria accepted a UN ceasefire on October 22nd, it had lost some 1,150 tanks. Iraq lost over 100 tanks and Jordan over 50, whereas Israel had lost only 250.

The war in the south, between Israel and Egypt, did not affect Hussein greatly. In meetings with Arab political and military leaders, Hussein could convincingly defend a policy of inaction. First, he could describe how he had been down this route in 1967 and fought Israel under an Egyptian general with disastrous results. Second, he could point out Israel's potentially devastating air superiority.

This is not the place for a detailed account of the October war. Suffice it to say that it had two results. In the Golan Heights, Israel ended up controlling more land than it had done since its gains in 1967. In the south, there was a sort of checkmate: the Egyptians had established a bridgehead across the Suez Canal and into the Sinai desert whereas the Israelis had also crossed the Canal and had trapped Egypt's third army.

The situation was ripe for negotiation. An ambitious American stood ready to mediate: Henry Kissinger. First, troops would have to withdraw from ceasefire lines. Second, peace talks could start. But would it be a regional peace, including Hussein's Jordan and Hafez Assad's Syria, and – just possibly – the Palestinians, or a separate Egyptian-Israeli one, without them?

Hussein was worried. In speculation about a peace settlement, Jordan's claim to reoccupy the West Bank, Gaza Strip and East Jerusalem had received scant attention. Would he be excluded from a settlement? Kissinger reassured him that it was inconceivable that the interests of Jordan would not be fully protected; the king's views would be given the full weight that they deserved. How reliable were these promises?

19   WHAT KIND OF PEACE?

E ver since the end of the 1967 war, attempts had been made to draw
up a peace pact for the region in line with UN Security Council
resolution 242 of the same year. It called for the withdrawal of Israeli
forces from "territories" seized in 1967 in return for guarantees by Israel's neighbours that it could live in peace within secure and recognized boundaries free from threats or acts of force. Resolution 242
amounted to a swap of "land for peace". If implemented, it should have
restored the West Bank and East Jerusalem to Jordan.

It did not do so. The troubles were manifold. The words of resolution 242 seemed refreshingly simple and straightforward, but they
could be interpreted differently. And the intentions of the Arabs and Israelis differed.

First, PLO leaders were in no mood to give their recognition to a
state responsible (as they saw it) for the uprooting of hundreds of
thousands of Palestinians from their ancestral homes (who were not
mentioned in the resolution). Second, Israel, having fought off an Arab
attempt (albeit bumbling) to destroy it, was in no mood to give back
Arab East Jerusalem and the West Bank to Jordan.

The Arabs interpreted 242 simply: to them it clearly stressed the
"inadmissibility of the acquisition of territory by force"; it said the Israelis should withdraw from the Occupied Territories and the Arabs
would guarantee their existence; negotiations, preferably indirect
through a mediator, were needed only to tidy up the details.

Israel's moderately expansionist foreign minister, Abba Eban, disagreed. He took 242 to endorse continued Israeli control of the Occupied Territories until such time as a land-for-peace agreement was
approved. And he did not accept that the reference in 242 that "secure
and recognized boundaries" meant the pre-1967 ones, which offered

Israel little security, especially at its "wasp-waist". This would have to be negotiated.

Hardline Israeli nationalists had no intention of handing back anything to the Arabs, especially East Jerusalem and the Golan Heights: they wanted Israel to expand in hundreds of settlements that would eventually stifle the Palestinians and shove them into Jordan. One of Israel's hard men, Ariel Sharon, liked to say that "Jordan is Palestine". More moderate Israelis such as Yigal Allon, deputy prime minister, thought in terms of a compromise. But no Israeli was in a hurry: it would take time to digest the Occupied Territories. There was no pressing need to co-operate with the Swedish special UN envoy, Gunnar Jarring.

On April 28th 1969 King Hussein visited the White House and talked to President Nixon and Henry Kissinger about the prospects for a settlement. Kissinger found "the little king" one of the most attractive leaders he had met.[1] The national security adviser admired the king for keeping a foot in two camps: one Western and the other Arab. Kissinger thought Hussein stoutly defended the Arab cause even when his fellow-Arabs, as he saw it, did not. At the same time, Hussein "never bargained about his friendship with the United States".

In another revealing comment, Kissinger observed that while Jordan was "substantially dependent on American aid", the king put up with cumbersome and sometimes humiliating procedures (presumably signing CIA receipts) without losing his composure or adopting the role of a supplicant.

However, Kissinger also noted, somewhat disingenuously, that whilst Hussein was prepared to talk of making peace with Israel and to hold clandestine talks with Israeli representatives with this in mind, he would not sign a bilateral peace treaty with Israel. True, but Kissinger did not add the essential condition: Hussein (and Nasser) would sign an agreement that also comprised a settlement of the Israel-Palestine and Israel-Syria disputes and the future of Arab East Jerusalem.

Like his grandfather, however, Hussein was always on the look-out for a clandestine deal that would help the Hashemites and Jordan as well as the Palestinians: he told Kissinger that if Israel ceded the Gaza

Strip to Jordan, he would agree to substantial frontier changes of the West Bank frontier in Israel's favour. Nothing came of it.

In a speech to the National Press Club in Washington on the day of his White House visit, however, Hussein made no mention of such a deal. But he did offer a peace proposal enlarging on resolution 242. The Arab side would not only guarantee secure frontiers for Israel, if necessary through the use of demilitarized zones, but also freedom of navigation through the (closed) Suez Canal and the Strait of Tiran. In return, Hussein asked the impossible of an expansionist Israel: the return of "all" occupied territories and a settlement of the refugee problem.[2]

In December 1969 the American secretary of state, William Rogers, launched a peace plan comprising Israeli withdrawal from occupied territories and Arab recognition of Israel. The plan clarified resolution 242's call for the return of "territories" seized by Israel in 1967. To this Rogers added that "any changes in the pre-existing lines should not reflect the weight of conquest and should be confined to insubstantial alterations required for mutual security. We do not support expansionism." Egypt and Jordan cautiously accepted it; Israel rejected it a day after its publication and launched a campaign against it. The Rogers plan was, nonetheless, seen by the Arabs as offering the basis for a deal. It slid into oblivion.[3]

The next peace move came on March 15th 1972 when Hussein launched his federation plan. This was carefully crafted to contain something for everybody except the PLO. The idea was to create a united Arab kingdom comprising the West Bank with its capital in Jerusalem and the East Bank with its regional capital in Amman, where the federal capital would also be based. The king would retain wide powers over the executive and the army but the two parts of the federation would have their own parliaments.

If given a healthy shove by the United States, this might just have proved acceptable to the Israelis, assuming a deal could be struck with Hussein over frontiers. Hussein was viewed by the Israelis as a safe Arab, with whom they could do business; they could never do business with Arafat. To the PLO, however, Hussein's proposal was a direct challenge to its leadership of the Palestinians. To Egypt and Syria it would have meant the restoration of an unwanted conservative, pro-Western monarch to a position of greater influence over the Middle Eastern power game.

It is anybody's guess what the West Bankers thought of the idea. Many had for years been the bitter enemies of Hussein and his grandfather, King Abdullah, whom they regarded as outsiders imposed on them by the British. No Palestinian had forgotten Hussein's 1970 war against Palestinian guerrillas based in Jordan. Few supported the king, and his plan came to nothing. It did, however, inspire others to place a permanent block in the way of his ambitions.

Nonetheless, many West Bankers including teachers continued to receive their salaries from Jordan after the 1967 war, and were duly grateful. And in 1972, Israeli-sponsored elections of local councils on the West Bank were won by conservative, pragmatic notables, giving an impression of normality.

In February 1973 Hussein visited Washington and again won over Nixon and Kissinger by his legendary courtesy, pro-Western moderation and sound judgment. Hussein told his hosts, for example, that Sadat's expulsion of Soviet advisers and trainers did not presage lower tension in the region: the Egyptian president was clearing the decks for a limited war with Israel.

After the fighting in the Yom Kippur war stopped, because Egypt and Israel were locked in a checkmate, a Geneva conference on the Middle East got nowhere in December 1973. On the Arab side, only Egypt and Jordan turned up. As Zeid al-Rifai, the Jordanian prime minister and Hussein's representative, put it afterwards: "It was the most peculiar conference I ever attended – no terms of reference, no rules of procedure and no agenda." Jordan and Egypt wanted Palestinian representatives to attend in the two Arab delegations but the Israeli prime minister, Golda Meir, would have none of it, and Kissinger did not challenge her. The inaugural session at the Geneva conference turned out to be its last.[4]

On January 19th 1974 Jordan presented another formula for a deal for Jordan-Israel troop disengagement (as part of an overall settlement) in which the two governments would withdraw their forces

5 miles from the banks of the Jordan. The king thought it would bring more peace to the area. It would test the Israelis' sincerity. Golda Meir turned it down. When the formation of an Israeli-Egyptian working group was proposed, to deal with troop withdrawals, al-Rifai suggested one for Israel and Jordan. The idea was ignored.[5]

Kissinger put priority on deals between Israel and both Egypt and Syria. Why? First, he was a pragmatist. He knew that the Sinai and the Golan were not part of the Land of Israel as it existed at the time of the dispersal of the Jews by the Romans in AD 135. The two territories could therefore be partially given up, as a *quid pro quo*, without difficulties from Jewish fundamentalists.

Second, a deal with Egypt above all would fatally undermine Soviet influence over the Cairo government, doubly enhancing the reputation in Washington of Kissinger the miracle-worker and cold warrior.

Thirdly, East Jerusalem, Judaea and Samaria (the West Bank) were very much part of the Land of Israel; the Jews would hold on to them tenaciously. Kissinger never brought the full weight of American influence to bear on Israel in favour of a land-for-peace deal over the West Bank. Suspicious, conspiracy-minded Jordanian leaders drew their own conclusions.

Kissinger launched his famous shuttle diplomacy which led to troop disengagement agreements between Israel and both Egypt (in January 1974) and Syria (in May of the same year). A second Israeli-Egyptian agreement was signed in September giving Egypt another slab of the Sinai desert in return for conciliatory gestures by President Sadat, including a promise to send advance information to Israel about any unusual troop movements. Jordan was not involved: its borders were not changed by the 1973 war.

In the summer of 1974, perhaps sensing that the moment was propitious with all the talk of peaceful Israeli troop withdrawals, Hussein took a daring step. He conferred secretly with the top Israelis: Yitzhak Rabin, then prime minister; Yigal Allon, then foreign minister; and Shimon Peres, then defence minister. Accompanied by his prime minister and confidant, Zeid al-Rifai, the king flew by helicopter to a secluded spot in the Arava valley where the Israelis had prepared "a modest caravan". Nothing of substance was decided.

For Peres it was the first of many meetings. "The king made a powerful impression me," he wrote later. "Though short in height, his ramrod posture and swift athletic movements radiate a strong presence. His smile is warm and captivating and his manners are impeccable. He seems in control of his every muscle."⁶

Peres viewed the king as the "epitome of Hashemite pride" who saw himself as the "personification of the Arab destiny". Nonetheless, he also saw an Arab monarch worried about strategic threats to his small and poor desert kingdom. Hussein's basic attitude to Israel, Peres thought, was one of admiration. With Israel, Hussein's Jordan was in a *de jure* state of war and a *de facto* peace. This was symbolized by the twin towns at the head of the Gulf of Aqaba: Israel's Eilat and Jordan's Aqaba, which lived cheek by jowl and never fired a shot at each other. Already in 1974 Peres's fertile imagination was racing ahead of events. He suggested an agreement on three entities: Israel, Jordan and the West Bank/Gaza strip. Israel and Jordan would jointly administer the Occupied Territories. It was wishful Israeli thinking, but nonetheless a demonstration of a politician in search of solutions. Hussein politely said he would think about it.

The opportunity for Hussein's rivals and adversaries to block his ambition to continue representing the Palestinians arose on October 29th 1974 at an Arab summit in Rabat. It proved to be the king's worst setback since the war of 1967.

The final statement contained an apparent allusion to Hussein's plan for a united Arab kingdom. "All are aware of Zionist schemes still being made to eliminate the Palestinian existence and to obliterate the Palestinian national entity," it said. In order to strengthen the Palestinians, the summit resolved "to affirm the right of the Palestinian people to establish an independent national authority under the command of the Palestine Liberation Organization, the sole legitimate representative of the Palestinian people, in any Palestinian territory that is liberated. This authority, once it is established, shall enjoy the support of the Arab states in all fields and at all levels." Hussein said that if the statement was approved (which it was), Jordan would consider itself as having no direct involvement in the Palestinian question. He accepted the summit's decision.

In the same year, Hussein dissolved Jordan's national assembly on the grounds that its West Bank members had no further place in it. (Two years later, he prorogued it indefinitely. A national consultative council, appointed by the king, thereafter rubber-stamped government decisions.)

Arafat went from strength to strength in 1974. On November 13th, he addressed the UN General Assembly as a special guest, wearing military fatigues and with a revolver at his hip. "I have come bearing an olive branch and a freedom-fighter's gun," he declared. "Do not let the olive branch fall from my hand." The American and Israeli delegations walked out. The General Assembly gave observer status to a PLO delegation and approved a resolution affirming the Palestinians' right to self-determination, national independence and sovereignty. Hussein's role in the Middle East was again diminished.

The king was surprised by the decision of the Rabat summit. He had thought that at least President Sadat and King Hassan of Morocco would support him. But *realpolitik* had intervened. Arafat the master-publicist had indefatigably travelled the world, Arab and non-Arab, seeking support for the Palestinians' cause. He was persuasive. His theatrical manner, his unusual hat, conveniently covering his bald pate and the permanent revolutionary-style stubble on his chin did him no harm. It was murmured in the Gulf that at times the PLO's requests for money were, if not threatening, heavy-handed. That too did no harm: security-conscious rulers of rich oil-producing amirates willingly signed on the dotted line. Many of the cheques were said to be made payable to a bank account which Arafat alone controlled.

The Arabs' decision to recognize the PLO as the sole legitimate representative of the Palestinian people was not only deeply undemocratic but also stupid. All the heads of state and government who approved the Rabat resolution knew that it would be many years before Israel and the United States would agree to talk to the PLO, which they regarded as a terrorist organization. Israel would, on the other hand, talk to Hussein; America already did. In making a meaningless rhetorical declaration, the Arabs were damaging the interests of the Palestinians. They were handing Israel a ready-made excuse for not negotiating a land-for-peace deal for the West Bank and East Jerusalem and they were giving the Israelis more time to expand their settlements there.

At the same time, however, a Jordanian government which had in 1970 destroyed or expelled the Palestinian fighters based in its territory could scarcely claim the right to represent them.

The Israeli cabinet spelled its views on July 21st 1974, well before the Rabat summit. It wanted a peace agreement with Jordan. "The peace will be founded on the existence of two independent states only – Israel, with a united Jerusalem as her capital, and a Jordanian-Palestinian Arab state east of Israel with borders to be determined in negotiations between Israel and Jordan."

Kissinger made America's view clear in a memorandum of understanding attached to the second Egypt-Israel troop disengagement pact of September 1st 1975. He promised that American representatives would not talk to PLO representatives until the PLO recognized resolution 242 (which was unacceptable to them because it made no reference to the rights of Palestinian refugees). This famous memo inhibited contacts between America and the PLO for many years while the Israelis systematically "created facts" on the ground.

After the Rabat summit, Yitzhak Rabin, then prime minister, observed with characteristic bluntness that "the Rabat conference decided to charge the organisations of murderers with the establishment of a Palestinian state....There is no basis for negotiation with the terrorist organizations. It does not enter our minds to negotiate with a body that denies our existence as a state and follows a course of violence and terrorism." The Arabs had handed Israel the best possible justification or excuse (depending on your vantage point) for delaying tactics.

Why did Sadat vote against Hussein at the Rabat summit? Was it perhaps because Sadat, like Kissinger, may have concluded that while an Israel-Egypt agreement was feasible, an Israel-Jordan one was not? At the same time, Sadat must have felt he needed the radical Palestinians on his side to establish his credentials while engaged in bilateral negotiations with Israel. (In fact, the Palestinians turned against him.)

Hussein was anxious to work out some sort of an agreement with Israel. The Israeli government, on the other hand, had little interest in an agreement with Jordan under which it would give up part of the West Bank. The idea in 1976 of a senior cabinet minister, Yigal Allon, to restore Jordanian rule over much of the Occupied Territories but not over the actual western bank of the Jordan river valley, was considered by some to be too generous. In what appeared as a variant of the Allon plan, the Israelis offered to let Hussein administer local government on the West Bank while maintaining military control themselves. This was unacceptable to Hussein and the rest of the Arab world.

To many hard-headed Israelis, there was nothing to be gained from a land-for-peace agreement with Hussein that they did not have already: a *de facto* peace with quiet borders enabling expansionists to "create facts" in Judaea and Samaria which could be destroyed only with great difficulty. The settlers believed they had a God-given right to reoccupy the Land of Israel that outweighed the rights of peoples who had lived there since 135 AD. The settlers were intrepid and tough. But the longer that Israel refused to deal seriously with Jordan, the more Arafat's PLO was strengthened.

By continuing to control the West Bank and Gaza strip, colonial-style, and expanding Israeli settlements there, they eventually drove the Palestinians to their sticks-and-stones revolt, the *intifada*. By trying to crush the Palestinian protesters "like grasshoppers", in Prime Minister Yitzhak Shamir's endearing phrase, they created a generation of young Palestinians whose attitude to Israel and Israelis was one of undiluted hatred.

After too many years of violence and death, it eventually became clear that the Palestinians would never be totally subdued: there would always be would-be martyrs ready to wrap themselves in explosives and blow themselves up in a bus in Tel Aviv or a marketplace in Jerusalem, or hijack an airliner. The national security of the state of Israel could be achieved only by Jews and Arabs living together in peace and harmony, as they had done in the Middle East and North Africa for centuries. The Jews could never impose peace on the region. In the end, unwillingly, Israel would have to talk to Arafat.

At this point, the prevailing Arab view favoured a comprehensive, multilateral peace conference with Israel, its neighbours and the PLO all represented. There were to be no separate peace deals. However, experience had shown that in the Middle East it was hard enough to get two governments to agree. What chance, therefore, for negotiations simultaneously covering the Israeli-occupied Sinai desert, the Gaza Strip, Arab East Jerusalem, the West Bank and the Golan Heights? And what chance of Israel agreeing to talk to the PLO?

The idea was unrealistic. Sadat knew this, and broke ranks with his Arab brothers to achieve a separate, bilateral peace pact with Israel. Hussein knew the idea of a comprehensive settlement was more dream than reality. But this cautious survivor also knew that a bilateral deal was politically unacceptable to the Arab world; if he signed a bilateral deal with Israel that was not preceded by, or signed simultaneously with, an agreement between Israel and the PLO, he would be accused of betraying the Arab cause. For a peace treaty with Israel, Hussein had to wait until 1995.

After Gerald Ford had succeeded Richard Nixon as American president, as a result of Nixon's resignation over the Watergate scandal, the peace process ran into the sand and Hussein was a beneficiary. At issue were a partial Israeli withdrawal in the Sinai desert and guarantees for Israel. President Ford found Israel's prime minister, Yitzhak Rabin, to be obdurate.

Ford threatened to abandon Kissinger's step-by-step approach, which the Israelis liked, and convene a Geneva conference, which the Israelis would hate, since the Palestinians would somehow be involved. This led to a new Kissinger shuttle and a framework agreement which, Ford wrote later, came apart because Rabin "didn't seem to understand that only by giving do you get something in return" and "made me mad as hell".[7]

Ford decided in March 1975 to reassess American policies in the Middle East. While this was going on, he froze new aid for Israel but made an agreement with Jordan for the supply of missiles and other weapons.

Hussein had asked in November 1974 to buy three types of American surface-to-air missiles: Hawks, the biggest of the three, Chaparrals and portable Redeyes. He asked for Vulcan radar-guided anti-aircraft guns and a command-and-control system. The administration made an offer in April 1975 and withdrew it three months later in the face of opposition from the pro-Israeli lobby in Congress.

The lobby, Ford wrote later, was "made up of patriotic Americans" and was "strong, vocal and wealthy". Many of its members had "a single purpose". They accused him of being anti-Israel or anti-Semitic (and Kissinger of "out-Gentiling the Gentiles"). Ford denied it all vehemently and insisted that "the leaders of Israel and the American Jewish community simply can't hold up a legitimate settlement and expect me as president to tolerate it". But they did. On May 21st 1975, 76 American senators signed a letter to Ford urging him to "be responsive" to Israel's request for $2.59 billion in military and economic aid. The Ford administration's reassessment came to nothing. "It really bugged me," Ford wrote.[8]

Eventually, American military aid to Israel was resumed and Kissinger negotiated a second Israel-Egypt agreement for a partial Israeli withdrawal in the Sinai, to be monitored by a team of American technicians, on September 1st.

Meanwhile, the radicalization of the Palestinians and the Jews continued. Local Palestinian elections in 1976 in the West Bank resulted in victory for pro-PLO candidates in about three-quarters of the seats contested.

Jimmy Carter came to the White House convinced of the merit of a comprehensive settlement in the Middle East. But his first meeting with an Israeli leader, Yitzhak Rabin, on March 7th 1977, was "a particularly unpleasant surprise".[9] Rabin offered the idealistic new American leader nothing in the way of fresh ideas; he was ill at ease and timid yet stubborn. A subsequent meeting with Anwar Sadat was much more encouraging; the Egyptian president was open to agreements with Israel. "There was an easy and natural friendship", Carter wrote afterwards. "We trusted each other."

On April 5th Carter wrote in his diary that "King Hussein of Jordan came. We all really liked him, enjoyed his visit and believe he'll be a strong and staunch ally for us as we approach the time for a Mideast conference later on this year."[10] The king told the president that for the first time in 25 or 30 years he felt confident that in 1977 it might be possible to make some agreements.

There followed later that evening an incident that did credit to both men as they relaxed, with Mrs Rosalynn Carter, on the White House's Truman balcony watching airliners landing and taking off at National Airport, on the other side of the Potomac river. Hussein began to tell Mrs Carter how much he had appreciated her husband's handwritten note of condolences for the recent death of his wife, Queen Alia, in a helicopter accident, when he broke down in tears. Carter thought Hussein "was still emotionally drained". He gently asked the king if he would like to visit the coast of his native Georgia for a few days of rest. Hussein accepted, and Carter arranged for two family friends to be his hosts.

In May a political earthquake shook Israel: the general election was won by the hardline expansionist Menachem Begin at the head of the Likud bloc, ending the moderate Labour party's long tenure of office. Begin had been a terrorist in the days of the British mandate when the Stern Gang and the Irgun Zvai Leumi attacked British targets and, in the 1948 conflict, when they slaughtered Palestinians at Deir Yassin. He had become a tenacious nationalist political leader. With him at the helm, any kind of peace settlement seemed improbable. In the same year, however, attempts were made to launch a peace process in which Hussein was involved.

The idea was to revive the unsuccessful Geneva conference under the co-chairmanship of the United States and the Soviet Union, with the aim of achieving a comprehensive settlement. To avoid it becoming a useless talking-shop, committees would be set up to deal with bilateral negotiations.

Israel was opposed. It feared that the Arabs, grouped together, would start a contest for which leader could be the most anti-Israeli and radical; that the Soviet Union would cause trouble; and that such a conference would underline the different approaches of Carter and Begin. American Jews began to put pressure on Carter.

Among the Arabs there was much debate over how they would be represented, given America's refusal to talk to the PLO. Would there be a joint Arab League delegation including Palestinians (which Jordan and Syria favoured)? If not, what?

Sadat was showing signs of wanting to go it alone with Israel. At one point Syria's Assad authorized Hussein to act on his behalf and convene a meeting with Sadat to get Sadat to sign a statement promising not to go it alone. He made no such promise.

Then, like a bolt from the blue in November 1977, Sadat announced his readiness to visit Israel and address its parliament. Begin invited him and he accepted. The groundwork had been laid by Morocco's King Hassan and Moshe Dayan, Israel's foreign minister, who visited Morocco secretly, in disguise, to see Sadat's envoy. Dayan wore a false moustache, a wig and sun-glasses. Sadat's Arab brothers accused him of seeking a separate peace through a third pact with Israel under which all of the Israeli-occupied parts of the Sinai desert would be returned to Egypt. Sadat denied it, but his denial looked thin.

Nonetheless, Sadat's speech to the Israeli parliament gave nothing away in terms of policy. He called for a durable peace between Jews and Arabs but insisted that this could not be achieved in the absence of "a just solution of the Palestinian problem". However, Sadat gave away part of his bargaining position by going to Jerusalem and seeming to grant de facto recognition to the state of Israel in return for nothing tangible. (Begin subsequently visited Egypt and spent two days of talks with Sadat in Ismailia.)

Sadat loved the grand gesture and he had a sense of history. He knew the peace process needed another shove in the right direction. But did he have a strategy? Hussein tried to find out. Hussein's prime minister, Mudar Badran, says the king was "stunned to find that Sadat had gone to Jerusalem without a single plan in his head, without a diplomatic deal behind the scenes, without something – anything – in return. He went off just to break the stalemate and to embarrass Israel."[11] True, but these were not bad ideas. They changed the course of the history of the Middle East.

20   CAMP DAVID'S CONSEQUENCES

President Carter invited President Sadat of Egypt and Israel's prime minister, Menachem Begin, to an open-ended negotiating session at Camp David, the presidential retreat in the Catoctin mountains outside Washington, starting on September 5th 1978. It lasted until September 17th. By Carter's account it was a tense and exhausting experience.

Eighteen months before, when Hussein and Carter met for the first time in Washington, the king had told the president that he would take part in negotiations with Israel provided that they were on the basis of the return of the West Bank and East Jerusalem (the two formerly Jordanian bits of the Occupied Territories). If this could be achieved, the West Bank and East Jerusalem could be placed under international control for several years while the Palestinians decided who they wanted to rule them. The PLO would have to be included. For Israel this was a non-starter and got nowhere, as the king must have expected.

Camp David was run on a different basis. Hussein and Arafat were not invited. It was a three-way affair between Carter, Begin and Sadat. The reason for the exclusion of Arafat was clear: Kissinger's promise to Israel not to talk to the PLO unless it recognized two key Security Council resolutions (242 and 338). But why not Hussein?

Sadat was subsequently quoted by the Cairo newspaper *Al Ahram* as saying: "I refused to allow King Hussein to join us at Camp David because of his style of escalating demands and opportunism." Carter's national security adviser, Zbygniew Brzezinski, told the historian Madiha Rashid al-Madfai: "We refrained from inviting the king to avoid complicating the process. I don't think there would have been any Camp David agreement if there had been a larger number of participants."[1]

In 1977 the Carter administration had found it impossible to construct a common Arab front for a re-launched Geneva conference. So in planning for Camp David, Brzezinski said, "We had the choice of waiting for the slowest party to move forward, or to moving forward with the party that was prepared to move more rapidly, because that served our interest."

On the final day, Begin, Sadat and Carter agreed on a "Framework for the Conclusion of a Peace Treaty between Egypt and Israel" and a "Framework for Peace in the Middle East"; in the following year, on March 26th, the two former enemies signed a peace treaty.

In the short run Begin, tough, tenacious and at times tiresome and unpleasant, emerged as the winner. He achieved a peace agreement with Egypt that neutraliized Israel's southern front, giving the Jewish state greater freedom to deal with its other neighbours. The Suez Canal and the Gulf of Aqaba were opened to Israeli shipping and the two countries exchanged ambassadors. Israel undertook no hard-and-fast commitments over the Occupied Territories, including Jerusalem. The Arabs suspended Egypt's membership of the Arab League and moved its headquarters from Cairo to Tunis; the Arab world was in disarray. For Israel, it was a master-coup.

In return, Begin had to hand back the Israeli-occupied Sinai desert to Egypt over three years. This had never been in the Land of Israel and, apart from an oilfield, consisted of some Israeli military airfields, some farming settlements – and sand. Israel would buy the oilfield's output from Egypt in a special deal and America would provide Israel with large loans to pay for new substitute airfields.

At Camp David, Begin caused a hullabaloo about withdrawal from Sinai, spending long bargaining sessions going through texts word by word. It may be that his concerns were genuine. But the effect of this performance was to distract Carter and Sadat from paying sufficient attention to the areas where concessions were needed from Israel and where Begin had no intention of surrendering anything: the Israeli-occupied West Bank, Gaza strip, Golan Heights and Arab East Jerusalem. The result: the Framework for Peace in the Middle East was vague.

Up to a point, this was inevitable: full negotiations would have to be conducted by the Palestinians, Syrians, Lebanese and – so the Camp David leaders earnestly hoped – Jordan. All that Sadat and Carter could lay down was a framework. So the future of the Occupied Territories was left undecided. In the eyes of many Arabs, Sadat's actions amounted to treason; but many Americans and West Europeans regarded the Egyptian leader as a brave man who wanted to take the road to peace in the Middle East.

Both Sadat and Carter wanted something to show from Camp David, and a land-for-peace deal between Egypt and Israel was within reach. So they worked hardest for it while protesting their desire for an overall settlement.

The document dealing with a regional framework provided for an interim period of five years during which the final status of the West Bank and Gaza would be negotiated. In this period, the West Bank and Gaza would have full autonomy under a self-governing authority whose members would be freely elected. In the first step, working out the best way of setting up the authority, Jordan would take part, as well as Egypt and Israel; and both Jordan and Egypt could include Palestinians in their delegations as mutually agreed. Israel would obviously rule out PLO officials but not necessarily PLO sympathizers (although this issue was not apparently raised explicitly).

In the second step, once the authority was set up, the Israeli civilian and military administrations would be withdrawn; some Israeli forces would be "redeployed" in "specified security locations"; and negotiations would begin on the "final status" of the West Bank and Gaza.

There would be two committees: the first would negotiate and agree on the final status of the West Bank and Gaza strip; the second would negotiate a peace treaty between Israel and Jordan. This latter negotiation would take into account "the agreement reached on the final status of the West Bank and Gaza". In other words, there would have to be a decision on who ruled the West Bank – perhaps its elected representatives, King Hussein, friends of the PLO and, to a certain extent, Israel – before Jordan could sign a peace pact with the Jewish state.

Much of it is reminiscent of the negotiations in Oslo in the 1990s that led to a partial peace settlement for the West Bank and Gaza with

a self-governing authority. There was, however, one important difference: in the Camp David framework Jordan was offered a significant
role and did not take it, and the PLO was not mentioned; at Oslo, Jordan was excluded and the Palestinians were represented by a sanitized
PLO, which had abjured violence. There were more references to Jordan. First, a new police force for the two territories "will maintain continuing liaison on international security matters with the designated
Israeli, Jordanian and Egyptian officers". Second, during the transitional period, "representatives of Egypt, Israel, Jordan and the self-governing authority will constitute a continuing committee" to deal with
the Palestinian refugees.

It all sounded eminently sensible and level-headed. But while Begin
would negotiate, exactly as he had promised, he would go on until he
was blue in the face before agreeing to surrender any part of what he
and his followers thought was the Land of Israel.

Nonetheless, a vital principle was established at Camp David and in
the Israeli-Egyptian peace treaty that would be applied with limited
success in the 1990s in the West Bank and Gaza: an exchange of "land
for peace": Israel would return occupied Arab land and the Arabs would
make peace with their old enemy. In the long run, Begin was the loser.

Sadat had wanted to link the implementation of the two agreements
to make sure that Begin kept his promises over the Palestinians. The Israelis refused. Indeed article 6 of the peace treaty said implementation
was to be independent of any "external instrument" (for example, the
regional framework). Having accepted this apparent loophole, Sadat
and Carter persuaded Begin to approve a "minute" attached to the
peace treaty saying article 6 would not contradict the Camp David
agreements. This still left room for Israeli manoeuvre. Also, Begin was
persuaded to sign a joint letter with Sadat to Carter promising to
proceed with negotiations over the West Bank and Gaza. But a letter
was not a treaty, and a promise to negotiate meant little.

Where did this historic but ambiguous about-turn leave Hussein and
Jordan?

From the outset, the king had been doubtful about Sadat's gesture.
He was not consulted in advance about it. He tried to keep the Arab

world together after Sadat's visit to Jerusalem but was given short shrift by Syria's President Hafez Assad, who smelled a separate Egypt-Israel peace deal in the offing. Hussein did not take part in the Camp David talks. Since the Rabat Arab summit, it was the PLO and not their former Hashemite ruler who represented the Palestinians on the West Bank. If the king had tried to usurp the PLO's role, however tempting this might have been, he would have landed in deep trouble in the Arab world.

One of the flaws of the framework was that Carter and Sadat assumed that Hussein could somehow be won over or pressured into agreeing to play a key role representing the Palestinians. The Jordanian government issued a tetchy statement on September 19th insisting that it was not bound by any statement mentioning Jordan that had been prepared at Camp David. It reaffirmed its support for a comprehensive rather than a bilateral solution; condemned Sadat's actions (without naming him); demanded a complete Israeli withdrawal from the Occupied Territories; and insisted on the Palestinians' right to self-determination.

When the American secretary of state, Cyrus Vance, visited Jordan to brief its leaders, he was bluntly reminded of America's former commitment to a comprehensive solution. Referring to Sadat's acceptance of a bilateral deal with Israel, Vance said: "When one party says 'I agree', we cannot say 'No you don't'. We can't be more Arab than the Arabs themselves."[1] He had a point.

After Camp David was over, the king sent President Carter 14 questions seeking clarification, on behalf of himself and several fellow-Arab rulers. "What does paragraph A mean?" he asked, with more than a hint of exasperation. He also asked under whose sovereignty would the West Bank and Gaza fall at the end of the five-year transitional period. Negotiate a solution, Carter replied. After the five years, would Israeli forces remain? They might, for a while, Carter replied. Negotiate it. What about East Jerusalem? "The Jerusalem issue was not discussed at Camp David," Carter admitted. "It must be discussed at subsequent negotiations." What about Israeli settlements in the Occupied Territories? The framework said nothing. Begin was to claim he had agreed only to a three-month suspension of the building of settlements.

King Abdullah, Hussein's grandfather, with Glubb Pasha.

Hussein and his mother Zain in 1952.

Hussein at Sandhurst in 1953.

At the opening session of the Jordanian parliament on October 21st 1954.

A taste for fast cars.

The king with Muna, his second wife, on their wedding day in 1961.

The king and Alia, his third wife, on their wedding day in 1972.

Queen Noor, the king's fourth wife, whom he married in 1978.

The White House, March 25th 1959: the king meets Dwight Eisenhower, his first American president.

With Egypt's President Nasser, a dangerous enemy and unreliable friend.

On a visit to Paris the king meets Charles de Gaulle, his first French president.

French president Valéry Giscard d'Estaing with pilot in 1980.

Peace-makers and chain-smokers: the king and Yitzhak Rabin in 1994.

The "plucky little king", as the Israelis called him, in 1984.

The world's two longest serving heads of state in 1984.

King Hussein trying out a Kalashnikov, watched by Saddam Hussein.

Peace at last: Crown Prince Hassan, Yitzhak Rabin, President Clinton and Israel's President Ezer Weizman at Wadi Araba for the signing of the peace agreement between Israel and Jordan on October 26th 1994.

The rivals: the king with Yasser Arafat on a visit to the West Bank in 1996.

The new king, Abdullah, and the new crown prince, Hamzah, carrying their father's coffin at his funeral in February 1999.

It was unacceptable to the Arabs, who seemed determined to make the best the enemy of the good. It was too late for Hussein, who had decided that Jordan would not take part in the first stage and would join the Arabs in condemning Camp David. The Saudis joined the rejectionists. President Carter wrote: "All of us were angered when Hussein subsequently became a spokesman for the most radical Arabs."[2] It would not be the last time that the pro-Western king upset his good friends in Washington. .

The Arabs seem to have taken the view that Sadat and Carter, having embarked on such a perilous voyage, should at least have brought home something for them. Instead, the Egyptian and American leaders had agreed with Begin only that there should be more face-to-face negotiations between the Arabs and the Israelis. As for East Jerusalem, they had not even mentioned it. Since negotiations can be dragged out, Sadat and Carter were to a certain extent implicitly accepting the *status quo*.

That at least was the Arab view. The Americans dismissed it. Looking back, Brzezinski argued that at Camp David they had created a pragmatic framework for the future that had to be made to work. The United States had thrown the ball to the Arabs and they should have run with it. He emphasized his point to Rashid al-Madfai: "If the Arab side had half a brain inside its head it would realise that the creation of autonomous institutions over a five-year period on a territory defined by the 1967 lines would make it more difficult subsequently to have any peace settlement other than on the 1967 lines."[3]

Thanks, but no thanks, replied the Arabs at a summit in Baghdad, the Iraqi capital, on November 2nd-5th 1978, attended by 21 of 22 Arab League members (excluding Egypt). The summit participants urged Sadat to abrogate the Camp David agreements and vowed that, if he failed to do so, they would boycott Egypt. Sadat refused, and this was the fate of the leading nation of the Arab world. As a political act, the Arabs' boycott was as obtuse as the decision of the Rabat summit naming the PLO as the sole representative of the Palestinian people. (It should be added that for obtuseness, Kissinger's extraordinary promise in writing to Israel not to have any dealings with the PLO until it recognized Security Council resolutions 242 and 338, reaffirmed by Carter, takes some beating.)

As it was, the expansionist Israelis shrugged their shoulders and went on building settlements, "creating facts", in the West Bank and Gaza. By the end of 1977 more than 5,000 Jews had settled on the West Bank; by late 1980, there were 12,500 settlers there plus 6,500 on the Golan Heights and 6,000 in Sinai (who would leave under the terms of the Israel-Egypt peace treaty). By 1997, some 52 per cent of the West Bank was in Israeli hands. Begin did not hide what was going on; he boasted about it, thereby adding to the bitterness felt by Israel's neighbours. The economies of Israel and the Occupied Territories mingled; East Jerusalem became part of the Jewish capital. The Israelis seized control of water resources and were using some 20 per cent of the West Bank's supply by 1980; they either bought or confiscated large areas of Palestinian land.[4]

As the Israeli economy grew, so did that of the West Bank and Gaza, but much more slowly. The Israelis did next to nothing to improve the infrastructure of the Occupied Territories. They invested little in roads, bridges, ports and railways there. It was not in their interest to do so and thus to make the territories a more pleasant place to inhabit. After all, the hardliners really wanted as many Palestinians as possible to abandon their homes, leave the territories and settle somewhere in the diaspora.[5]

If the Arab world had not dropped a large rock on its own feet by nominating terrorists to represent the Palestinians, and instead given the job to Hussein, the king could have been able to marshal world opinion against Israeli expansionism. If nothing else he could have slowed down its pace. But Hussein was ignored. His experience, his excellent relations with the United States, Britain and France and his sound working relationship with the Soviet Union went for nothing.

Unsurprisingly, there followed a long and sterile period in which Israel talked to Egypt (five fruitless Sadat-Begin meetings by 1980) but to no other Arab leader (except Hussein, clandestinely, and without any breakthrough). Sadat suspended the meetings in 1980.

In 1978 Carter made soundings to see if a meeting between him and Hussein would be fruitful. The answer came back: no. Carter was a qualified admirer of Hussein. Looking back on this period, the president described the king's short stature and quiet, almost deferential, manner. He found the king to be shrewd and thoughtful and a good listener. "Hussein has much more personal strength than his weak kingdom permits him to exhibit," he wrote.[6]

But he also found the king to be "Hamlet-like" in his inability to "make a decision on Jordan's role" in representing the Palestinians at a time when the PLO was caught up in internal squabbles. Carter leaves the impression that, in the king's place, he would have sought to retake the leadership of the West Bank and Gaza and ignore the Rabat decision of 1974. However the king knew that such an action would be fraught with danger for him and the Hashemite dynasty. The situation was bad enough as it was.

Hussein's main worry was that under Begin some 12,000 Palestinians a year were being induced or forced to leave their ancestral homes on the West Bank and move out, "either to Jordan or to join the many wandering refugees in other countries". If this went on, Hussein told Carter, it would undermine the Israeli-Egyptian peace treaty and wreck any chance of a permanent and overall peace settlement. It might also destabilize and radicalize Jordan.

For the cautious king there was a middle way between trying to seize the leadership of the Palestinians from the PLO and doing next to nothing. This was to be available as a modest, helpful and constructive force for peace in the Middle East, accepted on all sides. If the Palestinians wanted him to represent them, in a confederation of Jordan and a liberated Palestine, he would be instantly available. He might try some of his own initiatives. But the PLO would have to be included.

Carter tried to apply pressure on the king to join post-Camp David talks with Israel but without the PLO. Jordan's request to buy F-16 aircraft in 1978 was disregarded. In the following year, the American House of Representatives approved a military aid bill that deprived Jordan of any aid until it played the part it was given at Camp David. There was so much haggling over a contract for 300 American M-60 tanks that the exasperated king bought 274 British Chieftain tanks instead, with the help of Saudi Arabia. Carter also cut American budget support aid from $40m in 1978 to $20m in 1980.[7] Nonetheless, Hussein did not give in, although tensions and pressures did not stand in the way of a visit to the White House by Hussein in 1980.

Ronald Reagan, who became president in 1981, found the Israelis just as difficult as Carter, Ford and Nixon had. Although they exercised great influence in Washington, they were unpopular. The Arabs could have tried to take advantage of American exasperation with Israel. Hussein tried to offer the sane and moderate face of the Arab world to the United States, but his fellow-Arabs did not co-operate.

At the outset of Reagan's presidency, Begin called in the big guns of the Jewish-American lobby to oppose the sale by the United States of early-warning intelligence aircraft (AWACS) to Saudi Arabia. "He lost the sympathy of powerful figures in the administration, and sorely tried the tolerance and understanding of the president," the American secretary of state, Alexander Haig, wrote afterwards.[8]

Sending the AWACS bill to Congress for approval in October 1981, Reagan wrote: "It is not the business of any other nation to make US foreign policy." The vote in favour was 52 to 48. Haig, with a reputation for being pro-Israeli, commented sharply: "Begin nearly won."

That was not all. In June 1981, without telling the Reagan administration, Begin ordered the bombing of Iraq's Osirak experimental nuclear reactor just before it became operational. Begin explained that if he had told Reagan or Haig they would have tried to stop him. Begin feared that the Iraqis were planning to make nuclear weapons for possible use against Israel. (The Iraqis were indeed doing so, partly because they believed that Israel had developed nuclear weapons for possible use against them.) After some governments voiced concern over the Israeli action, the issue was forgotten; several influential powers were privately pleased to see the Iraqi reactor blown up.

On October 6th Sadat was assassinated at a parade in Cairo and succeeded by his vice-president, Husni Mubarak, a former air force general. Mubarak promised to keep Sadat's ideas alive. But the peace process, such as it was, began to slow down, with much assistance from Israel.

In December 1981 Begin infuriated the Arabs and the Americans by deciding on the *de facto* annexation of Syria's Golan Heights, seized by Israel in the Six-Day War of 1967 and consolidated after the Yom Kippur war of 1973. Begin's action blithely disregarded UN resolution

242's assertion of the "inadmissibility of acquiring territory by war". To penalize Israel for damaging the prospects for peace, Reagan mildly suspended a memorandum of understanding on strategic co-operation between the two countries.

"What kind of talk is this, 'penalizing Israel'?" a furious Begin asked the American ambassador in Tel Aviv. "Are we a banana republic? You have no right to penalize Israel." The Israeli defence minister, Ariel Sharon, shouted at Haig: "We are your ally and friend and should be treated as such!" Haig says Sharon "pounded on the table so that the dishes jumped" and that he replied: "If you act like an ally, general, you'll be treated like one."

Israeli-American relations improved on April 25th 1982, when Begin kept his promise at Camp David and returned the Sinai desert to Egypt. But not for long. In June, again with no advance tip-off to its only ally and benefactor, Israel invaded Lebanon, to destroy the PLO's state within a state there. For months the Palestinians had been using Lebanon as a base for a small-scale war of attrition against Israeli targets, and local people as well as guerrillas had fallen victim of disproportionate Israeli reprisals. Lebanon did not have the equivalent of a King Hussein to expel the *fedayeen*. So the Israelis did the dirty work.

Hussein was one of many who warned Arafat of the coming blitz. In early 1982 he sent his foreign minister, Marwan Qasem, to Arafat. "The Israelis are going to hit you once and for all, so be careful," Qasem told the PLO leader. "Don't give them a pretext."[9]

Haig had repeatedly told Begin and Sharon that the United States would support a military action against the PLO in Lebanon only if there was an internationally recognized provocation and the retaliation was commensurate with the crime. The provocation picked by Begin as his *casus belli* was an attempt by an Arab terrorist (not from the PLO but from a renegade faction led by the extremist Abu Nidal) to kill the Israeli ambassador to Britain, Shlomo Argov; the ambassador was badly injured in a London hotel.

The invasion started on June 5th 1982, and by June 13th the Israelis had surrounded Beirut (having at first said they would go no further than 40 miles into Lebanon); they had linked up with their Maronite

Christian allies in East Beirut; and they had inflicted devastating damage on the Syrian armed forces. ("Are you losing patience with Israel?" Reagan was asked. "I lost patience a long time ago," the president replied. "The bloodshed must stop.") Eventually, after the Israelis had shelled and bombed suspected PLO bases in Beirut and elsewhere in Lebanon, the PLO marched on board ships in the harbour on the start of a journey which took them to Tunisia, Yemen and other Arab countries that would have them. The PLO was dispersed and much weakened. Israel was condemned by the UN General Assembly and shrugged its shoulders: enough powerful people in the world were quietly pleased to see the PLO get a bloody nose, although the loss of civilian lives in Lebanon was appalling.

It looked like a triumph for Israel, but it did not last long. On September 16th-18th 1982, with Israeli knowledge and possibly approval, forces of the Lebanese Phalange Party, comprising Maronite Christians led by President-elect Bashir Gemayel, entered Sabra and Chatila, Palestinian refugee camps on the edge of Beirut (which were encircled by Israeli forces) and systematically slaughtered hundreds of defenceless civilians, many of them women, children and old people. The Israelis observed but did not intervene. It was noted that Sharon and Gemayel had conferred on the night before the killings began.[10] Begin shrugged his shoulders. "*Goyim* are killing *goyim*," he said, "and the world is trying to hang the Jews for the crime."[11]

The bombing and shelling of Beirut and the massacres did great damage to Israel's international reputation. Some Israelis, like Sharon, may have thought this was a price worth paying to demolish the Palestinian movement. They were wrong. These tragic events were just more episodes in the struggle of the Palestinians for survival and, they hoped, for statehood. There would inevitably be more. Only after it made peace with Arafat's PLO would Israel begin to feel secure.

Already the next episode was beginning. It was during this period that Palestinians, not the foot-soldiers of the PLO but youths, began to demonstrate and cause disturbances on the West Bank. It was the first indication of what would become the Palestinian *intifada*.

King Hussein must have observed the defeat of the PLO and the humiliation of Arafat in Beirut with mixed feelings and a sense of *déjà vu*. Above all, he must have felt frustrated. He thought, rightly, that he and his family were a key to unlocking the door of peace in the Middle East. He could offer, and indeed had offered, to unlock the door. The trouble was that this door had a second lock which only the PLO could open. And although the PLO had its key in its hands, it was not only weakened by defeat but also, as usual, hopelessly divided between radicals and pragmatists; it could not decide to open the door.

Into this gloomy atmosphere the Reagan administration tried to beam a shaft of light on September 1st 1982. The president launched his own peace plan. He and his secretary of state, George Shultz (who had succeeded Haig), realized that the peace process, such as it was, had been almost destroyed by Israel's shelling and bombing of Beirut and the slaughter at Sabra and Chatila. It had to be revived. Also, although Reagan and Shultz were appalled by Israeli actions, they emerged in public as Israel's worried supporters. America needed to restore its reputation in the Arab world. Hussein would have one of the main parts to play.[12]

Shultz's assessment of the king echoes Kissinger's. He found him "the most engaging of monarchs", short, fit and muscular, and he observed that he addressed his male interlocutors, in a deep baritone, invariably as "Sir". He could at times be sad or petulant, Shultz noted. He managed to combine the dignity and gravity of a hereditary monarch with the charm of a father interested in his children. But although he had a deep sense of history and personal mission, "he has a weak hand to play in regional politics".

In secret preparations for the new initiative, the Americans consulted Hussein. One of Shultz's aides, Nicholas Veliotes, flew secretly to London and thence, aboard Hussein's own aircraft, to Amman. Hussein listened intently. He repeated to Veliotes what he understood the plan entailed: that the United States would oppose a Palestinian state; that it would oppose Israeli sovereignty over the West Bank and Gaza; and that it would favour a link between the Palestinian authorities in those territories and the kingdom of Jordan. "Do you mean it? Will you carry it through?" he asked.

Veliotes replied in the affirmative and returned home believing that Hussein was "a potential player". The canny Shultz said he would await Hussein's considered response.

This arrived in a day. The king urged the United States to seek widespread Arab support, to go far towards meeting the PLO's needs and make clear that the initiative was not linked to Camp David (which remained unpopular in much of the Arab world). Shultz writes in his memoirs that he took this to be a way of saying no. He drafted a letter for Reagan to send to the king saying, in effect, "We have stood up to be counted; now so should you."

In his "Fresh Start" initiative, Reagan said the time had come for a new approach in the Middle East, based on the Camp David agreements and with King Hussein playing an important part. On Israel, Reagan said: "The security for which she yearns can only be achieved through genuine peace, requiring magnanimity, vision and courage." (Such qualities were in short supply among Begin's hardliners.) He called on the intractable Palestinians to recognize that "their own political aspirations are inextricably bound to recognition of Israel's right to a secure future". He also called on Arab leaders, who had boycotted the Jewish state, to accept "the reality of Israel and the reality that peace and justice are to be attained only through hard, fair and direct negotiation".

Reagan's formula was vague. Only Egypt was talking to Israel, he said, and only through "broader participation in the peace process, most immediately by Jordan and the Palestinians", could Israel feel secure. This could be done, he thought, by activating the five-year period of Palestinian autonomy while a final settlement was being negotiated, as envisaged at Camp David. At the same time, construction of Jewish settlements in the West Bank and Gaza would be frozen.

It was the "firm view" of the United States, Reagan went on, that self-government by the Palestinians of the West Bank and Gaza, "in association with Jordan", offered "the best chance for a durable and lasting peace". He ruled out a separate Palestinian state. Reagan said he "fervently hoped" that the Palestinians, Jordan and the rest of the Arab world would "accept this opportunity". Unlike Carter at Camp David, Reagan and his aides kept Hussein briefed as the plan was prepared.

The next day, the Israeli cabinet replied. Its response bore the imprint of Menachem Begin. In harshly undiplomatic language, Israel rejected Reagan's plan. It consisted, Israel said, of "partial quotations from the Camp David agreement or are [sic] nowhere mentioned in the agreement or contradict it entirely". Since the American proposals "seriously deviate from the Camp David agreement, contradict it and could create a serious danger to Israel, its security and its future", the statement added, "the government of Israel has resolved that on the basis of these positions it will not enter into any negotiation with any party".

Begin was right in that the Reagan proposal was not an affirmation of the terms agreed at Camp David but a considerable change. The prime minister, who had both the cold logic of a lawyer and the dreams and nightmares of a fanatic, felt he had every right to reject them.

As for Reagan's proposal for a link between Jordan and the West Bank and Gaza, Begin was brutally dismissive. "Were the American plan to be implemented," the statement said, "there would be nothing to stop King Hussein from inviting his new-found friend, Yasser Arafat, to come to Nablus and hand the rule over to him."

Six days later, the Arab leaders replied. At a summit meeting in Fez, they affirmed an apparently hardline negotiating position which, according to Jimmy Carter's analysis, contained carefully crafted circumlocutions that supported the Reagan statement and implied recognition of Israel.

It had eight points: "Israel's withdrawal from all Arab territories occupied in 1967 including Arab Jerusalem" (that is, the Arab leaders accepted Israel within pre-1967 borders); the removal of Israeli settlements; guarantees of religious freedom; confirmation of the Palestinians' right to self-determination, with the PLO as their "sole legitimate representative"; the placing of the West Bank and Gaza under UN supervision for several months (presumably while a transfer of power took place); "creation of an independent Palestinian state with Jerusalem as its capital"; the drawing up by the UN Security Council of "guarantees of peace for all states of the region including the independent Palestine state" (translatable as a guarantee of peace also for Israel); and Security Council guarantees that the principles were accepted.

This was a reworking of the land-for-peace formula. It was unacceptable to the Israelis because they refused to talk to the PLO and also because the hardline Likud government had no intention of giving up Judaea and Samaria (the West Bank); on the contrary, Begin wanted to take over more Palestinian land, preferably the entire West Bank, and to tell the world that "Jordan, not the West Bank, is Palestine". The Fez response was a deep disappointment to the Americans because the Arab leaders had ignored the Jordanian option, which was essential to the success of both the Camp David agreement and the Reagan plan. For all its flaws, however, it could form a base for negotiations, requiring much give-and-take.

For the Reagan administration, Jordan was an essential part of the peace process. Hussein would be an acceptable negotiating partner for both the Israelis and the Americans. If only he would agree, the Americans, fed up to the back teeth with Begin and Sharon, would be in a position to press them to negotiate land for peace and moderate their behaviour. (Shultz complains that, in addition to pressing on with West Bank settlements, Begin was arrogantly treating President Gemayel of Lebanon like an Israeli puppet.)[13]

"If we actually could produce a genuine Arab partner to negotiate directly with Israel," Shultz wrote later, "I was convinced that the Israelis would be drawn into those negotiations by the sheer force of Israeli public opinion."

A message arrived from Hussein voicing his unhappiness with the Fez response and suggesting that he might imitate President Sadat and fly to Jerusalem to address the Israeli parliament. "I was sceptical", writes Shultz, as well he might have been. In this message, Hussein seems to have been impulsively talking from the heart. He knew only too well how much depended on the PLO's approval.

Reagan launched his initiative as the PLO was completing its withdrawal from Beirut. Arafat's first stop, in a rebuke to the Arab world for failing to come to his aid, was Athens. There, one of his first visitors was Jordan's foreign minister, Marwan Qasem, who invited the PLO chairman to Amman. He arrived in October 1982. Hussein may well have been hoping to catch Arafat at his weakest and to persuade him to agree to a joint approach to the Reagan initiative. It was an impossible task. Hussein could never pin Arafat down; the PLO chairman was probably playing for time.

Arafat's biographers, Andrew Gowers and Tony Walker, quote Hussein as saying privately of the PLO chairman: "The man's a liar. He can't be trusted. He's a shadow leader. How can he claim to speak for the Palestinian people?"[14]

Nonetheless, Hussein and Arafat pressed on, with Hussein seeking to persuade Arafat to accept Security Council resolution 242. He succeeded in getting the PLO chairman to agree to a much diluted draft agreement. According to the version received by Shultz on February 6th 1983, Arafat agreed with Hussein to a joint PLO-Jordan approach to Middle East peace based on Reagan's "Fresh Start"; a negotiating team of Jordanians and non-PLO Palestinians; an undertaking not to link any "non-PLO" negotiator with the PLO; and a joint effort to convince the Arab world of the rightness of this approach.

This meeting, and the apparent Jordan-PLO agreement, was the result of firm prodding of Hussein by Reagan and Shultz. When Hussein visited the White House in December 1982, Reagan wrote and gave him two letters setting out the rewards that he would receive from America, including arms, if only Jordan would enter negotiations with Israel. Reagan also promised to persuade Israel to freeze its settlement-building and to agree that the five-year transitional period during which a final solution was to be found for the West Bank and Gaza, as provided by the Camp David accords, would be shortened. The king said he needed Palestinian support. Hence the meeting with Arafat.[15]

On February 22nd 1983, however, the Palestinians again shot themselves in the foot. A meeting of the Palestine National Council, a loose, non-elected but fairly representative body, met in Algiers and issued an other-worldly declaration of radical demands that must have delighted Israeli strategists looking for an excuse not to negotiate but to carry on colonization schemes. Indirectly alluding to the Reagan initiative and Hussein's ideas, the closing Council statement emphasized, among other things: "rejection of all plans aimed at encroaching on the right of the PLO as sole legitimate representative of the Palestinian people in any form such as power of attorney or agent or participant in the right of representation".

In another bout of foot-shooting, the Hussein-Arafat draft was also rejected at meetings in Kuwait in April 1983 of the PLO's executive committee and the central committee of Fatah, Arafat's own mainline faction of the PLO. Radical Palestinians could not abide the idea of having King Hussein, their old enemy, representing them, even if such a tactical move would encourage support for their cause in America and Europe.

On April 10th Jordan's government announced the end of the PLO-Jordan initiative and declined Reagan's invitation. "We in Jordan, having refused from the beginning to negotiate on behalf of the Palestinians, will neither act separately nor in lieu of anybody in Middle East peace negotiations," Hussein declared.[16]

Reagan and Shultz lost interest; after all, they had achieved their minimum goal of taking the moral high ground by being on record with a constructive proposal. They did not have to face the wrath of Israel and the pro-Israeli lobby in Washington although, had Hussein broken with the PLO and the Arab League and joined "Fresh Start", Shultz might have been prepared to do so. However, it was not clear how far Shultz and Reagan would go to help Hussein, if the king followed the example of Sadat and made a separate peace with Israel, in securing a land-for-peace deal with Israel's hard men, Begin and Shamir.

Hussein and Arafat did not meet again for a year. It was back to a stalemate that could not last. Meanwhile, Israeli expansionism in the Occupied Territories, "creating facts" with new farms and housing estates, continued unabated. Palestine was being taken over by the Israelis.

21 FOURTH WIFE, EXTENDED FAMILY

Hussein's fourth wife, Queen Noor, was a remarkable contrast to the king. Tall, willowy, with a shock of long hair, flashing eyes, an open smile and two rows of perfect teeth, she looked all-American, bursting with vim and vigour and earnest good intentions. Hussein was balding and he had a silver moustache and silver hair; four decades of danger and tension had left their mark on him. He was born in 1935, she in 1951. And yet this odd couple seemed to have worked out a relationship. He seemed pleased to have married such an attractive and vivacious woman; she enjoyed being a queen and promoting Jordan's international standing by her membership of various international organizations. Or so it seemed. The trouble was that the king had a roving eye.

Noor grew up as Lisa Halaby, daughter of the head of America's Federal Aviation Administration under President Kennedy, Najeeb Halaby. She graduated in architecture and urban planning with a BA from Princeton in its first co-educational class. After working in Australia, Iran, the United States and Jordan on planning urban development projects, she travelled through the Arab world doing research on aviation training facilities in order to prepare a plan for an Arab Air University based in Amman. She subsequently joined Royal Jordanian as the airline's director of planning and design projects. In the late 1970s Amman was a small place and in upper-class west Amman everybody knew everybody, so it was not long before the lanky American came to the attention of the king, who was available. The fact that Ms Halaby was much taller than Hussein was of no consequence. They were married in 1978.

She was a total stranger to the life of a monarch: the living conditions, the mentality, the people, the protocol and the way a royal court in Arabia worked. Yet she quickly got the hang of it. She did not try to exert any wifely influence on the king in order to promote, for example, political ideas which she espoused. At the start of the marriage she was very much the wife of the king, doing everything in tandem with him.

"Sometimes the king would be irritated by her," says a close observer. "He could show that in front of his aides. But she is a strong character too, ambitious, and she wanted, and she got, to establish herself as the queen – not equal to the king but not lower than the king. After a few years, she started to create her own personality, her own office. And now, she is working not in competition with the king but parallel to the king in non-political matters."

The queen was very modern: she had a site on the World Wide Web with two photographs and a run-down of her activities.[1] She was also politically correct. She wanted to make the world a better place. She was, for example, president of United World Colleges which is an equal opportunity international secondary education programme designed to foster cross-cultural understanding and global peace. She was also chairperson of the advisory board of the United Nations International Leadership Academy; on the board of the Near East Foundation, helping the poor in the Middle East and Africa; a trustee of the Mentor Foundation, campaigning against drug abuse; and a director of the Hunger Project, committed to the sustainable end of world hunger through the empowerment of women. In July 1998, she began to serve as a substitute for the late Princess Diana in an international campaign against land-mines.

She was also active in the International Commission on Peace and Food and the Centre for the Study of the Global South. The Noor al-Hussein Foundation works in Jordan on projects in the same fields and to preserve and promote historic sites.[2] It was all light years away from Hussein's daily diet in 1998 of Benjamin Netanyahu, Hafez Assad and Yasser Arafat.

However, the queen was politically aware as well. On Arafat's wife, she said in 1997: "Suha Arafat of course has become a friend, a woman that I look upon as a sister, who is challenged by many of the things we are challenged by, and at the same time is in a very unique position. She is welcome any time, with her beautiful baby."[3]

Noor added four children to Hussein's large family: two sons, Hamzah (born on March 29th 1980) and Hashem (June 10th 1981), and two daughters, Iman (April 24th 1983) and Raiyah (February 9th 1986). She also tried to become a substitute mother for Queen Alia's two children: Haya and Ali. "Being stepmother is a difficult role but she has been fantastic," says Haya. "I owe a lot to her for bringing us up so normally. She was the one who was 'hands on' during our childhood and I don't think she could have done a better job."[4]

Hussein had a wife who gave him affection and four children but who could not speak, read or write Arabic fluently. She was, like Muna (Toni Gardiner), not appreciated by the leading families of the country; they thought that their monarch should have married one of their own offspring. She was not appreciated by the nationalists because she was American (and therefore presumably pro-Israeli).

Alia had been ideal. She combined roots in Palestine and the East Bank and she spoke perfect Arabic, Jordanian-style, as well as excellent English and Italian. But even she, by the account of an ultra-loyal aide, suffered because of the king. He had a particular interest, it seems, in foreign nannies.

Eventually, by two unconfirmed accounts, the royal eyes stopped roving and settled on a young journalist working in the royal palace, an attractive Palestinian-Jordanian. By one account[5] the Amman rumour mill was saying the king had fallen in love with her and had promised to marry her. He was 57 at the time; she was 25. Most Jordanians seemed to discount the story, according to this account. However, the story was so persistent that Jordanian embassies in London and Washington issued denials. There were no further developments.

But according to a second unconfirmed account, given to the author by two well-placed informants, the king was attracted and began to visit the young journalist's family at home. Nothing improper occurred. But the visits took place at a time when the relations between the king and queen were, according to the same account, tense. "She was outside the country, they didn't speak to each other, and they started to think about separation and divorce," one of the informants said. The country was always full of rumours and stories of his feelings for the journalist and the king's bad relations with his wife.

At Christmas 1991 the king and queen decided to go separately to London "to reach a conclusion, in or out". "They agreed that they would stay together." Meanwhile, the journalist's mother was indiscreet about the king's visits. The king was angry. There was a lot of pressure on him to dissuade him from taking a fifth wife, as he was not young any more. It was in the interests of both partners for the marriage to continue, and so it did. The journalist went to study in the United States and disappeared from circulation in Amman. She later returned and is now working in the Jordanian capital. The story faded away. But it may have left a residue of coolness.

Hussein seems to have been a good father as well as a demanding one, if results are anything to go by. Alia, daughter of his first wife, Dina, graduated from the University of Amman in English literature. Of the children of Muna, Abdullah, the eldest, had graduated at Oxford University, taken a Master's at Georgetown University and trained at Sandhurst, and then gone on to become a major-general in the army. His brother, Feisal, was a lieutenant-colonel after having graduated in engineering at Brown University.

Princess Aisha, one of the brothers' twin sisters, was like Feisal, a lieutenant-colonel and a high achiever. Aisha went to school in the United States and graduated at Oxford University and Sandhurst. She was the first woman in the Middle East to complete five parachute jumps and to receive her wings, and to attend Sandhurst. She hoped to be the first woman soldier to attend Jordan's own staff college. She was in 1997 in charge of the army's Directorate of Women's Affairs; she was also married with two young children. "I want to prepare my children the way my parents prepared me," she said in an interview. "I was taught that being a princess carried with it a great responsibility in the way I acted and in giving back to my country."[6]

Aisha had no plans to give women a role as actual combatants: that would be pushing her luck. However, she aimed to assign women to more active roles such as in radar control, military intelligence and the military police. "They're young, experienced, ambitious and full of the vitality that their jobs require," she said. But their working hours are between Saturday and Wednesday (Friday is the Muslim day of rest) between 8 am and 2 pm. This allows mothers to spend quality time with their children and lessens the guilt that they feel for being working mothers, Aisha believes. Aisha is a feminist in a *macho* world but she is no rabble-rousing radical. It is difficult for a woman to pursue a military career, she says, but she respects Middle Eastern culture. She thinks she knows the way to advance the role of women in this minefield. How? "With time, hard work, respect and patience."

Queen Alia's son, Ali, attended Sandhurst in 1995 and went on to study medicine at Bristol University. Prior to Hussein's death Alia's daughter, Haya, had been writing a book about her father. What did he think of that? "He keeps nodding and raising his eyebrows when I mention it." What does Haya admire most about her father? "Probably his humility and that he's down-to-earth and incredibly generous," Haya said. "I remember once when I was riding on a motor-cycle with my father. A boy came over and asked for money at the traffic lights. My father didn't have any on him at the time, so he took off his watch and gave it to him." Haya also mentioned her father's sense of humour and his "total perfectionism".

Haya revealed that her father had suffered from intestinal cancer (he had also had a kidney and a testicle removed). "The idea of it was terrifying for us all," she said.

Haya was determined to do well in show-jumping and hoped to represent Jordan at the Sydney Olympics. She and her father owned some of the horses in the stable in Britain where she was based. Before her life took this turn, she gained A levels in classical Arabic, English language and literature, politics and government, and history. She subsequently read politics, philosophy and economics at St Hilda's College, Oxford.

Ali's and Haya's adoptive sister, Abir, graduated from a Washington university.

Of Noor's children, by 1998 Hamza had completed his A levels at Harrow School, Hashem and Iman were studying at the Fay School in the United States and Raiyah was in school in Amman.

Hussein's children grew up in a world of privilege where their father was the king and they were Hashemites. However, they also gave the impression of being able. Aisha summed up the relationship in 1997: "I won't be a hypocrite and tell you that being His Majesty's daughter didn't help me push through some important projects."

Hassan, the king's brother and appointed successor until Hussein changed his mind at the last minute, was another high achiever. After graduating at Christ Church, Oxford, he returned home and embarked on a dizzying round of activities: chairing committees on the national economic plan; founding learned societies; trying to bridge the gaps between the world's religions; and writing books. In addition to speaking Arabic, English and French, he studied Hebrew and understood German and, it is claimed, Turkish. A keen sportsman and a proficient helicopter pilot, Hassan was frequently by his brother's side at important events, went on foreign missions for him, saw ambassadors and substituted for the king when he travelled abroad.

However, a Jordanian who knows him well says that the former crown prince "is loquacious and speaks in generalities". A former palace employee who handled his speeches, in impeccable English, says: "His sentences are so long that by the time you've got to the end of them, you've forgotten what he was saying at the start."

Hassan's wife, Sarvath Ikramullah, the daughter of a Pakistani diplomat, has also been seen as a problem. The patrician lifestyle she adopted while her husband was Crown Prince did not go down well with ordinary Jordanians, who in any event do not hold Pakistanis in high esteem.

22 A DEAL WITH ARAFAT

From time to time, Syria's president Hafez Assad, who regarded himself as arbiter of the Levant, tried to destroy Arafat and Hussein, his two rivals. Assad prodded an independent-minded PLO officer, Abu Musa, to mount a revolt against its chairman, Arafat, in May 1983. Abu Musa favoured only the armed struggle against Israel. Negotiations, to him, meant capitulation. Syria declared Arafat to be *persona non grata* and expelled him to Tunis. His presence was still acceptable in Lebanon, however. He returned there, and led the remnants of PLO forces in the Bekaa valley to the one remaining PLO enclave, around the northern port of Tripoli.

In Tripoli the PLO was starved of supplies by two odd allies brought together by their hatred of Arafat: Abu Musa and his "rejectionist" guerrillas plus Assad's armed forces on land, and the Israeli navy off-shore. It looked like curtains for the PLO chairman, who was trapped.

However, after mediation by the Saudi foreign minister, Prince Saud, Arafat was allowed to leave Tripoli with the remaining PLO fighters aboard a Greek ship under a French naval escort. Once again Arafat – unique, extraordinary, irrepressible, elusive and unreliable – had survived. Not only had he survived but he sailed to Egypt (not to Tunisia, as he had announced) and was given a red-carpet welcome to the country of his birth by President Mubarak. Arafat's visit meant that the Egyptian leader might be coming in from the cold. The Arab boycott of his country, imposed after Egypt's Camp David peace pact with Israel, might be ending. The PLO chairman, sensing his weakness acutely, cast around for other potential allies. In the first week of 1984 the central committee of Arafat's PLO faction, Fatah, authorized him to re-open negotiations with King Hussein. Another stage in the peace process was about to start.

Arafat in 1984 was at one of the lowest points in his fortunes. He needed a venue for a meeting of his Palestine National Council, an *ad hoc*, unelected but broadly representative "parliament" comprising most Palestinian organizations involved in the "struggle" against Israel. Syria was hostile, Egypt was still isolated and South Yemen and Algeria were unenthusiastic. Assuming a modest pose, Arafat asked Hussein if he could hold the council meeting in Jordan. The king agreed immediately. It was not just an act of charity, however. If Arafat had been unable to arrange the council session, his position and that of his faction in the PLO, Fatah, would have been diminished. It would have been a victory for Syria's President Assad, Arafat's and Jordan's long-standing adversary. Syria issued dire threats but the show went on.

Hussein had an advantage. The PLO had been beaten not only in Beirut but also in Tripoli. Arafat had to base himself in distant Tunisia and some of his soldiers were based in the even more remote Yemen. But Hussein was very much in charge in Jordan and tempted to take some risks in order to seize the initiative. He was an acceptable negotiating partner for the Israelis and the Americans, who kept on urging him to put his head above the parapet. But he could do little unless he had Arafat and the PLO by his side. This seemed a good opportunity for Hussein to try to achieve the near-impossible.

As for the United States, "all our efforts were focused on getting King Hussein to enter direct talks with Israel despite the threats of Arab radicals," writes Shultz. "Sometimes the king talked boldly of doing so; at other times he sank into despair."[1]

The king might have wanted to enter direct negotiations and he might well have got the best available deal from the Israelis, possibly with the help of Shultz. But it was out of the question. Arab leaders at their Rabat summit of 1974 had formally declared the PLO to be the sole legitimate representative of the Palestinian people. Hussein had accepted this decision. Therefore, if Hussein was to act for the PLO because neither Israel nor the United States would have anything to do with it, he would first have to obtain Arafat's assent. Attempts to obtain this assent, on terms acceptable to Israel and America, took up many hours in the 1980s. The effort failed. But it was not a wasted exercise. Many of the ideas that were proposed and discarded bore fruit in the 1990s.

The king's approach was consistent. In view of the PLO's non-acceptability to America and Israel because it declined to recognize resolution 242 and abjure violence, Hussein proposed that Jordan and the PLO be represented initially at a peace conference by a mixed delegation of Jordanians and "non-declared PLO Palestinians", headed by the king. This delegation would, he hoped, be an acceptable negotiating partner. But there would be no Camp David-style separate deal between Jordanians and Palestinians and Israel, negotiated by America. Any negotiation would take place only after receiving the stamp of approval of an international conference. To be accepted as a negotiating partner, the PLO would have to recognize resolution 242 and abjure violence. The king also reaffirmed his support for resolution 242 which, he said, he had helped to draft. As a state, Palestine might be part of a confederation with Jordan.

There were two hidden signals here. First, the word confederation is vague and defined differently in different parts of the world. However, while a federation is usually a collection of regional governments in control of all but foreign policy, defence and finance, a confederation is a collection of states with strong powers linked to a weak central government. Switzerland, officially known as the Helvetic Confederation, is probably a good example of the latter.

King Hussein was calling for two quasi-states and a loose central government. This should have gone a long way to recognizing Arafat's understandable insistence on the Palestinians' right to self determination.

The second hidden message was support for resolution 242, which calls for "respect for and acknowledgement of the sovereignty, territorial integrity and political independence of every state in the area". While Hussein was not asking Arafat to say precisely "I hereby recognise the state of Israel and its right to exist", recognizing resolution 242 was coming close.

Arafat, however, would not come that close. To be fair, it would have been hard for any leader in Arafat's shoes, defeated twice in Beirut and Tripoli and facing a challenge to his authority from Syrian-backed radical extremists, to agree to let Hussein represent the Palestinians even temporarily and to have no seat at the negotiating table at least at the start.

Hussein became restless again in the autumn of 1984. In talks with a special American envoy, Richard Murphy, he spoke in terms similar to Ronald Reagan's still-born "Fresh Start" proposal, which gave him a key role.

Hussein hoped to make the PLO internationally respectable and at the same time to win for himself a special and decisive role in achieving peace in the Near East. The king also had a strategic motive for seeking partnership with the PLO. It was that the two parties closest to the issue were the PLO and Jordan. If they could reach a solid working agreement they could build Arab support and gain greater support on the international level. If the PLO could be persuaded to accept resolution 242 and abjure violence, the way would be clear for America and Israel to recognize it and for a peace conference to be held.

Hussein set about achieving this goal methodically. First, he took advantage of the session of the Palestine National Council in Amman to set out his wares in a speech of welcome in November 1984. "The internal situation is one that largely perceives the possibility of restoring the Occupied Territories through a Jordanian-Palestinian formula, which requires commitments from both our parties considered by the world as necessary for the achievement of a just, balanced and peaceful settlement," he said. "If you find this option convincing – recommended further by our ties as two families linked together by a united destiny and common goals – we are prepared to go with you down this path and present the world with a joint initiative for which we will marshal support. If on the other hand you believe that the PLO is capable of going it alone, then we say to you: 'Godspeed, you have our support.'" The king put it bluntly: acceptance of resolution 242 as a framework for a peace conference was "non-negotiable".[2]

The Palestine National Council responded positively. "With respect to Jordan," its final statement said, "the PNC decided to continue the efforts to develop relations with Jordan in order to co-ordinate joint efforts to achieve our common objectives – the liberation of the Palestinian land and individual."[3]

This cleared the way for a meeting in Amman on February 11th 1985 between Hussein and Arafat. As reported to Shultz, they agreed on a common approach: there should be a joint Jordanian-Palestinian confederation and a joint delegation to negotiate with the Israelis. The PLO would be "out at the beginning, in at the end". In return the PLO would recognize resolution 242. However, Hussein and Arafat wanted the negotiations to take place as offshoots of an international conference.

Shultz was dubious about the idea of a conference but sent Murphy to the Middle East to see if he could meet a prototype joint Jordanian-Palestinian delegation that not only excluded the PLO but also included "non-declared PLO Palestinians" that was acceptable to Arafat as well as to Israel. It proved to be impossible.

That is Shultz's version. According to another, negotiations continued all morning and during lunch at the king's residence. At one point, the king scrawled a formula on the back of a menu and handed it to Arafat, who said: "This is excellent." When officials subsequently tried to turn it into a document, however, they found it to be nonsense. This did not stop the two men from trying to market it, but Arafat soon found many of his PLO colleagues were opposed.[4]

Another version is that the terms agreed in February were those recommended by the king together with the idea of some "non-declared PLO Palestinians" meeting Murphy. The Jordanian prime minister, Zeid al-Rifai, four times pressed Arafat to confirm that after the meeting with Murphy took place, he would announce his support for resolution 242, Increasingly irritated, Arafat agreed. Afterwards, al-Rifai said that he did not believe him. Nonetheless, Arafat was taken at his word and the news was sent to Washington.[5]

Oddly, the text of the Hussein-Arafat agreement says nothing about a Murphy meeting after which Arafat would recognize resolution 242, nor is there a mention of the idea of keeping the PLO out at the beginning of the projected peace conference and bringing it in at the end, with a peace settlement at hand. Such proposals must have been discussed without reaching a conclusion.

The key point of the Jordanian-Palestinian agreement of 1985 was that Jordan and the PLO agreed to "move together" towards the achievement of a peaceful and just settlement in the Middle East. This joint action derived from "a common understanding on the establishment of a special relationship between the Jordanian and Palestinian peoples". The agreement emanated from the spirit of "United Nations resolutions relating to the Palestine question" (translation: resolution 242). The agreement reaffirmed support for land for peace (Israel would give back land taken in 1967 in return for peace with Jordan and the PLO). It also reaffirmed support for self-determination for the Palestinians "in the context of an Arab confederation, to be established between the two states of Jordan and Palestine". This phrase was subsequently amended to emphasize the Palestinians' role: it called for self-determination "for the Palestinian people in a Palestinian state confederate with the Hashemite kingdom of Jordan".

The king and the chairman favoured "a resolution of the problem of Palestinian refugees" and "a resolution of the Palestinian question in all its aspects" without being specific. They called for an international conference to be attended by the five permanent members of the Security Council and the parties to the disputes "including the PLO, the sole legitimate representative of the Palestinian people, within a joint delegation". This was subsequently amended to state that the joint delegation would comprise equal representatives of Jordan and the PLO.[6]

The agreement seemed acceptable to the PLO leaders, but it was not. True, it referred to Palestine, like Jordan, as a state. But Palestine plainly was not one and would not become one in the near future. So the PLO would inevitably go into any conference in a subordinate role. Nor was the PLO ready to accept resolution 242, with its omission of any reference to the Palestinian refugees. So, going against their leader, the PLO executive committee, meeting on February 19th, rejected "all the plans of capitulation and separate deals such as the...Camp David accords, the Reagan Initiative and resolution 242" and the granting of "the right of representation...to any other party". Once again, pragmatic common sense had been thrown out of the window.

During a visit by Hussein to Washington in May, Shultz, misunderstanding political realities in the Near East, pressed him to do the impossible to clear the way for negotiations with Israel and for congressional approval of military assistance: this was to declare a state of non-belligerency with the Jewish state. To the Americans it seemed an easy and reasonable gesture to make. However, by making it, Hussein would throw away one of his very few bargaining chips to be used in peace negotiations with Israel and he would make himself more vulnerable to criticism in the Arab world for having done a Sadat-like bilateral deal with Israel.

The king went almost all the way, expressing "a genuine desire for negotiations, proceeding in a non-belligerent manner". To which Shultz commented: "This was not enough for Congress, not enough for Peres, not enough for me."[7] It should have been.

Still alive after this setback was Hussein's plan to form a delegation of non-declared PLO Palestinians to meet Murphy and for this to be followed by a declaration by Arafat accepting resolution 242. There would be a one-day international conference to give Hussein some cover, followed by serious negotiations. The names of the proposed delegation members were sent to Washington by Hussein on behalf of the PLO.

The king promptly learned that only two names were acceptable to the Israelis when Peres announced their names in Israel's parliament. "We were furious," says the then foreign minister of Jordan, Taher Masri. "We had given the names to the United States, not to Israel." Hussein came to distrust Peres.

Murphy shuttled through the Arab world and agreement on the non-declared PLO Palestinians who would attend the near-mythical Murphy meeting seemed close. However, Hussein declined to meet Reagan's demand for a clear commitment to the opening of talks with Israel after the Murphy meeting, perhaps worried about winning PLO support, and the idea was dropped.

In a speech to the UN General Assembly the king offered to open direct negotiations with Israel "under suitable, acceptable supervision". But that meant an international conference or the UN Security Council or both, and could bring in the Soviet Union. Unacceptable to the Americans, the king's proposal went nowhere.[8]

Shultz describes a frustrating experience with Hussein when the two men met at a dinner in New York on September 24th 1985. Shultz says he had prepared a carefully crafted plan for step-by-step mutual recognition ending up with negotiations including Israel, the United States, Jordan and the PLO (after it had accepted Security Council resolutions, recognized Israel's right to exist and abjured violence). The king was recovering from influenza, insisted on a cheeseburger rather than lobster for dinner and was not interested in Shultz's ideas. Six days later, after Hussein had held a fruitless meeting in the White House with President Reagan, Shultz observed to his chief: "Sometimes the king acts like a spoiled child." To which Reagan replied: "George, he's a king."[9]

Next to try to achieve a Middle East breakthrough was Britain's prime minister, Margaret Thatcher, who behaved as if she was impatient with Reagan, Shultz and Murphy. In September 1985 she joined King Hussein in trying to engineer a meeting of PLO Palestinians, provided they were known to have no terrorist blood on their hands, and Britain's foreign secretary, Sir Geoffrey Howe. The big difference between this projected Howe meeting and the much-mooted Murphy meeting was that Murphy's brief was to meet non-declared PLO Palestinians whereas Howe would meet the genuine article. In return for this gesture of recognition and encouragement for moderates, the PLO representatives would have to sign a statement recognizing the state of Israel and abjuring terrorism.

The meeting was to be held in London on October 12th–13th. Two members of the PLO's executive committee, Muhammad Milhem, a deported West Bank mayor, and Bishop Elias Khouri, arrived. So did Taher Masri and King Hussein, who would hover in the background.

However, when Milhem was shown the draft London declaration it was clear that this was the first time he had seen it. He refused to sign and tried to get the British Foreign Office to rephrase it. It refused. He also tried to talk to the peripatetic Arafat, who happened to be in Sudan, where the telephone service barely functioned. Eventually he got through. Arafat claimed it was the first time he had heard the text and told Milhem not to sign. Hussein was furious and deeply embarrassed.

How had it happened? On the face of it, there was a shambolic breakdown in communications. Yet Milhem and Khouri must have asked before leaving for London what they were expected to do, and the well-briefed Arafat must have been told. By one account, however, Zeid al-Rifai, Jordan's prime minister, briefed only Bishop Khouri, who was non-political, and mistakenly assumed that Khouri would brief Milhem. Nobody briefed the PLO's man in Amman. "The king thinks Arafat betrayed him in front of Thatcher," says a well-placed source. "The king values his relations with Thatcher. So he hates anybody who spoils them." But Arafat, far away in Khartoum, must have assumed that his royal rival was up to his old tricks again, trying to regain a role in the West Bank by bypassing the PLO. The incident added to the mistrust between the two men that had begun in the late 1960s.

In any event, the Howe meeting did not take place. What did take place was yet another outbreak of violence that brought Hussein's dealings to a temporary halt.

Israeli success in frustrating seaborne PLO attacks reached a climax on the night of April 20th–21st 1985 when Israeli patrol boats blew apart the *Atavarius*, which was taking a PLO unit on a hare-brained expedition to seize control of the headquarters of the Israeli armed forces in Tel Aviv, take hostages and obtain the liberation of Palestinian detainees.

Perhaps as a reprisal, three gunmen from Arafat's well-trained Force 17 guerrillas broke into an Israeli yacht at a marina in Larnaca, Cyprus, on September 25th and killed a woman and two men on board. The PLO subsequently described the victims as employees of the Israeli secret service, Mossad. Israel predictably reacted with an act of disproportionate state terrorism.

In a display of brilliantly accurate firepower on October 1st, Israeli airforce F-15s destroyed the PLO headquarters near Tunis, killing 70 Palestinians and Tunisians. Shultz was told by the Israeli ambassador to Washington, Simcha Dinitz, that Ariel Sharon had called for an attack on Jordan because Force 17 had an office in Amman. The government had decided against this idea (which would have ruined Israel's relations with the king and destabilized Jordan) and had picked Tunis instead.

By one account, Israel was able to carry out its Tunis attack because it had used top-secret information provided by Jonathan Pollard, who was a Jewish-American working for the Office of Naval Intelligence in Washington and reporting, via an Israeli embassy contact, directly to the prime minister's office in Jerusalem. Pollard was subsequently arrested (on November 21st) and given a long jail sentence for spying.

Shultz says he found the case shocking and chilling and adds that it marked "only the beginning of a long effort to come to grips with the reality and implications of Israeli attempts to steal secrets from its one true friend in the world. American Jews, sometimes accused of being more pro-Israeli than pro-American, were particularly anguished."[10] Shimon Peres was one of the prime ministers to benefit from Pollard's information and it was Peres who apologized to the Americans.

However, Hussein and Arafat were unable to take advantage of Israel's discomfiture. This proved to be a passing phenomenon: indeed, a campaign was eventually launched in vain to obtain Pollard's early release. His arrest had been dwarfed by an event on October 7th that damned Yasser Arafat in the eyes of many, yet paradoxically underlined the fact the PLO simply would not go away or be definitively smashed, and had to be bargained with.

The Italian cruise ship *Achille Lauro*, lying off Alexandria, was seized by four young Palestinian terrorists. They belonged to the Palestine Liberation Front (PLF), a PLO faction whose leader, Abul Abbas, was a member of the PLO's executive committee. The PLF, though small, was part of the loose PLO establishment.

One of the *Achille Lauro*'s 19 American passengers, out of a total of some 400, was a wheelchair-bound Jewish-American, Leon Klinghoffer. He was callously shot and pushed overboard.

For once, Jordan was not directly involved. Egypt's president, Hosni Mubarak, negotiated a deal: the terrorists would hand over the *Achille Lauro* at Port Said and they would be flown to Tunis to be "disciplined", along with Abul Abbas. A furious Ronald Reagan ordered the American air force to hijack the EgyptAir Boeing 737 on which the group was flying from Cairo to Tunis. It was buzzed by F-14s and obliged to land at the Sicilian NATO airbase at Sigonella, where it was surrounded by American troops ready to transfer the terrorists to an aircraft bound for

America. However, the Americans were surrounded by many more Italian troops, and Italy's foreign minister, Giulio Andreotti, insisted that the terrorists be tried in an Italian court. Abul Abbas was later freed and disappeared into Yugoslavia; the four terrorists were jailed.

This was a distraction for leaders who might otherwise be caught up in the peace process. In January 1986, however, some hardy souls including Hussein, Murphy (by this time promoted to assistant secretary of state) and Shimon Peres were seeking an acceptable formula for the international conference so desired by Hussein. He wanted it to convene once to give subsequent negotiations the stamp of international respectability. That was acceptable to America and Israel. But he also wanted it to serve as a sort of court of appeal, to be convened if there was deadlock. This was unacceptable because such a court would include Soviet and Chinese "judges". However, the supple mind of Peres saw a solution. Nobody could stop Hussein from seeking help from the conference but Israel would not go back to it. That seemed to be a positive step forward. There seemed to be general agreement on the format of the proposed conference.

Next came another effort to get Arafat to accept resolution 242, to recognize Israel's right to exist and to abjure violence. On January 25th 1986 Hussein received a written reply from Shultz to his questions about PLO representation. It said: "When it is clearly on the public record that the PLO has accepted resolutions 242 and 338, is prepared to negotiate peace with Israel and has renounced terrorism, the United States accepts the fact that an invitation will be issued to the PLO to attend an international conference."[11] At last, the way ahead to a conference and a settlement, with a central role for Hussein, seemed clear.

But it was not enough for the PLO. In return for accepting resolution 242, it wanted America to recognize the Palestinians' right to self-determination within the context of a confederation with Jordan. Hussein argued that this could be settled later: the important thing was to get the Israelis to withdraw. Nonetheless, Hussein put it to the Americans and received a fudged reply which left matters as they stood.

At this point, the United States put pressure on Hussein in two ways: first, it said that if the PLO could not accept resolution 242, the peace process could proceed without it; and second, President Reagan was sorry but he could not win congressional support for the long-delayed sale of American arms to Jordan. Nonetheless, the Americans also came up with a phrase designed to please the PLO, according to Hussein. They favoured "the realization of the legitimate rights of the Palestinian people".

Arafat sat down with Hussein in Amman on February 5th 1986 with three PLO texts which the latter later described as "bad, worse and worst". Arafat sought from the Americans, as a *quid pro quo*, their recognition of the Palestinians' right to self-determination rather than their legitimate rights. Not an unreasonable request, perhaps; Woodrow Wilson would have approved. But this was seen in Washington and Tel Aviv as opening the door to the creation of a Palestinian state controlled by terrorists.

Arafat left Jordan on February 7th refusing to recognize resolution 242 and American phraseology. A Reagan administration official compared Arafat with an American fish called a mud puppy, a denizen of the bottoms of canals in the south that "flaps about to muddy the waters whenever anything approaches".[12]

Maybe, but Arafat's manoeuvrings had a purpose. His constituency among the Palestinians and in the Arab world was, for better or worse, suspicious of Hussein's ambition to regain the influence over the West Bank which he had lost in 1967.

Many did not want to have Hussein as the monarch at the head of a confederation of Jordan and Palestine with one army and one police force. No prizes for guessing who would be in charge. And many in Arafat's constituency did not want him to accept resolution 242, with its implicit recognition of Israel, without receiving a substantial *quid pro quo* from the Jewish state. If he recognized resolution 242, he would immediately become vulnerable to the charge of treason, especially from Syria-based Palestinian extremists. He was to win *a quid pro quo*, a swap of land for peace, only at Oslo in 1993. But in 1986 there was no meeting of minds.

His dream shattered, Hussein delivered a measured, sober three-hour litany on television and radio, on February 19th, recording what he had tried and failed to do. He ended all collaboration with the PLO "until such time as their word becomes their bond, characterized by commitment, credibility and constancy". On July 7th, Hussein, angry at the language of critics in Fatah, ordered the closure of additional PLO offices which he had allowed to open. The PLO formally ended the Amman agreement in April 1987.

A month later, Hussein remembered his youth. Glubb Pasha died in his sleep at the age of 88. Hussein told the British at the last minute that he intended to speak at a memorial service in Westminster Abbey. The event provided the king with an opportunity to honour the man who had dedicated his professional life as a soldier to Jordan and the Hashemites (after his expulsion from Jordan, he became a writer specializing in the Arab world). However, on the day before Hussein's departure for London, American bombers based in Britain raided Tripoli and Benghazi in Libya as a reprisal against the Libyan leader, Colonel Muammar Qaddafi, and the Arab world, regardless of Qaddafi's reputation, was in an uproar. It was assumed that Hussein would cancel his journey to London However, risking criticism in the Arab world, Hussein did not alter his plans. The British saw this as yet another example of Hussein's bravery.

23 WASTED EFFORTS

By April 1987 Shimon Peres was again impatient with the lack of progress in the peace process. He was at the time foreign minister under Yitzhak Shamir, the hardline Likud leader who had succeeded Menachem Begin. Shamir, diminutive, wiry, stubborn and an anti-British terrorist in 1948, had become prime minister at the head of a national government after an inconclusive general election. Hussein still wanted an agreement with Israel and was prepared to make another effort.

Hussein and Peres, each accompanied by an aide, met at the London home of Victor (later Lord) Mishcon, a successful London lawyer and friend of both the king and the foreign minister (who sported a brown wig for the occasion as a disguise). The Mishcons' servants were given the day off and Mrs Joan Mishcon cooked lunch herself. Afterwards, writes Peres, "the king suggested that the two of us go into the kitchen to help with the washing-up".[1]

Hussein was in sparkling form, "weaving hilarious anecdotes into his pithy political assessments". One of them was the story of Ronald Reagan asking about fishing in the Dead Sea. There was a poignant note: the two men found out that they both had sons who flew Cobra helicopters in their respective air forces. Zeid al-Rifai raised a laugh by recounting his attempt to gain entry to the official guest-house in Cairo to which he had been assigned on a recent visit. The guard stolidly refused him admission until he hit on a ruse; knowing that Peres had recently occupied the same guest-house, he proclaimed himself to be Peres and the door was opened immediately. It was a story with a pleasing internationalist flavour which might become commonplace in the new Middle East, if it was ever built.

The talk lasted seven hours. When it was over, Hussein and Peres thought they had made history, until the old Middle East reared its ugly head. The two men agreed that a new process should begin with a day-long international conference giving what followed a stamp of approval; the conference could reassemble only with the approval of all the parties (thereby giving Israel a veto); there should be a Jordanian-Palestinian delegation excluding PLO members; and after the one-day plenary session, the conference would break up into bilateral, face-to-face negotiations on specific issues.

For reasons that Peres does not make clear, both men wanted the initiative to appear to come from the United States. Presumably, Hussein did not want a proposal that he should head a Jordanian-Palestinian delegation, excluding the PLO, to be seen to have come from him. Peres may well have thought that if the proposal came from him, Shamir, his political enemy, would automatically reject it.

On his return home, Peres mishandled Shamir. (The two men could not stand each other.) He says he briefed his prime minister on what happened in London and read out the draft agreement to him twice. However, Peres says he declined to leave a copy with Shamir, fearing that one of his aides might leak it. "I had to wait several days until the then American ambassador to Israel, Thomas Pickering, arrived to present me with the text of the document," Shamir wrote afterwards.[2] "Thus it looked as though it were an American initiative, which would have exonerated Hussein in Arab eyes of the sin of talking to us."

Ominously, Shamir said nothing, and Peres makes no mention of pressing the prime minister to give the green light to the initiative. Peres seems to have forgotten that Shamir's Likud bloc opposed any international conference that could lead to a land-for-peace deal that could in turn lead to the handover of any part of the West Bank (Judaea and Samaria) to the Palestinians.

The foreign minister may have been more euphoric than vigilant, for without telling Peres Shamir secretly sent a hardline aide, Moshe Arens, to Washington to see George Shultz. On Shamir's authority, Arens told him that if he were to present Israel with the Hussein-Peres plan as if it were an "American proposal", it would amount to a crass interference in Israel's domestic affairs. Shultz dropped what seemed to be a promising idea.[3]

The secretary of state seems to have had the impression that he was being used by Peres to support a plan that the Israeli foreign minister had not even presented to Shamir. Shultz evidently feared getting enmeshed in Israeli domestic politics. However, Peres insists that he did indeed brief Shamir fully. But it was oral: he did not do so with a text and covering report. Shamir blocked the initiative with a speech in January 1987 opposing an international conference and calling for direct negotiations between Hussein and himself (which he knew were politically impossible for Hussein). This was a victory for the hard men, Shamir and Arens. "King Hussein's disappointment and disillusionment were boundless – as were my own," Peres writes.

However, even assuming that Shamir and Shultz backed the idea strongly, there must still have been doubts about the king. Once again he was being asked to put his head above the parapet. Until this point he had followed the ruling of the Rabat summit that the PLO was the sole legitimate representative of the Palestinian people and he had sought Arafat's approval for any major move. This time he would not do so. What might have happened if the crunch came? Would he have stood firm and faced the critics? Hussein was a man of his word, so the answer ought to be yes. But might the sober restraint of Zeid al-Rifai, waved away by an impulsive monarch in the Mishcons' home, have prevailed in the end? Shultz reports that "by early May Jordan had disclaimed the London agreement, leaving Peres out on a limb, testy, and tending to blame me". Hussein had remained below the parapet.

As Arab-Israeli-American exchanges were quietly going ahead, the frustrations of the Palestinians, especially of those in refugee camps, exploded. It was the start of the *intifada*. It made matters worse in the short run, but it clarified minds. Israel's defence minister, Yitzhak Rabin, ordered the army to make a tough, even brutal, response. But time and again he repeated the refrain that there could be no military solution to the *intifada*; the solution would have to be political.

Possibly envious of his foreign minister's clandestine royal encounter, Shamir unexpectedly accepted an invitation from Hussein to have lunch at his country home outside London on July 18th. Hussein had arranged a kosher meal. The talk lasted for five hours. The two men talked around the issues: Shamir favoured pressing on with the Camp David formula while Hussein pointed to his need for an international conference paving the way to separate bilateral negotiations. They reported to Shultz differently: Shamir thought he could work with Hussein; the king did not think he could work with Shamir. The Israeli prime minister tried to line up more meetings for himself, or an emissary, with Hussein: the idea got nowhere in Amman.

Shultz tried a radical new approach on September 11th. There should be an international conference coinciding with and launched at a summit in Washington between Ronald Reagan and the Soviet leader, Mikhail Gorbachev. But its basis would not be the principle of land for peace. Instead, "sovereign control" in "various patterns" in the Occupied Territories over such issues as security, health, water and education should be "dispersed" among Israel, Jordan and the Palestinians. It seemed to be an attempt to blur the issues that had caused so much conflict and disagreement in the past.

The advantage for the Israelis was obvious: they would not have to give up land for peace or talk to the PLO. They could talk about sovereign control in various patterns until the cows came home, or, more precisely, until they had colonized as much of the Occupied Territories as they could. The advantage for Hussein was less clear: the Arabs would not regain control over the territories; the Palestinians would not be guaranteed the right to self-determination; and the PLO would kick up an almighty fuss at being left out of a highly complex deal which offered little that was tangible.

Shultz also proposed that Hussein should agree to bilateral talks with Shamir, endorsed at a summit meeting of Reagan and Gorbachev.

Shamir authorized Shultz to pursue his ideas further. When the secretary of state visited Hussein at his residence on Palace Green, London's exclusive embassy row overlooking Kensington Palace and Gardens on October 20th, he was given a blunt no for an answer. Perhaps out of politeness towards the chief of American diplomacy, Hussein did not criticize Shultz's concepts; he explained that he could not abide Shamir and did not believe he would ever give up land or sovereignty, or discuss the final status of the territories. Again, the

Hashemite monarch's head had stayed below the parapet.

Hussein had every reason not to expose himself to criticism and controversy: he was in the final stages of preparing an Arab summit to be held in Amman in November 1987. Already he had engineered a desert meeting between two long-standing rivals of the Middle East: Syria's president, Hafez Assad, and Iraq's president, Saddam Hussein, together with Arafat. The summit went well. At the summit, Hussein managed to snub Arafat in several ways.[4]

Hussein greeted all heads of state or government personally at the airport, but the man who greeted Arafat was his Jordanian nemesis, Zeid al-Rifai, the prime minister. The king became improbably friendly with another old adversary, Assad (both men were rivals of Arafat in the struggle for leadership over the Palestinians in the West Bank).

In the English version of the final statement, there was no mention of the PLO's status as the sole legitimate representative of the Palestinian people. Arafat had to fight to include a recommendation that the PLO attend any Middle East peace conference.

The Arab boycott of Egypt, for having signed the Camp David agreements, was ended. The summit also consolidated the reputation of Jordan and Hussein, as a legitimate partner in the Arab world rather than an Anglo-American puppet who was too close to Israel for comfort. But there was no suggestion of amending the 1974 Rabat summit declaration: the PLO stayed as the sole legitimate representative of the Palestinian people. (That role would become hard to play: the poor Palestinian masses, throwing stones, were themselves in charge of the *intifada*, not Arafat or the PLO, when it started in December. Nonetheless, Arafat, always ready to seize an opportunity, was posing as their leader.)

Although Hussein had rejected Shultz's latest peace proposal, the United States and Israel had not given up the Jordan option. To Shultz, leaving Tel Aviv for Amman in February 1988, Shamir said: "Tell King Hussein that when I say I'm ready to negotiate final status, I am. And what does final status mean? It means sovereignty."

On March 4th, Shultz launched a new initiative. There would be the brief international conference followed by bilateral negotiations. And who would represent the Palestinians? There would be a Jordanian-Palestinian delegation. There was no mention of the PLO, and no Murphy meetings. There would be a negotiation on Palestinian autonomy in the Occupied Territories twinned with a negotiation on final status. Shultz called it interlock. He was in a hurry.

The Jordanian response at first was that this was "basically a PLO matter". On April 6th the king handed Shultz a document outlining Jordan's basic position, with five points. First, it was impermissible to seize the territory of other countries; the basis for peace would be the return of land seized by Israel. Second, peace should cover all aspects of the problem including the Palestinians' right to self-determination. Third, peace negotiations should be comprehensive and take place at an international conference, which should not be a one-day wonder but remain in session, reflecting the "moral and constant weight" of the five permanent, veto-wielding members of the UN Security Council. Fourth, the principles of resolution 242 should apply to all occupied Arab territories (the resolution itself refers enigmatically to "territories"). Fifth, Jordan would attend an international conference but would not represent the Palestinian people there and would not negotiate for the PLO. But Jordan would form part of a joint Jordanian-Palestinian delegation "if the concerned parties accept this arrangement".[5] This meant that, while deferring to the PLO, Jordan would still have a special status.

Shamir was opposed, Hussein prevaricated, unwilling to turn Shultz down flatly, and Syria was opposed (as usual). The Shultz plan and the Hussein response got nowhere.

The king still wanted to play an important role in Middle East peace-making, however, and he wanted to regain Hashemite influence over the West Bank. For this reason, he had been paying about a third of the teachers and other municipal employees of the West Bank and he had encouraged the circulation of the Jordanian dinar there. He had held secret meetings with Israeli leaders and public ones with American leaders, and been seen as a key player in the peace process. But it had not worked: when the time came to take a decision and act on it, Hussein could not do so. On another occasion he would impulsively indicate a readiness to go it alone with America and Israel, only to draw back when the time for a decision arrived. On occasion he would defer to the PLO and seek its permission to deal with America and Israel on the PLO's behalf. But neither Arafat nor his fellow Arab leaders would authorize Hussein to represent the Palestinians, even temporarily.

For better or for worse, it was the PLO and Arafat who were perceived as the true representatives of the Palestinians. At an Arab summit in Algiers in June 1988, the leaders decided that extra money for the Palestinians should go through Arafat, not Hussein. This was galling and humiliating. Ever since 1967 Hussein had been pumping money into the Occupied Territories, as he reminded the summit. Jordanian currency and passports were still being used. Jordan still paid salaries to 18,000 civil servants on the West Bank and another 6,000 in the Gaza Strip. But Jordan was not mentioned in the final statement as the conduit of aid to the West Bank and Gaza Strip. There was in Amman, said Crown Prince Hassan, a "genuine feeling of resentment".[6]

The king seems to have decided, or to have been persuaded, that he was in an impossible position. There was no point in going on. America and Israel would have to abandon the Jordan option. The next stage in the peace process would have to be handled by the PLO itself. Accordingly, Hussein announced on July 31st 1988 that Jordan was cutting legal and administrative ties to the West Bank, including salaries to civil servants. "Since there is a general conviction that the struggle to liberate the occupied Palestinian land could be enhanced by dismantling the legal and administrative links between the two banks [of the Jordan], we have to do what is expected of us," the king said.[7]

He seemed to rule out the idea of a Jordanian-Palestinian delegation to a peace conference. This put paid to the Shultz initiative – and Hussein's head remained below the parapet.

Although the Jordanian disengagement was apparently thorough, it did not affect the 3,000 employees of the ministry for religious endowments and religious affairs, including the Islamic religious court system. Thus a significant Islamic strand still tied the West Bank to Jordan. Jordan's constitution and the 1950 parliamentary resolution unifying the East and West Banks were not changed. And the weather forecast on Jordanian television still covered the West Bank. Asked at a news conference in August if Jordan had irrevocably renounced sovereignty over the West Bank, the king replied: "Did I say that?"

The theory cannot be discarded that the king was trying a long-range gamble. While he himself had little more than contempt for Arafat (and did not consult with him prior to or during Jordan's disengagement), his fellow Arab heads of state appeared to think highly of him. All right, Hussein may have said to himself, let Arafat take over the full representation of the Palestinians, wages and all, and let us see how he botches the job. There will be no dialogue between Arab and Jew. Arab leaders will see the error of their ways and turn for help to a man of proven experience with all the necessary contacts: himself. If this is accurate, it was a dangerous ploy. Arafat, given an opportunity, never missed it.

In a message to Shimon Peres, Hussein said he took his decision hoping the PLO would "see the light and come to terms with reality".[8] This seemed to be happening. In the previous month, an aide of Arafat, Bassam Abu Sharif, had published an essay indicating that the PLO might be ready to negotiate directly with Israel.

But on what terms? Same three points as usual, said Shultz: accept resolution 242, abjure violence and recognize Israel's right to exist. The PLO responded through a third party with a question: in return, would America hold a dialogue with us and recognize our right to self determination? Shultz's answer: yes to the first part of the question but no to the second on the grounds that self-determination was a code-word for an independent Palestinian state (which Shultz and the Israelis rejected).

In November, Arafat persuaded his parliament, the Palestine National Council, to approve what seemed to be a meaningless gesture: the proclamation in Algeria of "the establishment of the state of Palestine on our Palestinian territory with its capital holy Jerusalem". There was more to this than propaganda, however. First, Arafat was implying that the borders of Palestine would be those at the end of the Six-Day War of 1967, that is, the PLO was recognizing Israel without actually saying so. Second, the PLO was making its ultimate move in fending off Jordanian claims to the West Bank. (Some Jordanian officials had been trying to fudge the issue: they argued that Jordan's role in the peace process as a state whose territory in the West Bank was occupied did not conflict with the PLO's role as "sole legitimate representative of the Palestinian people".)

At the same time, Arafat was seeking an American visa to attend the General Assembly of the UN. Under strong international pressure to grant the visa, Shultz nonetheless refused, citing Arafat's working relationship with Abul Abbas, organizer of the hijacking of the *Achille Lauro*.

Arafat appears to have thought it essential to establish a dialogue with America and Israel, now that it looked as if Jordan had withdrawn from the fray. If Shultz would not drop the price Arafat had to pay, then he would pay in full. Apparently out of the blue, Arafat told a Swedish intermediary that he would meet Shultz's three-point terms and handed him the statement that he intended to make on December 13th. The three-point letter said the PLO was ready to negotiate a comprehensive peace settlement with Israel, within the framework of an international conference and on the basis of resolutions 242 and 338. It undertook to live in peace with Israel and respected its right to live in peace with secure and recognized frontiers "as will the democratic Palestinian State which it seeks to establish" in the Occupied Territories. And it condemned individual, group and state terrorism.

There was only one snag: Arafat failed to make the statement as promised. Shultz says he told Reagan: "In one place Arafat was saying 'unc, unc, unc' and in another he was saying 'cle, cle, cle', but nowhere will he yet bring himself to say 'uncle'."[9]

The next day, at a press conference in Geneva, Arafat did say uncle, reading from a text prepared by Shultz, who promptly announced: "The United States is prepared for a substantive dialogue with PLO representatives". It was a victory for Shultz and a clear sign that henceforth the PLO option would replace the Jordan option. The dialogue would take place in Tunis with the Americans represented by their ambassador to Tunisia, Robert Pelletreau. And that, for the time being, was that.

In April 1989 Arafat promoted himself to president of the state of Palestine, largely so that he could claim equal status with genuine heads of state. In May he declared the Palestinian covenant, which called for the destruction of Israel, to be lapsed, using the French legal word *caduc*.

Hussein of Jordan had faded away into the background. Arafat had the stage, front centre.

In the same month, Hussein took his disengagement one stage further: he decreed a change in the electoral law to delete the West Bank and in November he held elections in the East Bank for the first parliament since 1950 to have no West Bank representation. The king was leaving centre stage. Or so it appeared.

24   WAR IN THE GULF

When Ronald Reagan was succeeded as president of the United States by George Bush, his vice-president, in 1989, George Shultz was succeeded by James Baker as secretary of state. Baker was a close friend of Bush and manager of his presidential election campaign. He had been Reagan's chief of staff and treasury secretary and was a quintessentially pragmatic politician. Bush and Baker got on well with another pragmatist, retired air force Lieutenant-General Brent Scowcroft, Bush's national security adviser. They might have lacked what Bush famously called the vision thing and Scowcroft called overarching concepts, but they thought they knew how to deploy power and fix crises. There was almost an exception. His name was Yitzhak Shamir.

Baker took time to become involved in the peace process but when he did, King Hussein did not figure prominently among his negotiating partners. Baker knew where power resided, and it was not in Amman. Having abdicated responsibility for the West Bank and East Jerusalem, at least for the time being, the king was not a key figure. He would again matter if and when Israel and the Palestinians agreed to sit down at an international conference. The Palestinians would in all likelihood form part of a joint Jordanian-Palestinian delegation at the outset. But the king's support for such an undertaking was well known and not an issue.

From his vantage-points inside the Reagan White House and next door at the Treasury, Baker had watched Shultz's struggles to work out a generally accepted formula for peace in the Middle East with Hussein as a key but ultimately indecisive figure; Baker thought it had been a quagmire for Shultz and could be for him. He tried to keep out but he was sucked in.

The impediments to progress persisted. The Palestinians were led by a man who was unacceptable as an interlocutor to the United States and Israel. After all the brouhaha surrounding Arafat's statement in Geneva, recognizing resolution 242 and Israel's right to exist and abjuring terrorism, he had precious little to show his supporters as a *quid pro quo*. The PLO had a formal point of contact with the United States through Ambassador Pelletreau in Tunis, but this was designed for middle-rank officials and not Arafat personally. There was no prospect of negotiation with Israel.

Shamir was not interested in a settlement with the Palestinians on the basis of resolution 242 and land for peace. His periods as prime minister were marked by increases in the numbers of Jewish settlements in the Occupied Territories. When Soviet Jews were allowed to emigrate to Israel in large numbers, Shamir talked openly of the need for a big Israel. He thought it was the natural God-given right of the Jews to live in the Land of Israel, that is, Israel and the West Bank. This unabashed and tenacious expansionist dealt with Bush, Baker and Scowcroft with delaying tactics and evasions. Like Jimmy Carter with Menachem Begin, Bush came away from meeting Shamir believing he had been promised an indefinite suspension of the establishment of new Jewish settlements, only to hear of new ones shortly afterwards.

Shamir did come up with an apparently innocuous proposal to hold elections in the West Bank and Gaza. Hussein at first dismissed this as a procrastinating tactic, a method of turning the West Bankers into rivals of the PLO in Tunis and of delaying an international conference. He later gave the idea his approval if it led to the convening of an international conference (which Jordan would attend).

There was also the power of the Jewish-American lobby. In a revealing observation, Baker described the principal Jewish lobbying group, the America Israel Public Affairs Committee (AIPAC) as the "lion's den".[1] Baker said that in 1989 he discussed with Bush and Scowcroft a hardening of Reagan's mild criticism of Israeli settlement-building as an "obstacle to peace" since there was a strong case for calling it "illegal". They concluded that nothing would be gained by a confrontation with Shamir on this point. Baker added: "To the contrary it would create domestic political problems for us, thereby making any peace initiative more difficult." (For domestic political problems read AIPAC.)

While American officials bent over backwards to treat Israel politely and to couch rebukes in the mildest possible language, Israel did not return the compliment. After Baker addressed AIPAC and said Israelis should give up the vision of a Greater Israel, forswear annexation and "reach out to the Palestinians as neighbours", Shamir described the speech of the American secretary of state as "useless". On another occasion, Benjamin Netanyahu, then Israel's deputy foreign minister, accused the Bush administration of "building its policy on a foundation of distortion and lies". Baker refused thereafter to see Netanyahu in the State Department building.

After sporadic soundings in the Middle East in which the Egyptian president, Husni Mubarak, played a useful role, Baker presented a five-point plan encompassing an entirely new approach on September 28th 1989. It excluded Jordan. The idea was for an Israeli and a Palestinian delegation to meet in Cairo to discuss elections and even the final status of the Occupied Territories. The Palestinians would be non-PLO, approved beforehand by Israel. This was an adaptation of a proposal by Shamir to hold elections in the West Bank. Baker says he sold his idea to Mubarak and, through him, to the PLO.

At first Shamir was said to approve the idea but then Bush and Baker made strong statements opposing additional Jewish settlements in the Occupied Territories at a time when Jewish emigrants from the Soviet Union were flooding in. This caused "an instant firestorm within the American Jewish community", says Baker, and Shamir was furious. He opposed inclusion in the Palestinian delegation of people from Arab East Jerusalem and deportees. When the foreign minister, Shimon Peres, presented Shamir with an ultimatum setting a day for approval of Baker's plan, "I fired him," Shamir wrote afterwards.[2]

This brought down the government. In its place, Shamir set up a government on June 11th 1990 (three months later) without Peres's Labour Party. He said he would talk only to Palestinians who accepted his concept of Palestinian autonomy, a concept which fell far short of self-determination and statehood. On July 5th Shamir tightened his terms in a speech to his Likud party: elections were possible only after the *intifada* had ended; East Jerusalem Arabs would be excluded; construction of new Jewish settlements could continue; and there would be no possibility of a Palestinian state. These conditions looked tailor-made for rejection by the PLO. "I felt battered, beaten and betrayed," Baker wrote afterwards. "The peace process was dead, the victim of a suicide."[3]

Once again, the Palestinians failed to take advantage of strains between the Israelis and the Americans. On the contrary, they committed an act of crass stupidity that actually eased these strains. On May 30th 1990, two boats (four others having already broken down) carrying Palestinian guerrillas towards Israel were intercepted by Israeli patrol-boats. They either intended to attack a private bathing resort for senior armed forces officers (according to the Palestinians) or defenceless civilian bathers (according to the Israelis). The attackers were members of the Palestinian Liberation Front, led by Abul Abbas, based in Baghdad and sponsored by President Saddam Hussein.

Arafat said (probably truthfully) that he knew nothing about the planned attack, but refused to condemn it outright. Shamir immediately demanded that Bush end the PLO-American dialogue in Tunis. "Painfully aware that the dialogue was all that remained of the shattered peace process, neither the president nor I wanted to end it," Baker wrote. "But when Arafat's silence continued, we had no choice." The secretary of state thought Arafat had squandered any chance of establishing his "credibility or even a scintilla of moral authority" by refusing to condemn the terrorist attack. Angry with everybody, Bush and Baker suspended the dialogue on June 20th 1990.

In Arafat's defence, there were mitigating circumstances. First, Abul Abbas was the chairman's old comrade-in-arms; second, Arafat did not want to annoy Saddam Hussein, who was one of his most generous and regular financiers; third, Arafat drew a distinction between "terrorist" attacks on civilian targets and "legitimate" attacks on military ones such as an officers' club; and fourth, the attack was timed to coincide with an Arab summit in Baghdad. It was designed to assert the influence of Saddam Hussein and to remind America and Israel that the Palestinians could do more than throw stones at the Israelis (which they continued to do, against all the odds).

Saddam Hussein had caught the imagination of the Arab masses and some of their leaders in a speech in Amman in February 1990, when he began to use the harsh language of confrontation: "Given that the influence of the Zionist lobby on American policy is as powerful as ever, Israel might embark on new stupidities in the next five years." There was "no place in Arab ranks" for those who proposed to submit to the United States; the Arabs should close ranks and confront the superpower.

This went down badly with Mubarak, whose relations with and cashflow from the United States were excellent. But it went down well with the Palestinians and stirred Hussein and Arafat. Hussein's speeches adopted a harsher tone.[4] For the time being, at least, he and Saddam Hussein became friends.

Nonetheless, Hussein went to the Baghdad summit in a gloomy mood. He was going nowhere. He had abandoned his role as a participant in the peace process and given it to the PLO but had nothing to show for it. He was dealing with an economic crisis at home and badly needed to distract the attention of angry Jordanians from it. A foreign adventure might help.

Arafat too was in a gloomy mood. He had got next to nothing out of his soft line with George Shultz and the hard men of Israel's Likud would have nothing to do with him. He and the PLO were going nowhere too. It seemed that Shamir, defended and promoted by the Jewish lobby in Washington, was single-mindedly and successfully pressing on with his policy of expansionism in the West Bank, the Gaza strip, the Golan Heights and Arab East Jerusalem. And there was nothing that Hussein or Arafat could do about it. Nothing, that is, until Saddam Hussein invaded Kuwait.

Hussein and Arafat had become dependent on Saddam Hussein's largesse. Since the Israelis had murdered Arafat's close friend Khalil al-Wazir (Abu Jihad) in Tunis in 1988, he had spent much of his time in the relative safety of Baghdad, where three Iraqi airliners were at his disposal. His house was heavily protected. Arafat became more dependent on Iraq when it emerged that some of the money being sent to the

West Bank from Kuwait and Saudi Arabia was bypassing the PLO and being sent to other organizations for distribution. This was Arafat's lifeblood. His frustration with the United States grew when it again refused him a visitor's visa (as a result a Security Council session was held in Geneva, not New York). Meanwhile, Jewish immigrants from the ex-Soviet Union poured in to Israel and asked for housing, increasing the need for Israeli expansionism. Arafat's one dependable friend, it seemed, was the Iraqi dictator.

Both Hussein and Arafat had welcomed and supported Saddam Hussein's initiative in 1989 in setting up the Arab Co-operation Council (ACC), comprising Egypt, North Yemen and Jordan as well as Iraq. It excluded Syria, Iraq's traditional rival, and the Gulf states, which had their own Gulf Co-operation Council. The Saudis, sensing that they were being surrounded, were unhappy.

"The ACC was formed without King Fahd being informed, still less consulted," says the Saudi prince Khaled bin Sultan, who was subsequently the joint commander of Operation Desert Storm. "On the day before its formation was announced, King Hussein of Jordan called on King Fahd at Dhahran but failed even to mention it before going on to Baghdad."[5]

At the start, the ACC was portrayed as an economic grouping but Saddam Hussein subsequently tried to give it a military dimension. The Saudis worried when they were told that King Hussein, whose family has a claim to the Hejaz, had energetically persuaded North Yemen, which has a territorial claim to Saudi territory north of its border, to join the ACC.

At one point, Saddam Hussein offered to give fellow-members of ACC some of his Mercedes-Benz cars. President Mubarak told Baker that he and his delegation had politely declined. "Go to Amman," he added, "and you'll see all the Mercedeses."[6] Egypt dropped out of the ACC.

In ordinary circumstances, the growing dependence of Hussein and Arafat on the Iraqi dictator might not have mattered. But Saddam Hussein had turned into a megalomaniac. And Iraq, weakened by war with Iran and a slump in the oil price from $21 a barrel in January 1990 to

$14 a barrel in May 1990, was nearly bankrupt. Saddam Hussein sent his prime minister to Kuwait to demand $10 billion; he was offered a measly $500m.

At the Baghdad summit Saddam Hussein talked in tough terms not only to the distant United States but also, in a closed session, to Arab oil-producing countries which he thought were over-producing and thereby keeping prices down. He named no names, but looked pointedly at the amir of Kuwait and the president of the United Arab Emirates and said: "You're virtually waging an economic war against my country".[7]

On July 17th Iraq presented a bill of particulars to the Arab League, charging Kuwait with over-production, theft of oil reserves and two off-shore islands; he demanded that Kuwait write off the huge loans it had made to Iraq during its war with Iran.

When Hussein spoke to President Bush by telephone on July 28th, Bush expressed the hope that the dispute "will not exceed limits of reason". Hussein replied: "There is no possibility for this, and it will not reach this point."[8]

Two days later, King Hussein flew from Amman to Baghdad to assess Saddam Hussein's thinking and continued to Kuwait, where he saw the crown prince, Sheikh Saad, and passed on what he had learnt. "He is very angry with you," the king said, according to one account.[9] Saad asked: "But is there a military threat?" Hussein is said to have replied: "Oh no!" Saad asked: "Then why has he massed troops on our frontier?" Hussein did not believe the troops were there, and Saad offered to show them to him. On July 31st Hussein alerted Bush that the situation was serious.[10] Iraq invaded on August 2nd 1990.

After the invasion, Hussein was quoted in an American newspaper as saying that the amir of Kuwait had disregarded his warning about Iraq's military threat to Kuwait. The Kuwaitis subsequently suspected that Hussein had betrayed them. King Fahd had his suspicions. When the Saudi monarch telephoned Hussein on the morning of the invasion, he was told that he was asleep and could not be disturbed.

"Rightly or wrongly, we came to believe that Jordan, the PLO, Yemen and even Sudan had conspired with Saddam to control the Gulf," Prince Khaled writes. "The reluctance of King Hussein, Chairman

Yasser Arafat and President Ali Abdullah Saleh [of Yemen] to condemn Iraq's aggression aroused our deepest suspicions." It was "not far-fetched", the prince adds, to fear that King Hussein dreamed of retaking the Hejaz, President Saleh dreamed of retaking Saudi Arabia's Asir province and Arafat dreamed of turning Kuwait, where many thousands of Palestinians lived and worked, into a Palestinian-led Iraqi state pending the recovery of Palestine itself.

British officials also believed that Hussein felt deeply the loss, as a result of the Six-Day War of 1967, of his guardianship over the Holy Places of Jerusalem. This highly prestigious post had been gained for the Hashemites in 1948–49 by his grandfather. Since the Six-Day War, the king had exercised a long-distance concern for maintenance of the Holy Places but only under Israeli authority. If Saddam Hussein's rash adventure had succeeded, and Israel had pulled back from the West Bank and East Jerusalem, Hussein might well have expected to resume his full guardianship of and authority over the Holy Places. He might have dreamed of this outcome, but the hypothesis was extremely far-fetched.

(In 1994, Hussein's active interest in the guardianship became clear when he was accorded a special role in Jordan's peace treaty with Israel. "Israel respects the present role of the Hashemite Kingdom of Jordan in Muslim holy shrines in Jerusalem," the treaty says in article 9. "When negotiations on the permanent status will take place, Israel will give high priority to the Jordanian historic role in these shrines." This sparked a row with Arafat and the king had to retreat, somewhat ambiguously, from this position.)

Excited by such territorial and spiritual ambitions, the king at times exceeded his customary caution. His description of Saddam Hussein as an Arab patriot, two days after Kuwait was invaded, would not be quickly forgotten by suspicious fellow-leaders. Jordan, along with the PLO, voted against a resolution of the Arab League foreign ministers condemning the invasion of Kuwait and calling for an Arab summit. (The resolution was approved by 14 votes to six.) Jordan and the PLO expressed reservations at the summit about approving the sending of foreign troops to help defend Saudi Arabia.

And had not King Hussein told a meeting of tribes people and parliamentarians that if he were not king he would still be sharif (descendant of the Prophet Muhammad), and asked his audience to call him Sharif Hussein, like his grandfather, Sharif Hussein of the Hejaz? There was no direct proof of a plot, Prince Khaled admits. But he and many Gulf leaders believed there was one.[11]

An incident at the start of the war may well have damaged Hussein's relationship with Mubarak, who was seeking an Arab solution. By agreement, Hussein flew to Baghdad to ask Saddam Hussein to attend a mini-summit. Hussein said Saddam Hussein agreed on August 3rd but the project failed when the Arab League condemned Iraq's invasion. Mubarak said he asked Hussein to set two conditions for holding the mini-summit: the immediate withdrawal of Iraqi forces from Kuwait and the restoration of the amir. But King Hussein "told me he had been unable to discuss details". Possibly scenting a trap, Mubarak told a news conference on August 8th that this was unacceptable. How could he and King Fahd attend a summit "while we still did not know what we were going to achieve"? The summit would fail and the situation would worsen, he added.[12]

Thereafter, Hussein and Arafat tended to side with Saddam Hussein while assuming the role of peace-makers. They warned of a devastating war and urged the Iraqi dictator's critics to back down and let him off the hook.

The king had to take a painful decision: to side with the American-led anti-Saddam countries or to side with the Iraqi dictator. If he chose the first approach, he knew he would stir up a hornet's nest at home for himself and the Hashemite family among the Palestinians living in Jordan. They adored Saddam and loathed the Kuwaitis (who were widely perceived as being greedy, rich and selfish people accustomed to treating their servants badly). In a statement on August 12th which had electrified the Palestinians, Saddam Hussein had hinted that Iraq might withdraw from Kuwait if Israel would withdraw from the Occupied Territories. Since he controlled Kuwait, he seemed to be speaking from a position of strength.

The Iraqi dictator's terms were ridiculously lopsided. He wanted the "immediate and unconditional withdrawal of Israel from the occupied Arab territories...as well as the withdrawal of Syria from Lebanon and the withdrawal of Iraq and Iran [an allusion to the Iraqi-Iranian border at the end of the Gulf war]". After these questions had been solved, said Saddam Hussein, "the formulation of provisions relating to the situation in Kuwait" could similarly be worked out, "taking into account the historic rights of Iraq to its territory and the choice of the Kuwaiti people".

Having in the eyes of the rest of the world cast his lot with Saddam Hussein, the king did his utmost, along with Arafat, to persuade him to modify his behaviour. This effort bore fruit on December 6th when Saddam Hussein freed all foreign hostages.

Mildly echoing Saddam Hussein, Hussein said in a speech on December 9th that the settlement of the Kuwait dispute should in some way be linked to a settlement of the Israeli-Palestinian dispute. The king also said that from the outset, "our pan-Arab duty dictated that we should not be dragged into taking sides".[13] In this way, he claimed, he could work with both sides in trying to mediate a solution. His emphasis on compromise ran counter to the absolute rejection of Iraq's invasion of Kuwait by the Western powers, led by President Bush, and many Arab countries, led by Egypt and Saudi Arabia. But Saddam Hussein's proposed solution, echoed by the king, was pure honey to many Palestinians.

Hussein also made the seemingly innocuous but explosive remark: "The resolutions of the Security Council pertaining to the Arab-Israeli contact, of which the Palestinian problem is the root cause, must be implemented with the same vigour with which the implementation of the resolutions on the Gulf crisis is being pursued." He suggested: "The Gulf crisis, the world economy in its oil dimension, the Palestinian problem and weapons of mass destruction are all inter-related Middle Eastern problems. Any effort to resolve only one of these problems in isolation from the others would fail to produce security, stability and peace in the region."

The king also indirectly criticized the United States. "Disagreement between two sister countries," he said, "turned into a wider chasm in the Arab system which foreign powers, in pursuit of their interest, hastened to penetrate and to interfere directly in our own Arab affairs."

At one point in the air war to wreck Iraqi defences before Operation Desert Storm began, when Saddam Hussein claimed that mosques were being destroyed, the king voiced his support for the dictator and accused the American-led forces of "committing war crimes under the guise of UN resolutions".[14]

For his part Saddam Hussein warmed the hearts of Palestinians and Arab nationalists by standing up to Israel, declaring: "I swear by God that we shall let our fire consume half of Israel if it tries to wage anything against Iraq."

Hussein was reflecting his people's feelings by seeming to side with Iraq. "At home, his popularity has reached a peak," the fortnightly paper *Middle East International* reported.[15] "The harmony between the official and popular positions against Western intervention has accelerated the democratization process and fostered national unity."

On February 15th, when the American-led coalition forces were about to launch a land battle to liberate Kuwait, Saddam Hussein raised his price for withdrawing from it. He added the cancellation of Iraq's foreign debts of $80 billion and the economic reconstruction of Iraq at the allies' expense.

If Saddam Hussein had lost touch with political reality, so had Hussein, who declared: "With happiness and joy we received your reasonable peace initiative, which is based on your genuine commitment to the supreme Arab interests. The demands contained in your peace initiative are legitimate pan-Arab and national demands which are in harmony with our Arab hopes and with international legitimacy. We do not believe a single Arab state can stand against or reject these demands."[16] These were rash words. They were, perhaps, the first evidence of the "new" Hussein, a king disinclined to listen to his courtiers' advice, stirred to action by emotional impulses.

According to James Baker, King Hussein was a "long-time acquaintance and personal friend" of President Bush, and his support of Saddam Hussein during the war was "an act of personal betrayal that had caused the president enormous anguish. It also elicited uncharacteristic anger from the man who prefers to give friend and foe alike the benefit of the doubt." Bush was so furious with the king that he turned down several requests for meetings.[17]

However, Baker knew that the United States would need Hussein's help in forming a Palestinian-Jordanian delegation to a peace conference. He had to stay on good terms with the Hashemite monarch. At the same time, Hussein needed American benevolence. After Kuwait was liberated, the angry amir expelled most of the small state's large Palestinian population and the exiles went to Jordan where some were a burden on the treasury. Jordan's aid donors in the Gulf stopped sending money to the king.

Nonetheless, Baker was not going to let the king off the hook easily. During a visit to Aqaba after the liberation of Kuwait, completed with a ceasefire in March 1991, the shrewd Texan lawyer told him: "It's a rough row to hoe to repair Jordan's relationship with the United States", but promised: "We'll do what we can to help you patch things up with the Saudis." America would be prepared to let bygones be bygones but only step by step and with a royal commitment to helping the organization of the peace conference. Hussein immediately promised to help, and did.

Unlike previous secretaries of state, Baker was not enchanted by the king. He found him to be a "very gracious person" but, in Aqaba, reminded himself that here were people who had said "terrible things" about the United States and were behaving as if nothing had happened. The king launched into a long justification for his behaviour before and during the war that the secretary of state found to be "wholly unconvincing".

In a visit to Amman on May 14th, Baker stressed to Hussein that he needed a joint Jordanian-Palestinian delegation with no PLO links to attend a peace conference. Hussein would have to be seen to be organizing it; Arafat "cannot show up in Amman during this process". No problem, said Hussein. As a thank-you gesture, Baker sent food aid worth $25m to Jordan.

When Baker returned to Jordan on July 21st, the king assured him that he was working on a list of non-PLO Palestinians who would form

part of a joint delegation. Baker concentrated on securing the atten-
dance at the conference of President Assad of Syria, Prime Minister
Shamir of Israel and some acceptable Palestinians. First was Shamir, the
man whom Baker and Mubarak had always suspected of not wanting
peace. He looked, thought the secretary of state, as if he had "bitten
into a sour persimmon".

Baker had painted him into a corner: no longer could Israel claim it
had no Arab interlocutors. As Avi Shlaim writes, the Palestinians "got
on board the bus that Baker had warned would come only once whereas
Shamir continued to quibble over the fare, the driver, the rights of
other passengers, and the bus's speed, route and destination".[18]

Assad agreed on October 15th. The Palestinians offered seven of the
agreed 14 names and promised the rest. Baker asked Hussein to send
the names to Shamir through his "private Israeli channel" in order to
rule out any surprises. He agreed. The king was at last fully on board,
Baker thought. He cabled Washington that it was time for substantial
American aid to Jordan to flow again.

The remaining seven names of non-PLO Palestinians were produced.
By that time the United States and Russia had invited those concerned
to attend the conference in Madrid. The conference opened on October
30th 1991. Its enduring legacy was, as Baker says, that it was held at all.
For the first time Arabs and Jews sat down at the same table. There were
two days of speeches and rebuttals and then the conference broke up
into bilateral and multilateral meetings on specific subjects. The next
stage would be vital.

The Madrid formula suited Hussein because Jordan's role as member of a joint Jordanian-Palestinian delegation at a conference attended
by several other Arab leaders gave him the cover that he needed. It gave
him a role as a peace-maker yet he was no more vulnerable than before.
Indeed, Jordan's presence in the delegation was essential for the conference to be sold to the suspicious Israelis. Once the framework for negotiating peace between Israel and the Palestinians was in place,
however, Jordan would no longer be needed. Henceforth, Jordan would
negotiate with Israel only for Jordan, and not the Palestinians.

Throughout this period the absence of an Arab effort to win over the

United States was evident. The Arabs, with the exception of Mubarak, failed to take advantage of the fact that relations between the United States and Israel were bad. In public, American officials treated Shamir politely as head of government of a friendly country but in private they thought he was committed more to expanding Jewish settlements in the Occupied Territories than to peace. In sharp contrast, Mubarak became a friend whose word counted.

For example, Baker had been infuriated when, on January 22nd 1991, six days after the coalition forces had launched air attacks on Iraqi forces in Iraq and Kuwait, the Israelis publicly and without warning issued a request for $13 billion from the United States in the form of housing guarantees, and proceeded to try to ram it through the American Congress with the help of AIPAC and in the knowledge that the Bush administration was opposed to it because it might upset the peace process. President Bush described himself as "one lonely guy" fighting "powerful political forces" amounting to "something like a thousand lobbyists".

In another incident Baker came close to declaring the Israeli ambassador, Zalman Shoval, *persona non grata* for having said in public that Israel had not received "one cent in aid" to compensate for damage caused by Iraqi missiles, conveniently forgetting the stationing of American Patriot ground-to-air missiles and their American crews in Israel. Baker also refused to see Ariel Sharon during his visit to Washington and he made sure that Sharon's meeting with Jack Kemp, Secretary of Housing and Urban Development, took place in the Israeli embassy and not in Kemp's office.

Apart from Mubarak, the Arabs were nowhere to be seen. Hussein's golden reputation in Washington had been badly tarnished by his apparent endorsement of Iraq's seizure of Kuwait, although he was very helpful in Madrid; Assad was suspicious, dictatorial and provided a home for terrorists; and the Saudis (apart from exceptions such as Prince Bandar) lacked Mubarak's openness, confidence and ability to get on with the Americans as well as with the PLO. Shamir could be as stubborn as he wished.

Everything changed on June 23rd 1992. Israeli voters threw Shamir out of office and brought back Labour with Yitzhak Rabin and Shimon Peres at the helm. The voice of reason and reconciliation was heard in the land.

25   PEACE AT LAST

The Madrid conference seemed to put an end to Hussein's hopes, almost abandoned, of wider Hashemite influence in the region. Palestinians and Jordanians formed a joint delegation to Madrid which could, on the face of it, enable him to wield influence. But the delegation was immediately divided in two for the ensuing bilateral talks. These were between Israel and the Palestinians and Jordan (and also with Syria and Lebanon). There were also to be multilateral talks between Israel and its potential regional partners on regional issues: economics, water resources, arms control and the environment. A fifth multilateral committee, on refugees, was added later.

The key bilateral was between Israel and the Palestinians, held in Washington. It went slowly. The chief Palestinian delegate insisted on referring back to PLO headquarters in Tunis on virtually every point that came up.

Both sides were in a hurry, however. Peres and Rabin wanted to sign a peace pact and win ratification in parliament before the next general election. Arafat was short of cash, his former supporters in the Gulf having cut him off following his apparent support for Saddam Hussein's seizure of Kuwait. Money was the lubricant of the PLO and a source of Arafat's power. Since the post-Madrid negotiations, excluding the PLO, were not working, the situation cried out for a back channel for direct Israeli-PLO contacts (which were illegal in Israel and limited to Tunis for Americans).

Some enterprising Norwegians proposed their own country, off the beaten track and ideal for secrecy, as the venue in September 1992, and they were accepted. Hussein knew nothing about this development, which was treated as top secret. The Palestinian delegation was led by Abu Ala'a, the PLO's shrewd "finance minister".

As the give-and-take bargaining sessions got under way, the idea emerged of an Israeli handover to the PLO firstly of "Gaza first", subsequently changed to "Gaza and Jericho first". These two would be the first components of Palestinian interim self-government. Key areas of civilian life, such as education, health, social welfare, taxation and tourism, were also to be handed over.

The first tentative opening of the back channel took place in December 1992. Jordan seems scarcely to have been mentioned. The only substantial issue affecting Hussein seems to have been over control of the Allenby bridge over the Jordan river. The PLO wanted to control the West Bank side of the bridge, adjacent to Jericho; the Israelis insisted on controlling it themselves, and for a revealing reason: to help Jordan.

"King Hussein and his key advisers knew that joint Israeli-Jordanian control of River Jordan bridges had prevented potentially hostile or disruptive elements from crossing into the kingdom," Shimon Peres writes.[1] "The Jordanians were sure to want this discreet but effective screening to continue, and would not want the bridges to be left to the fledgling Palestinian authorities."

In August 1993 the two sides, meeting in Oslo, reached agreement on a declaration of principles and an interim agreement. To some it proved Abba Eban's dictum that "nations are capable of acting rationally when they have exhausted all other alternatives".[2]

And King Hussein? "A few months after Oslo had got under way," wrote Mahmoud Abbas (Abu Mazen), a senior PLO leader, "we began to feel very embarrassed for not having informed Jordan, and in particular His Majesty King Hussein personally, of this development. Jordan had been our partner in the formal negotiations, had given us legal cover to go to Madrid and had helped us in 'corridor negotiations' in the first Washington sessions to separate the Jordanian from the Palestinian track." Moreover, the PLO had constantly talked of a confederation with Jordan.

Abu Mazen continued: "For these important reasons, we shuddered even to contemplate the consequences of King Hussein's anger if we were to reach an agreement with the Israelis which took him completely by surprise."

PLO leaders urged Arafat to brief the king at their next meeting and he returned saying that he had done so. Abu Mazen was not convinced because he knew that "when Arafat says something he does not really want to disclose, the person listening to him will understand nothing". Abu Mazen says he tried on three occasions to arrange a meeting with the king in order to brief him, but failed. Abu Mazen finally briefed the king thoroughly, but too late, on October 17th. "I do not know if he accepted my excuses or not," the PLO leader writes. "But I do say that he had every right to be reproachful."[3]

After the United States, in the person of Warren Christopher, was informed, the news broke. By all accounts, Hussein was indeed furious that he had been left out. The Americans were said to have been in the dark as well, but this cannot have been so. Peres describes several emotional telephone calls between PLO negotiators with him in Stockholm and their leaders in their Tunis headquarters, in which the " i"s were dotted and the "t"s were crossed. These calls must have been bugged by the CIA. The Americans, like the PLO, withheld their news from Hussein.

First, on September 9th 1993, came a historic letter from Arafat to Rabin. In it he said the PLO recognized "the right of the state of Israel to live in peace and security". The PLO recognised Security Council resolutions 242 and 338 and it renounced "terrorism and other acts of violence". Rabin's reply was terse and to the point: "In the light of the PLO commitments included in your letter, the government of Israel has decided to recognize the PLO as the representative of the Palestinian people and to commence negotiations with the PLO within the Middle East peace process."

On September 13th 1993 Israel and the PLO formally signed two pacts in Washington: a declaration of principles and an interim agreement. A Palestinian Council was to be elected, an administration was to be set up and a five-year transitional period would begin after Israel's withdrawal from Gaza and Jericho. Negotiations on the permanent status of the territories should start "as soon as possible but no later than the beginning of the third year of the interim period". To be negotiated: the future of Jerusalem, the Palestinian refugees, the Jewish settlements, security, and so on.

King Hussein did not get a look-in. "He felt that the Israelis and the Americans, especially Peres, had pulled the rug from under his feet," says a former foreign minister. He opposed Oslo immediately. One day later, he accepted it. Why? Perhaps because he had received assurances from his friend Rabin that, once the Palestinian agreement was tidied away, there would be a role for Jordan – and Hussein. And there was. "The king's ego grew big," says the ex-minister. "He felt so proud, so happy with the role that the peace treaty between Jordan and Israel gave him."

The Oslo agreement set the precedent for the king to make his own peace pact with Israel on behalf of Jordan alone. He could not be accused of making a separate peace and betraying the Arab cause since Arafat had preceded him. Assad did, however, feel isolated, but he had been the enemy of Arafat and the king for years. They owed him nothing. On July 25th 1994 the king and the prime minister of Israel signed the "Israel-Jordan Washington declaration". Hussein also addressed a joint session of the American Congress for the first time. He was often in tears when he spoke with pride about the Hashemite dynasty and Sharif Hussein. By doing a deal with Israel, the king was given a new role, going all the way with the Israelis.

The Washington declaration is redolent of King Hussein's caution. The declaration is described as an "initiative of President William J. Clinton", who receives effusive praise, rather than that of Hussein or Rabin. It continues: "Jordan and Israel *aim at the achievement* of a just lasting and comprehensive peace." The declaration says that "the long conflict between the two states is now *coming to an end*". As a result, "the *state of belligerency* between Jordan and Israel *has been terminated*". (Italics added)

Nothing in the first part of the Washington declaration seemed to say flatly that Jordan and Israel were at peace with each other. In the second half, however, the declaration mentioned specific measures by two nations at peace: a link between Israel's and Jordan's electricity grid; two more border openings; new international air corridors; cooperation against crime, especially drug-trafficking; and negotiations on trade, including an end to the trade boycott against Israel.

On October 26th 1994, however, the Jordanian prime minister,

Abdul Salam Majali, and Rabin signed a full peace treaty at the Wadi Arava border crossing-point. It was followed by a dozen sectoral agreements designed to make Jordan and Israel true working partners, increasingly prosperous as they consolidated peace.

This was the culmination of a long-standing and growing relationship between Hussein and the Israelis that had started with a clandestine meeting with Israeli representatives in September 1963 and was followed by some 700 hours of secret talks and 39 agreements, most of them verbal.[4] Henceforth, Jordan-Israel meetings would be in the public domain.

Unexpectedly, Hussein and Rabin became friends. Rabin said at the signing: "It is not only our two states that are making peace with each other today, not only our nations that are shaking hands in Arava. You and I, Your Majesty, are making peace here, our own peace: the peace of soldiers and the peace of friends."

In his emotional eulogy at Rabin's funeral in Jerusalem, Hussein, his head draped in a red-and-white *keffiyeh*, said: "I never thought that a moment such as this would come, when I would grieve the loss of a brother, a colleague and a friend, a man, a soldier who met us on the opposite side of the divide, whom we respected as he respected us, a man I came to know because I realized, as he did, that we have to cross over the divide, establish a dialogue, get to know each other and strive to leave for those who follow us a legacy that is worthy of them. And so we did, and so we became brethren and friends."

While this may have come from the heart, there was another reason for Jordan's speedy signing: fear that the PLO would become the principal interlocutor for Israel. Rabin insisted at a secret meeting with Hussein in late September 1993 that such a fear was unfounded. Shlaim argues: "King Hussein signed this treaty not simply in order to recover territory and water resources but to protect his kingdom against a takeover bid by the Palestinians and in order to forestall the emergence of an Israeli-Palestinian axis."[5]

The king was also happy to please the pro-Israel American government. After the signing, a delighted Bill Clinton addressed the Jordanian parliament, promising to write off Jordanian debts, to provide military aid and never to let Jordan down. Hussein had travelled a long way from the dog-house to which he had been consigned after the liberation of Kuwait.

Jordan-Israel relations worked well for a time. Jordan's parliament, caught up in the wave of euphoria after the signing and hopeful of a peace dividend, approved the treaty quickly. In April 1995 Jordan and Israel exchanged ambassadors: Jordan's Marwan Muasher and Israel's Shimon Shamir. Parliament also repealed two laws prohibiting trade with Israel in July. Three months later the two governments approved a pact on security co-operation. A parallel effort was made to co-operate on military issues with reciprocal visits by senior officers and by a joint air show marking the first year of peace in which the two air forces flew in a joint formation. In November, Hussein received a reward for good conduct from President Clinton: Jordan was declared to be a Major Non-NATO Ally of the United States.

Relations with Israel remained fairly good under Rabin's successor, Shimon Peres, except during and after Israel's lethal campaign against the Hizbullah guerrillas in south Lebanon, code-named Grapes of Wrath, in which innocent civilians as well as guerrillas died and some 300,000 Lebanese fled temporarily from their homes in the south to Beirut. The first green sprouts of peace were nonetheless appearing.

Tourism increased. In the first eight months of 1996 Jordan had 786,000 visitors, compared with 739,000 in the same period of 1995. Many of them were Israelis. In Petra, Jordan's best known tourist attraction, six new four-star and five-star hotels opened in the two years following the peace treaty. Fifteen more were planned in 1966, but these depended on the consolidation of peace.

Trade began. Jordan's parliament repealed two laws prohibiting trade with Israel in July 1995. The two sides cut import tariffs that would apply to each other as normal traders. Jordan cut the tariff applicable to Israel by 10 per cent for two years for products including pharmaceuticals, medical equipment, communications equipment, plywood, tyres and foodstuffs. For its part, Israel favoured imports from Jordan including cement, pharmaceuticals, toys, furniture and foodstuffs with three levels of tariff: zero, 20 per cent or 50 per cent reduction from

the normal rate. Fifteen Israeli investments in Jordan, in textiles, manufacturing and agriculture, were launched with Israeli know-how and
cheap Jordanian labour.[6]

Economic development was initiated. There was a $90m project to
produce bromine on the Jordanian shore of the Dead Sea and a $60m
plant to produce raw materials for a company in Haifa. The adjacent
airports and harbours of Aqaba (Jordan) and Eilat (Israel) were to
work together. Several water projects were under consideration and
Hussein boasted that Israel had pledged to help Jordan increase its
water supply by 215m cubic metres a year. However, Lori Plotkin, an
American researcher, writes: "Jordanian perceptions that Israel had not
taken sufficient steps to fulfil its commitment…have sharpened popular criticism of Israel and the peace treaty within the kingdom."[7]

In 1995 Jordan was the host for a well-attended regional annual economic conference, attended by Israel and most of the Arab world, at
which the Jordanians presented 137 projects costing $1.2 billion that
they thought merited foreign investment. It reflected the atmosphere in
the Arab world: cautious optimism outweighed long-standing suspicion, resentment and hatred of Israel. The caution came from the Egyptian foreign minister, Amr Moussa, who warned at the conference against
excessive speed in opening up to Israel. This brought King Hussein to
the microphone to insist that he would not walk but run to peace.

A year later, the next regional economic conference in Cairo was almost cancelled; it was held by the Egyptian government only under
strong American pressure. Its unofficial slogan with regard to Israel
was: "Contacts but no contracts." Only 40 Jordanian business people
attended; there were no Jordanian projects. There was a simple reason:
between the two conferences there had been a political earthquake in
Israel. Shimon Peres and the Labour Party lost a general election to
Benjamin Netanyahu and the hardline expansionist Likud bloc in
May 1996.

In less than a year Netanyahu destroyed the trust that had been
painstakingly built up between Arabs and Jews by Hussein, Rabin and
Peres, several American secretaries of state and their staffs, several
Norwegian officials and, at the end, Arafat (among many others).

Netanyahu brought Hussein close to despair, with uncompromising expansionism which not only kicked away the building blocks of peace but also undermined, with unpredictable consequences, the most moderate and pro-peace figure in the Arab world: Hussein.

Inexplicably, Netanyahu chose to open up a long-closed tunnel alongside Jerusalem's Temple Mount, a holy place of Islam, in September 1996. Hussein was not told in advance. Indeed, the king had conferred with Netanyahu's adviser, Dore Gold, on the day before the tunnel was opened, and Gold had said nothing. Hussein was furious.

Netanyahu's action contravened the spirit of article 9, paragraph 2, of the Israel-Jordan peace treaty, which says: "Israel respects the special role of the Hashemite kingdom of Jordan in Muslim holy shrines in Jerusalem. When negotiations on the permanent status shall take place, Israel will give high priority to the Jordanian historic role in these shrines." Arafat, who objected strongly to the Jordanian intrusion in Jerusalem that was set out in the treaty, joined the denunciations and demonstrations.

Opinion polls cited clearly chart the growing disillusion in Jordan over the peace treaty.[8] In one taken shortly after the Washington declaration in July 1994, 82 per cent of Jordanians polled believed that the economy would benefit from peace. In a poll in March 1995 among professionals, 71 per cent opposed trade ties with Israel. In another, in January 1996, 47 per cent of those polled said the economy had deteriorated in the first year of peace.

Suspicion snowballed. Opposition political parties, some of them made up of Palestinian radicals and Islamists, opposed deals with Israel from the start. So did many professional associations which had served as a cover for opposition groups before they were legalized.

After the opening of the Temple Mount tunnel, 38 Jordanian groups – political parties, professional organizations and non-governmental organizations – signed a statement calling for resistance to "all forms of normalization with the Zionist enemy". A senior officer of the royal court, asked by the author if he thought the king had "moved too fast" in opening ties with Israel, unhesitatingly replied: "Yes."

The king was able to undercut his critics in October 1996 when he and Arafat attended a summit in Washington with President Clinton and Netanyahu over the Temple Mount corridor and the Palestinian disorders after the corridor had been opened. The atmosphere was hostile and heavy with suspicion. The king accused Netanyahu of the "arrogance of power". Echoing the views of several earlier presidents of the United States, the king told Netanyahu in Clinton's presence that Israel could never live in security if it adopted a "fortress mentality".

For the king the Washington meeting served at least two useful purposes. First, he appeared to friends and critics alike to be standing up to Netanyahu (although the Temple Mount corridor remained open). Second, he was reaffirming his and Jordan's interest in Jerusalem's holy places.

Nonetheless, the gap between Hussein's pragmatic attitude to Israel and that of traditionally anti-Israel Jordanians was growing dangerously. When a mad Jordanian soldier killed seven Israeli schoolgirls in March 1997, King Hussein cancelled his schedule and went to Israel to comfort the families of the dead girls; radical Jordanian lawyers offered their services free of charge to defend the killer "hero".

Hussein's distrust of Netanyahu mounted as he showed his disdain for pacts with the Palestinians and Jordan that had been signed by the previous Rabin and Peres governments in the name of the state of Israel. Netanyahu kept Israel's word and withdrew Israeli forces from most of the predominantly Arab town of Hebron (as agreed at Oslo) only after coming under strong American pressure and a successful intervention by Hussein in January 1997. Hussein shuttled between Netanyahu in Tel Aviv and Arafat in Gaza and mediated a settlement which he announced after a talk with the former: "I leave here confident that everything will move in the right direction." The royal intervention was a valuable step forwards in the peace process; it was also a reaffirmation of Hashemite concern over the future of the West Bank and a reminder that Arafat was not the only player on the Arab side.

The troubles persisted, however. Disregarding criticism, Netanyahu, who had announced a vigorous colonization programme on the West Bank, went ahead with the construction of a housing estate at Har Homa in East Jerusalem, which until the mid-1990s had a majority

Arab population. The housing estate, which according to the American consul in Jerusalem was not needed, would cut off East Jerusalem from direct contact with the West Bank. Arafat suspended talks with Netanyahu until work on the housing estate was suspended. Hussein joined in the angry Arab chorus.

Playing to his Israeli audience and paying no heed to future ties with Israel's Arab neighbours, Netanyahu barely complied with Israel's promise of a troop withdrawal in the West Bank in March 1997 by deciding on pulling out of only nine per cent of the land area at issue. Reliable press reports in June that Netanyahu planned to annex more than half of the West Bank seemed to many Jordanians to be the last straw.

Many Jordanian business people who wanted to do deals with their Israeli counterparts were said to have decided not to do so, for fear of being boycotted by fellow-Jordanians as economic collaborators. As for trade between Jordan and the self-rule areas of the West Bank, Jordanian business people found this was restricted by Israeli officialdom. The excuse was Israel's need for high security; the real reason, many Jordanians thought, was to protect the sale of relatively high-priced Israeli goods in what had been a closed market.

In March Hussein's bitterness and exasperation with Netanyahu boiled over. He wrote an open letter to him that must be without precedent in relations between leaders of neighbouring states and is worth quoting extensively. "I am deeply pained by the cumulative tragic acts which you started, as prime minister of Israel, thus making peace look more and more like a distant mirage," he wrote. "I might have remained aloof had not the lives of all Arabs and Israelis and their future been swiftly sliding towards a swamp of blood and tragedies as a result of fear and loss of hope."

Hussein rejected Netanyahu's "repeated excuses" that he had been under "pressure and coercion" since he was the first prime minister to be directly elected by popular vote and therefore had political power. "The bitter reality", Hussein added, "is that I am beginning to see that I do not find in you a person standing at my side to implement almighty God's will to achieve a final reconciliation among all the descendants of Abraham. It seems that the path you have followed will lead to the destruction of all that I and the Hashemite family believed."

Displaying the depth of his distrust of Netanyahu, he continued: "If your intention is to draw our Palestinian brothers into an inevitable armed resistance, then you should go ahead and send your bulldozers to the area suggested for constructing settlements without regard for the feelings of the Palestinians and the Arabs, or for their anger and despair, without doing anything to improve the situation. You should also give orders to your strong armed forces, which surround the Palestinian cities, to commit crimes in a manner that may lead to a new displacement for the tormented Palestinians from the country of their fathers. By this you would wipe out the peace process for ever." In other words, the king expected the Israelis to provoke the Palestinians into acts of violence that would serve as justification of more Israeli seizures of Palestinian land and the expulsion of more Palestinians.

Later in the letter comes an extraordinary *cri de coeur* when he asks: "How can I work with you as a peace partner and as a genuine friend in this troubled and confused atmosphere, at a time when I feel there is an intention to destroy all that I have built between our two peoples and countries?"[9]

Netanyahu in his reply took the approach of a cold debater. The peace process was defective, he wrote. That was why he had been elected. The king should count his lucky stars, Netanyahu implied. At the time of the election, the peace process was "in its death throes", Netanyahu claimed. "Instead of letting the Oslo agreement die out after the election, however, I looked for a way to try to revive it." He was "surprised at the personal tone of the attacks against me". Netanyahu brushed off Hussein's heartfelt protest as one of the "inevitable difficulties that occasionally crop up in the peace process" and said that these should not cause "drastic fluctuations" in Israel-Jordan relations.

Netanyahu concluded with an odd suggestion that implied that the Jordan-Israel peace treaty did not matter much. "It is our duty to understand our joint historic role and not to allow the obstacles on the Palestinian track to overshadow the understandings reached back in the days of my predecessors," he wrote. Presumably he was not referring to Rabin and Peres, his immediate predecessors, or to the Arava peace treaty. Who, then? Begin and Shamir, or further back? And what under-standings?

He seems to have been alluding to the days when the king used to have clandestine meetings with Israeli officials to deal with routine problems, as well as to plan for peace, through "understandings". A return to those days would require a great leap backwards. Or was Netanyahu telling Hussein to stop complicating his life by helping Arafat and meddling in Palestinian issues?

In any event, by mid-1997 the king's worst fears looked likely to be-come reality. The peace process was widely described as dying or dead. Construction of the Har Homa housing estate was suspended but the expansion of some West Bank and Gaza settlements was going ahead. The Temple Mount tunnel was still open. The quiet but steady pur-chase by Jews of houses in Jerusalem from Arabs and Christians pro-ceeded. Few Palestinians took seriously a promise by the government to build thousands of flats for Palestinians in East Jerusalem. Among the Palestinians there was a quiet sense of growing desperation yet also a growing conviction that an outbreak of a new *intifada* would only hand the Israelis an excuse for delaying implementation of the Oslo agree-ments or even abrogating them.

As things stood in mid-1998, the failure of the peace process was undermining the position of King Hussein, its strongest supporter, whose head was well and truly above the parapet and clearly exposed. It must have been a tempting target to extremists of various persuasions. When he followed Arafat in making peace with Israel, it was with Yitzhak Rabin and it looked a safe move. Rabin would probably have won the next election and peace would have been consolidated. How-ever, the king had not imagined that his friend would soon be assassi-nated and replaced as leader of the Labour party by Peres, a statesman less respected at home than abroad, and that Peres would lose the election to the fast-talking Netanyahu.

26 DEMOCRACY AND SURVIVAL

At his death in 1999 Hussein was in his 46th year as king of Jordan. How, in such a volatile part of the world as the Middle East, did he manage it? There is no simple answer. A combination of many factors, some of them personal and others strategic or accidental, brought this about.

Hussein's personality helped. The king was canny but not an intellectual. He was a mixture of caution and impulsiveness, of ambition but also of realism; he could be passive but also an activist. Such a combination of opposites could have been fatal. In the king's case, the synthesis succeeded. The evidence is the length of his reign.

His education ensured that he would be no intellectual: modest schools in Amman followed by short spells at a school in Alexandria, at Harrow and at Sandhurst gave him little opportunity to develop a philosophy of government, for example. He was a contrast to his brother, Prince Hassan, who studied at Oxford University and has contributed to the inter-faith dialogue and to the development of science and education in Jordan. Hussein was very much the pragmatic politician and devout Muslim who scattered pious phrases through his speeches and news conferences.

Nobody could fault Hussein on religious grounds except activists who wanted to follow Iran in installing a theocratic state. Here, after all, was a man who claimed to be a direct descendant of the Prophet Muhammad and who until 1967 was the protector of Islam's Holy Places in Jerusalem.

Hussein did not hesitate to cause trouble occasionally for his neighbours, Syria and Egypt, by supporting the Muslim Brotherhoods in these two countries. In the late 1980s he allowed Islamic activists to form political groups, stand for parliament and hold ministerial posts. Hussein always made sure he had a defence against criticism, or attack, on religious grounds.

This did not mean that he espoused Islamic extremism, however. On the contrary, his stance as a devout Muslim gave him the strength to withstand extremist pressures and, for example, rule over a secular state and, among other things, respect women's rights.

Another essential factor in Hussein's success was his relationship with the armed forces, whose leaders in other parts of the Arab world have not hesitated to seize political power. In Jordan they did not do so. Jordan's Arab Legion, under Lieutenant-General Sir John Bagot Glubb, was imbued with the British tradition of service to the civilian authorities. Hussein won the loyalty of the Legion's Jordanian officers by ousting Glubb and replacing him and other outgoing British officers with newly promoted Jordanians. He won the loyalty of his soldiers, especially those in the Bedouin units, by treating them with respect and visiting their camps frequently. He won not only the loyalty but also the respect of the air force by learning to become a skilled pilot, flying jet fighters, airliners and helicopters.

He won the loyalty of many – though not all – civilian politicians and, in doing so, helped to convert Jordan, which is essentially an artificial country created by Winston Churchill, into a cohesive whole. He did this by ensuring that his cabinets, of which there have been many, brought together representatives from Amman and towns to the north and south.

Using the traditional tactic of a strongman, he switched around his governments frequently. No one man was allowed access to so much political power that he might consider imposing himself as the real ruler of Jordan. Many representatives of good families did their stint as a cabinet minister, won respect and were grateful.

In his early years as king, Hussein relied heavily on his uncle, Sharif Nasser bin Jamil, for advice and company. Sharif Nasser was a canny practitioner of *realpolitik*. Later, it was the turn of Wasfi al-Tall, until his assassination, and subsequently Zeid al-Rifai. All were loyal. They had good reason: their positions of power and privilege depended on Hussein remaining on the throne. Nobody stayed long as prime minister. By early 1998 the king had had 55 governments including several with the same prime minister.

As one ex-premier put it: "To be the prime minister of Jordan with the long-lasting and mature leadership of the king, it's not an easy job. You have to have a strong character and a convincing argument and support within your circle. If you know your job, if you are not worried about losing your job, you can deal with the king, it will be a smooth relationship, and it could be an exchange of authority and power. Of course, he is the source of power – nobody disputes that. But it has to be shared, and it depends on the character of the prime minister. The present prime minister [in 1998], Mr Majali, has nothing to do with running the affairs of state. The king is declaring, acting, agreeing outside the knowledge of the prime minister. He accepts that, and the king likes that, so this is how it is going."

A less well-known part of government, the General Intelligence Directorate (roughly equivalent to America's Central Intelligence Agency) and the Public Security Directorate (roughly equivalent to the Federal Bureau of Investigation), played a large role in Hussein's survival. They appear to have thwarted several attempted coups originating in Nasser's Egypt and Assad's Syria. The state security court and broad police powers remain in place as vestiges of martial law, which was imposed from 1967 to 1991.

Hussein defended the Hashemites with the style of a strongman. "There has been a steady improvement in the human rights situation", according to the American State Department's Country Report on Human Rights Practices for 1996, published in January 1997. But the report adds: "Nonetheless, problems remain, including: arbitrary arrest; abuse and mistreatment of detainees; prolonged detention without charge; lack of due process; harassment of opposition political parties; restrictions on the freedoms of speech, press, assembly and association. Human rights activists protested detentions, the arrest of journalists and opposition party members.... Citizens do not have the right to change their form of government, although in recent years the king has taken steps to increase participation in the political system, such as legalizing political parties. Parliamentary elections in 1993 and municipal elections in 1995 were largely free and fair although there were opposition accusations of government misconduct."

Apart from the free and fair elections, it sounds bad. However, Hussein's was not a regime built on fear and repression. It was geared to the survival of the Hashemites and a better life for Jordanians. Opponents were not ruthlessly tortured and killed (although there was a case in 1996 of a Palestinian guerrilla dying while in detention). The opposition was given considerable leeway. What it could not do, however, was challenge the Hashemites. These were Hussein's rules of the game. Most Jordanians could understand them.

Accused of a non-political crime, most Jordanians could be confident of getting a reasonably fair trial. In ordinary cases, the criminal justice system functions independently. Courts are usually open. However, there was damaging testimony in a case in July 1996 when the defendants were charged with plotting to carry out extremist attacks and illegally possessing and manufacturing explosives. The testimony showed that the defendants had been detained by security forces for five months without charge and without access to an attorney, before being transferred to a military prosecutor for questioning. All defendants claimed they were forced to confess during their five-month detention. Four of the 13 defendants were found to be innocent and nine were found to be guilty in varying degrees. The guilty defendants were given long jail terms and one was sentenced to death. This sentence was subsequently reduced to life imprisonment. The Jordanian press carried details of the trial including allegations of torture.[1] Elsewhere in the Arab world the treatment of the detainees could have been far worse.

Local police detention facilities are Spartan but clean, the State Department says. The International Committee of the Red Cross is allowed unrestricted access to prisoners and prisons. However, following riots over an increase in the price of bread in 1996, "the Committee was not allowed to inspect prisons or assess the condition of detainees until seven weeks after the first arrests". A regime that promises citizens a reasonably good chance of a fair trial merits support.

Hussein was a good fund-raiser. As an artificial country, Jordan cannot survive on its own. Under King Abdullah and during the early years of King Hussein, the essential cash came from Britain. As Britain faded, so did its remittances and Hussein found a new partner in the United States. Hussein presented himself to President Eisenhower as an anti-Communist and he was welcomed as such. American remittances have continued, on and off, ever since. Money has also come from Iraq, Saudi Arabia, Kuwait and the smaller Gulf states, which financed the so-called "frontline states" of Egypt and Syria as well as Jordan and the PLO.

Hussein paid dearly for his implicit backing of Saddam Hussein's grab of Kuwait: all of his backers stopped paying. Iraq had run out of money and the others wanted to punish the Machiavellian ruler. By 1997, however, relations with all the Gulf states except Kuwait itself had been restored, albeit without a cash-flow, after much eating of humble pie by Jordan. In that year, Jordan was relying heavily on aid from the European Union. The king found favour in America again by signing a peace treaty with Israel soon after the PLO had done so; the Clinton administration forgave Jordan some of its debts and arranged to send the king some F-16 jets.

In 1997 Jordan was approaching viability. It was receiving some aid. It had done a deal with the International Monetary Fund for a loan in return for adoption by the government of structural economic reforms. The government had enjoyed the inflow, albeit once only, of the savings of Palestinians who had been ousted from their jobs in the Gulf after Kuwait was liberated, out of vengeance for King Hussein's support for Saddam Hussein, and had settled in Jordan. There was still the hope that the mirage of the "peace dividend" of massive job-creating investments might become a reality.

King Hussein's survival was due also to his allies, overt and covert. One was, and probably still is, Britain. It sent in troops with no hesitation when, after King Feisal of Iraq was assassinated, Hussein pleaded, *in extremis*, for help. Whether it would do so again if, for example, Syria gave signs of planning an invasion, is a moot point. Some voices would be strongly in favour; others would advocate leaving it to America and Israel. A British prime minister might find some difficulty in persuading the House of Commons to approve sending land forces to Amman to support Jordan.

After ending its aid agreement with Jordan, British governments have played the role of discreet protector. "When the Saudis were slow on their aid payments, we expended considerable political capital persuading them to pay", a former minister of state at the Foreign Office said.[2]

The United States could usually be relied on at least to send an aircraft carrier battle group to the eastern Mediterranean if Hussein's regime was threatened. It would co-ordinate any further action with Israel. However, there have been times when the Central Intelligence Agency proposed that Hussein should be dumped, notably when he seemed to side with Saddam Hussein after Iraq had invaded Kuwait. The British say they persuaded the White House not to take this advice.

For years, Jordan's unwritten understanding with Israel was King Hussein's ultimate guarantee of survival; this guarantee may have been reinforced by the Israel-Jordan peace treaty. It is in Israel's interest, and always has been, for the Hashemites to rule over the land to its east. After Black September, when Hussein demolished the Palestinian guerrilla bases in Jordan, the Israel-Jordan border was quiet, *grosso modo*. For Israel, Hussein's Jordan was an excellent buffer state.

The Israelis would be most uncomfortable if the territory now forming the Hashemite kingdom were to fall under the control of Syria, Iraq or even Saudi Arabia. With their massive firepower, the Israelis could put up with any government on their borders, however radical or Islamist. However, the *status quo* worked very nicely. Should King Hussein's throne be in peril, the Israelis would probably have intervened in some way, as they did on occasions. When British troops flew in after the coup in Iraq, British aircraft were allowed to cross Israeli airspace to reach Amman. When Syria invaded, Israel (and the United States) told it to desist or, it is said, face the annihilation of its air force and tanks.

There is, however, another calculation: that Israel might force large numbers of West Bank people to move to the East Bank in Jordan. Such a tactic would have the merit that more West Bank land would be available for Jewish colonists. However, this would promote the establishment of a radical state based in Amman. So far, common sense has prevailed. In a speech in September 1997 Hussein warned that Islamist suicide-bombers ran the risk of provoking a massive Israeli retaliation causing the flight of the Palestinians in the Occupied Territories. "It will be only one or two or ten incidents after which one side will pounce on the other, and the victim will be the West Bank and its people as well as Gaza," he said. "Is it the object of the terrorists to repeat the tragedy of the years 1948 and 1967? Can we here in Jordan accommodate hundreds of thousands of new immigrants at a time when we are searching for water to meet our own needs?" One of the benefits of the Jordan-Israel peace treaty is that it should prevent such a disaster from occurring.

King Hussein's survival was not due to any help from Syria, Jordan's perennial rival and adversary. King Abdullah never forgot his brother Feisal's short reign in Damascus before he was ousted and transferred to become king of Iraq. Abdullah dreamed the impossible dream of being king of both Jordan and Syria, and made no secret about it. Successive Syrian regimes, all of them under the control of radical nationalists, had other ideas. One was that Jordan should belong to a Greater Syria along with Lebanon.

By having Syria as an adversary, it followed almost automatically that King Hussein would have an ally in Iraq, Syria's great long-standing rival. In Iraq's heyday before Saddam Hussein launched his wars, the king was a happy recipient of the dictator's largesse. Iraqi units were based in Jordan for a long period. If Jordan were to come under attack from Syria again, Iraq would face the possibility of having a Greater Syria on its borders. It might well intervene. There would be a question of which country intervened first: Israel or Iraq.

Although relations between the two countries have been repaired since the Kuwait war, Saudi Arabia cannot be regarded as a reliable prop for Jordan's survival. The opposite is also true. Saudi Arabian publications invariably referred to the monarch, in first reference, as "Keeper of the Two Holy Places King Fahd". It was King Fahd's father, Abdulaziz Ibn Saud, who seized Mecca and Medina, the two most holy places of Islam, from Hussein's great-grandfather, Sharif Hussein of the Hejaz. The rivalry, muted but real, persisted. The Saudis suspected, not perhaps without good reason, that if the cards had fallen another way during the Kuwait war, King Hussein would not have been averse to recovering the Hejaz for the Hashemites.

For example, Saddam Hussein's forces might not have halted their advance at the border with Saudi Arabia and might instead have overrun the "tripwire" contingent of American troops rushed there and seized the big Saudi oilfields nearby while the Iraqi air force tried to emulate the feats of the Israeli airforce in the six-day war of 1967. If the al-Saud family had been put to flight, their kingdom might have been shared among the partners: the oilfields and Riyadh, the capital, to Iraq; Saudi territory north of North Yemen, long claimed by that country's government, to North Yemen; and Mecca, Medina, Jeddah and the rest of the Hejaz to King Hussein. The prize for the PLO might have been a key role in the management of Kuwait, where Arafat once ran an engineering firm and many thousands of Palestinians had settled and prospered. It did not happen: Saddam Hussein blinked. But the Saudis remember what could have happened. Given a chance to stab Hussein in the back while maintaining their respectability, the al-Saud might have taken it.

King Hussein also survived by being seen by many Americans and Israelis as representing a key to peace in the Middle East and the voice of moderation. The Jordan option, in which the moderate and Westernized king would act on behalf of the Palestinians, was the favourite of several American presidents and Israeli prime ministers. At times, the king seemed like an activist for peace, albeit a cautious and sometimes a clandestine one. For years he seemed to be the essential man, but he was remarkably unwilling to take a risk for peace and show his head above the parapet.

In his defence it is argued that the king on one occasion did indeed offer to do a bilateral peace deal with Israel, bypassing the PLO and risking the unremitting fury of the rest of the Arab world. However, he told the Americans and, through them, the Israelis that he would do so only if guaranteed beforehand that the Occupied Territories would be returned to Jordanian control. Only thus could he have defended the deal to Arafat and his fellow-Arabs. The Israelis turned him down.

The king's personality also helped him to survive. His manner was a disarming mixture: regal yet modest. He addressed reporters at news conferences as "Sir". He won over Margaret Thatcher by his extremely courtly manner as well as his moderation. "Margaret deferred among politicians only to Reagan and Gorbachev, as representatives of superpowers," a cabinet colleague said. "But Hussein was a king, and she deferred to him too. And the king deferred to her. It was quite a sight."[3]

Workers at the royal court in Amman referred to Hussein with something akin to reverence. He was referred to as *sayyidna*, an untranslatable Arabic word roughly meaning "Our Lord", or as "His Majesty" – but never as "the king", Hussein or King Hussein. His wife was Her Majesty Queen Noor and his sons and daughters were all His or Her Royal Highness. There was a conscious effort to build a royal charisma. Indeed, the king was said to feel akin to some European royals and especially Britain's Queen Elizabeth. If the reign of the Hashemite royal family in Jordan had been short, the king could also claim with pride to be a direct descendant of the Prophet Muhammad – and did so frequently. All this has helped to buttress his authority, which was also emphasized by a low-key personality cult. His face was on Jordan's coins, banknotes and postage stamps, and it was his photograph on display in every government office. Defenders quickly pointed out that this was no different from Queen Elizabeth, for example. Yet there was a difference: the queen was above politics; the king had a packed political agenda. When he saw for the first time an equestrian statue of himself on display in Amman, he modestly ordered it to be dismantled. However, rumour-mongers said that he had previously seen and approved the statue. Nonetheless, as personality cults go, Hussein's was a modest one: it was not in the same league as, for example, Saddam Hussein's.

As the head of the Hashemites he believed he was a man of destiny, and he showed it. He was a strongman who told each new government what it should do. He cultivated popularity and often won it. He matured well: from being vulnerable, to being denounced as an Anglo-American puppet, he emerged as a leader in his own right. When he returned home a year after the war over Kuwait, after having been treated in America for cancer, many thousands of Jordanians lined his route from the airport to his mother's house and thence back home. It was a spontaneous outpouring of sympathy, affection and relief. The cheering crowds constituted a tangible proof that, in the minds of his people, Hussein had come of age: he was his own man. Those same crowds lined the streets despite ice-cold rain in January 1999 when he returned home after being treated with chemotherapy for six months in the Mayo Clinic at Rochester, Minnesota.

The king gained considerable prestige in the Middle East by negotiating an agreement between the Palestinian Authority and Israel over an Israeli troop withdrawal from the West Bank town of Hebron. Earlier, he attended a tense meeting in the White House including Arafat and Israel's prime minister Netanyahu to discuss Israel's sudden clandestine opening of a corridor past the Temple Mount, a holy place in Jerusalem.

Hussein also survived by combining being quasi-democratic with being a strongman. Having jailed a man for opposing him, or his policies, Hussein would disarm him by giving him a top job or at least granting him liberty. General Abu Nuwar, the man whom Hussein accused of responsibility for the Zerqa uprising, subsequently became Jordanian ambassador to France. In 1997, after one of his best known critics, Layth Shubaylat, had done seven months of a three-year jail term (which had been upheld on appeal) for slandering him, Hussein not only ordered his release but also drove him to his mother's home and handed her son over to her.

There were several subtexts to this action. First, here was the case of the magnanimous monarch. Second, here was a strongman-king who disposed of his critic almost wilfully, without any court of law's say-so. Third, here was a cunning messenger: it was said that the king returned the detainee to his mother and not to his wife because his mother was a monarchist whereas his wife was said by courtiers to be a radical.

By Arab standards, Hussein's control of the press was loose, but it could be tightened quickly. In 1996 the government controlled 61 per cent of the Jordan Press Foundation and 40 per cent of the Jordan Press and Publications Company, which together published the country's three main daily newspapers. These shareholdings were due to be reduced.

Reporters, editors and publishers used to have to obtain government licences and join the government-sponsored Jordan Press Association.

However, the government did not prosecute them if they did not do so. During 1996, 13 cases came before a special court involving alleged violations of the Press and Publications Law. Among the crimes: publishing information deemed to be offensive to the public; inaccurate or misleading reporting; slandering the king; and instigating public disorder. The law was amended and tightened in 1997. Two years earlier, of 20 cases involving the media only two resulted in guilty verdicts. The conclusion is that at least some of the cases might have been brought to harass the defendant.[4]

In 1998, however, the constitutional court ruled that the amendments, introduced as an emergency measure when parliament was not sitting, were unconstitutional. Its grounds were that there was no emergency. The ruling showed that Jordan was a fairly open society. "I don't agree with it," said Zeid al-Rifai, then president of the Senate. "But we will apply it." Another version of the law was approved by parliament in August 1998.

Jordanian television was flexible but depended on Hussein's national security concerns. Thus television news aired criticism of the government but rarely covered allegations of violations of human rights. During riots over a sharp increase in the price of bread in Kerak in August 1996, the authorities allowed foreign TV crews into the town but denied access to the Jordanian TV crew. Opposition parties boycotted parliament complaining that Jordanian TV did not cover their views on the issue. Opposition parties had access to radio and television to publicize their views but the cost was described as prohibitively high.

Jordanian practice clearly falls short of Western standards. But Jordan is not a Western country: it is located in a ruthless, violent part of the world. Leaders dare not let the reins fall slack: another horseman may seize control. The hard-nosed power-broker, Zeid al-Rifai, posed a difficult question for liberals. What if a Jordanian newspaper, financed by a foreign government and with reporters subsidized by its Amman embassy, insults a friendly Arab head of state, who complains to the king or prime minister and threatens to cut his programme of aid to Jordan?

For all their faults, in instances where national security or the king's personal security were not concerned, the Jordanian media were among the freest in the Arab world. This was not saying much. But it was no small matter.

Another way to win popular support was through holding freely contested elections. Hussein did this from time to time. One held in November 1989 was widely seen as fair. Criticisms were voiced of the previous government of Zeid al-Rifai over alleged corruption, economic mismanagement, intolerance and authoritarianism. (Under al-Rifai the government had in 1988 invoked the powers of the king's economic security committee to replace the editors and publishers of two of Jordan's three major daily newspapers.)

Hussein also tolerated trade unions while maintaining influence over them. More than 30 per cent of the workforce was organized in 17 unions. All unions belonged to the General Federation of Jordanian Trade Unions, which was subsidized and audited by the government. Disputes might be mediated or arbitrated. Workers had to seek permission of the labour ministry before striking. Strikes were rare, but unions were not averse to threatening to strike. The lowest minimum wage in 1996 was $150 per month.

Hussein's record on Jordanian women was good but there was room for improvement. Women were as free as anywhere in the Arab world, and this helped to promote the king's popularity. Women may vote and are encouraged to do so. In the municipal elections of 1995, 45 per cent of the voters were women. In 1996 there were two women in the Senate and one each in the cabinet and the House of Representatives. There are women engineers, doctors, teachers and lawyers. Women make up 14 per cent of the workforce and they outnumber men on the payroll of the education ministry.

However, the law requires that Jordanian women and foreign women married to Jordanian men obtain written permission from a male guardian to apply for a passport. Legal authorities enforce requests from fathers to prevent their children from leaving the country, even with their mother. A woman's testimony in family disputes, handled in Jordan by Islamic Sharia law, is worth half of a man's. Women in Sharia law receive half the amount of a male heir's inheritance.[5]

In 1997 the king was calling for a change in the law that turned a blind eye when a brother killed a sister who had disgraced the family by leaving her husband or having an affair.

Amateur radio enthusiasts frequently tuned in hoping to talk to a king, for Hussein, like Spain's King Juan Carlos, was a ham. He was given a radio when a young man and became a skilled broadcaster, "since my interest has always been in people and communicating amongst them", he told *RadCom*, the magazine of the Radio Society of Great Britain, in 1993. "It has given me the opportunity to know people throughout the world and, in many cases, to visit them later and to realise that we belong to a very large family that inhabits the global village which is our home now." In particular, he enjoyed talking to invalids restricted to their homes who spend their time making friends by radio. He claimed to have made contact with people in well over 150 countries. His proudest moment was a contact with the first amateur to operate from space, Owen Garriott, an American aboard the space shuttle *Columbia*. "We managed to arrange a schedule with him on his 92nd orbit," Hussein recounted to *RadCom*. "It was an excellent contact, something like three to four minutes horizon to horizon." His biggest problem? Pile-ups, when everyone roaming the airwaves tries to get a word in to him. "It's become almost impossible," he said. "Whenever one comes up, within a matter of minutes, more than usually you would have a pile-up and my hearing is not as good as it used to be." He added that he put his radio to practical use at the time of the 1967 war and the subsequent government campaign against the *fedayeen*. The king said: "In times of crisis and difficulty, it was a way to get in touch with friends throughout the world who were able to relay messages and to secure humanitarian help."

The gestures of kindness and thoughtfulness that the king made in Jordan are legion and are all part of an ancient tradition. An Amman policewoman, harassed by male colleagues, literally threw herself at the king's car when he was visiting a hotel. While her case was being investigated, he found her a temporary job in the royal palace.

The director of the Royal Institute for Inter-Faith Studies had met the king on one occasion before entering hospital for the removal of cataracts from his eyes. While in hospital, he received a post-operation telephone call from Hussein wishing him well.

These were gestures within the government which won or confirmed the recipient's loyalty. Much more extensive was the king's charity outside the royal palace, co-ordinated by the chief of the royal court, or *diwan*. This became a routine task of his kingship. Every working day when he was in town, Hussein first checked on overnight developments with his chief of *diwan* by telephone at about 10.30 am. Later, he would drive from his home in the quiet suburb of Hummar to his office in a multi-palace compound occupying some two dozen acres of parkland near the city centre. He often preferred to sit in the less formal office of his chief of *diwan* and in the chief's chair.

After dealing with affairs of state, decisions of the cabinet including foreign-policy issues and ambassadors' cables, he would get down to the job which he learned from King Abdullah: dealing with petitions. "In one morning, he might deal with a letter from President Clinton and a petition from a man whose daughter needs medical care at the King Hussein Medical Centre but he cannot afford it," said Awn Khasawneh, who in early 1998 was chief of *diwan*. "His Majesty sometimes has more interest in children than in very big political issues."

"In my two years' experience," Khasawneh added, "he has not said no to anybody." But the king did not always give people everything they wanted. More often than not they were given a helping hand to solve their own problems. In return, they supported the king.

Until the early 1990s, at least, the king had a reputation for listening and for giving the floor to a disparate collection of people. Some of those who reckoned they knew him said that, from about 1995–96 onwards, Hussein had become less of a listener and more impatient. "The king is one of the most patient people I have seen," said his loyal chief of *diwan*. "But this patience is outward. I have seen him on very rare occasions become angry but he has such exquisite politeness that even in his anger, he never shouts. But you can see the expression on his face change."

27 TAMING THE ISLAMISTS

Ever since the shah of Iran was ousted in a puritanical Islamic revolution which installed a theocracy dominated by Ayatollah Khomeini, Middle Eastern rulers have been anxious to ensure that they did not suffer a similar fate. Some rulers, such as the al-Saud family in Saudi Arabia, outdid the Islamic activists in public displays of piety. The rulers of Algeria and Tunisia tried to obliterate the Islamists. Egypt's presidents muffled them in Cairo and assaulted them in the South. The military boss of Sudan formed an alliance with them. Hussein conducted his relationship with the main Islamist organization in Jordan, the Muslim Brotherhood, and its political arm, the Islamic Action Front, with skill and *realpolitik* unmatched in the Arab world. Only in 1997 did the king's political instinct seem to be in danger of failing him.

Hussein's policy towards the Islamists was to pull rank on them by reminding them that he was a direct descendant of the Prophet Muhammad, and also to absorb them into his political system or to neuter them, but not to get into a political fight with them. He was following in the footsteps of King Abdullah, who had treated the Muslim Brothers with respect. This policy reached its high point in 1990 when the Jordanian cabinet included five Islamists.

The abiding reality in mosque-state relations was that the Islamists and the king needed each other even though, at times, they might exchange cross words. The king needed an organization of conservative, gentlemanly Muslims as a buffer against Islamic and Palestinian extremists. The Brotherhood needed the king as an insurance policy covering its continued existence as a political and religious force. If the Hashemites were to be overthrown, the vacuum would be filled quickly, either by Syria, Egypt or Israel; whatever happened, the Brotherhood would be worse off.

The king was a moderate and pious Sunni Muslim who had no sympathy for extremists. He visited Tehran three times in 1978, before the collapse of the shah's regime, hoping to bolster it. He was risking Islamist demonstrations at home (which were held and petered out). It came as no surprise when he supported his neighbour and aid-giver, Iraq, in its Gulf war against Iran under Ayatollah Khomeini, a Shia Muslim extremist, in 1980 (risking more Islamist demonstrations but keeping Saddam Hussein grateful and on his side in any Levantine difficulties that might have cropped up). Hussein made a point of distinguishing between "enlightened" and "fanatical" Islam.[1]

For some time the Muslim Brotherhood served a useful purpose. It had links to the Muslim Brotherhoods in Cairo, which had been its inspiration, and in Damascus, which it helped. The brotherhoods in Amman and Cairo had worked out how to get on with the government; Syria's had not. President Assad of Syria was not only brutal with opponents but also belonged to the Alawites, a sect which deified the Prophet Muhammad's son-in-law, Ali, and is viewed by many Muslims as heretic. Whenever he wanted to cause trouble for Assad, Hussein gave the Syrian Brothers a nudge and a wink; many of them were encamped in Jordan.

Hussein gave the Jordanian Brotherhood alone the right to exist as a political organization after he abolished parties in 1967. This may have been a policy of wise toleration or of cynically making it easier for state security police to keep track of trouble-makers – or both. Sensing the surge of Islam, the official media stressed the piety of the king and crown prince. The king went regularly on pilgrimage to Mecca. He made frequent references to God in speeches and press conferences. In return, from the 1950s to the 1970s, the Brothers supported the Hashemites. The Brothers went into business, did well and joined the establishment. Brothers in the bureaucracy won promotion like other state employees.

The Brotherhood's leader, Abdel Rahman al-Khalifa, said in February 1980: "In Jordan, nobody worries about the Islamic movement. The Jordanian leaders are wiser than the others." But they were worried, not least by al-Khalifa himself. In December, his line had hardened. "We would like to see the teachings of the Koran followed much more closely," al-Khalifa said. "The government...cannot stop our tongues."[2]

A split began to emerge in the late 1970s between the Brotherhood's old guard and young Islamists, many of them from the West Bank, who began to criticize the lifestyle of Amman's *nouveaux riches* and the development of widespread corruption.

In 1984 Islamic activists won three of six seats in a partial election to the House of Representatives. This apparently suggested to Hussein that the Brothers were becoming a threat; a firm hand was needed. Accordingly, he asked his loyal servant and resident hardliner, Zeid al-Rifai, to become prime minister in 1985 and remove that threat.

Immediately, the Jordan government sought a rapprochement with Syria. The king expressed shock to learn that a "criminal" and "rotten" group, hiding behind a "religious group" and provoking bloody events in Syria, "was actually living in Jordan". (The speech was reminiscent of Claud Rains, the police superintendent in the film *Casablanca*, expressing shock that gambling was going on in Humphrey Bogart's bar while pocketing his winnings.) Promptly, and somewhat ruthlessly, Jordanian security officers detained and extradited to Syria (and an uncertain fate) several hundred Jordan-based and anti-Assad Syrian Brothers. The Jordanian Brothers were untouched but warned. Undaunted, in a vote to reappoint the government-sponsored Speaker of the House of Representatives, most abstained.

In 1985 reasons for young Islamists to oppose Hussein rather than work with him, as their predecessors had done, grew. The economy began to experience a downturn and Hussein and Arafat failed to agree on a method of co-operation in dealing with Israel. In 1986, demonstrations at Yarmouk University were put down brutally. A by-election at Irbid was won by the regime's man only after the security service had blanketed the town and scared citizens so much that only a fifth of registered voters went to the polls. In 1984 Hussein disengaged from his old ties to the West Bank.

The king seems to have realized that it was time to relax political tensions. These arose again in 1989 when the government began to implement an economic reform programme in collaboration with the International Monetary Fund. It included cuts in subsidies and led to riots. In the same year, the first full and free parliamentary election since 1967 was held. A tactical retreat was in order. The distinguished Sharif Zaid bin Shaker, a childhood friend of the king's, former army commander and head of Hussein's private office, was prime minister.

The frequently critical correspondent of *Middle East International*, a London-based fortnightly newspaper wrote: "Jordan is witnessing public debate involving all sensitive issues ranging from the West Bank, the peace process and economic corruption to the power of the security services."[3] There seemed to be a consensus among dissidents. There was a call for the lifting of martial law, imposed far back in 1967; legalization of political parties; a halt to excesses by the security services such as the confiscation of passports; support for the *intifada* in the West Bank and Gaza Strip; the eradication of corruption; and the trial of officials involved in embezzlement.[4] Al-Rifai came under fire in 1988 for using the powers of the king's economic security committee to replace the editors and publishers of two of Jordan's three leading daily papers.

There were six groupings in the 1989 election campaign. The biggest was the Islamist trend led by the Muslim Brotherhood under the banner of the Islamic Movement. Its slogans included: "No to the West, No to the East, Islam is my path" and "Islam is the solution". Candidates of the Islamic Movement won 28 out of 80 seats; another 13 seats were won by various other Islamists.

The second biggest grouping comprised members of the Communist Party and the Jordanian wing of the extremist Democratic Front for the Liberation of Palestine. In third place came Arab nationalists linked to the rival Ba'ath socialist parties of Syria and Iraq. Fourth were the modernizers, favouring more economic reforms, a tougher fight against corruption and broader popular participation in Jordan's Hussein-dominated government. Fifth were the traditionalists, former conservative officials and "king's friends". There were also seats for minorities: eight for the Circassians, and six each for the Christians and Bedouins. However, only 40 per cent of the electorate voted, suggesting that many Jordanians thought parliament to be of little account when compared with the power of the king.

Nonetheless, it was a sea-change in Jordanian politics. What would the king do? A constitutional monarch would be expected to ask the Islamic Movement to form a government. This was not the case. First, in what looked like a divide-and-rule tactic, the king's friends, the leftists and nationalists joined forces to reject the Islamists' choice for Speaker (the Brothers reversed this situation later). Next came a conciliatory gesture: the government handed back thousands (it was said) of confiscated passports and released 49 detainees. Finally, the king picked a prime minister, and it was a curiously canny choice.

Mudar Badran was no Islamist but he had been Jordan's security chief in earlier years and seemed to be on good terms with the Brothers, two of whose leaders were married into the extended Badran family. Badran promised to lift martial law, to instal an independent judiciary and to lift the ban on the Communist Party. This did the trick. On January 1st 1990 parliament approved Badran as prime minister by 65 votes out of 80.

At first, the Islamists were not represented in the cabinet, perhaps because they had overplayed their hand and asked for too much. Later in the same year, Badran invited five Muslim Brothers and two independent Islamists to take seven ministries: education, health, justice, social development, Islamic endowments, transport and agriculture. They were not offered the key ministries of the interior, defence, finance or foreign affairs, but they accepted the deal. The king was undoubtedly running the show behind the scenes.

This remarkable situation lasted only until July 1991, when the Badran government was dissolved. The Brothers' performance as cabinet ministers was judged by their followers and others to be poor, and no Muslim Brother has held a cabinet post since.

Badran's successor, Taher Masri, a pro-Western liberal and veteran foreign minister, tried to persuade the Brotherhood to join his government but its leaders smelled trouble: Masri was too liberal and modern for their taste and the government was about to take part in the Madrid peace conference; they wanted to retain their freedom of action, and declined the offer. The Brothers argued among themselves about whether or not it was wise to have gone into government.[5]

In the next election in 1993 after the Madrid peace conference, the Islamic Action Front declined to take part, although many members did so in a personal capacity and were duly expelled. Islamists were represented in the 1993 parliament but there were roughly half the number in the 1989 parliament.

The Muslim Brothers and seven other opposition parties did not contest the general election of November 4th 1997, claiming it would be rigged and objecting to widespread corruption. They also objected to Jordan's restrictive press law, which Hussein endorsed in May 1997. The government claimed it had to rein in weekly tabloids whose "sensationalist" reporting was damaging Jordan's overseas image. However, it also prohibited any "news, views or analysis" that "disparages the king or the royal family, the armed forces and the heads of friendly states", which presumably included Israel's Benjamin Netanyahu.[6]

The Muslim Brothers complained of a "regression in public liberties, the marginalization of the House of Representatives [lower house] and the usurpation of legislative power by the executive authority" (translation: by King Hussein); increasing poverty; government favours for parties which supported it and restrictions on Islamic and pan-Arab parties. Most dangerous of all, the Brothers accused Hussein of "hurrying towards normalization with the Zionist enemy without getting anything in return, whilst this enemy continues its constant aggression against our sacred places and the Palestinian people's rights on their soil".

The Brothers were incensed by the king's refusal to withdraw the electoral law which hugely favoured rural constituencies, where support for the king was strong, over the towns. Amman and Zarqa, where nearly half of Jordan's 4.6m people live (including 2m Palestinians) and whence the Brothers drew most of their support, had only a quarter of the 80 parliamentary seats.[7]

There was also criticism of another aspect of the electoral laws that loaded the polls against the opposition in general. The laws had created large constituencies returning up to six members each. However, voters in these constituencies were allowed to vote for only one candidate. The opposition claimed, with some justification, that voters, given only one vote in a six-seat constituency, for example, would give priority to an independent candidate from their tribe or extended family. Candidates relying on a political or religious message would not win. Supporters of the law claimed that, without it, there was a danger that electors would give one vote to the tribal candidate and the remainder to just one party (translation: the Islamic Action Front) which could score a clean sweep. In 1998 the government was working on a new electoral law with constituencies electing only one member to the House of Representatives (British and American style). However, at least one high official was planning to gerrymander the constituencies to help the tribes.

At this point divisions in the Brotherhood were becoming sharper. On one hand, the old guard was still there, said an expert analyst, "still faithful, still polite, still understanding the position of the king and ready to concede and to behave themselves". But the great majority disagreed. They seemed to be represented less by the old guard and more by radical preachers of Friday sermons in the mosques. Hussein's ministers tried to muzzle some of them, and stirred up dissent.

There were three types of young Islamist: those still in the old chain of command; those in smaller and more radical groups such as Hamas and Islamic Jihad (Islamic Holy War); and those, more dangerous, confrontational and violent by nature and admirers of martyrdom. In 1998 the establishment still seemed to be in control, but weakened by the Arabs' failure to display any positive results from the moribund Middle East peace process and the Jordan-Israel peace treaty. Surveys carried out in 1997 by the movement to test the mood of its members showed about 85 per cent against taking part in the elections.[8]

To offset the Brothers' boycott, the king embarked on his own speech-making campaign even though he was far from being a candidate. Hussein urged the Brothers to take part. Corruption was certainly no worse than in other states and they could fight it best if they were based in parliament, the king said. Fears of vote-rigging, he added, were baseless. He suggested that the Muslim Brothers' decision was "born out of an internal crisis". Nonetheless, the Brotherhood was "an important part of the political spectrum", he said, adding that "the government appeals to the Muslim Brotherhood movement to reconsider its position".[9]

Both sides gained Pyrrhic victories. The king had presided over a contested election which was reasonably free, and he could claim that 54 per cent of the electorate turned out to vote. The result was a new parliament of malleable independents and tribal leaders which would cause him few headaches.

The Islamic Action Front could nonetheless claim that voter turnout in Amman and Zarqa was down to 35 per cent and in some cases to 20 per cent, amounting to a clear rejection of government policies. The results were: pro-government independents representing tribal interests took 62 of the 80 seats; the remainder were won by nationalist and left-wing candidates and eight independent Islamists.

By not taking part, the Brothers and their Front had moved out of the political mainstream. Outside parliament, their scope for action would be dangerously limited to demonstrations and continuing their existing policy of building up an efficient alternative government providing social services, schools, a university and a hospital, as well as support for small businesses. The king's long-standing policy of incorporating the Brothers into the Hashemite system seemed to have slipped. His short-term tactics in 1997 outmanoeuvred the Brothers; his long-term strategy seemed short-sighted.

At the same time, Hussein's support of moderate Islam went ahead. One example was the 4,000-student Al al-Bayt University in Amman, founded by the king and Crown Prince Hassan, which teaches moderate Islam, comparative religion, languages such as English and French, and seven different versions of Islamic jurisprudence in the spirit of positive toleration. The university opposes all forms of violence and suicide-bombers are condemned for being against life. Graduates become teachers, researchers, lawyers or preachers. Female students are left to decide whether or not to wear traditional Muslim garb.

The university was creating new members of the establishment, but what about the dissenters of Palestinian origin? It was hard to incorporate them because many of them looked to the PLO's leadership rather than King Hussein's. It would be easier to incorporate them if an alliance, or at least a clear understanding, existed between Hussein and Arafat. But it did not.

The king and the crown prince also sponsored a centre in Amman, the Royal Institute for Inter-Faith Studies, which was intended to promote the study and understanding of Christianity and Judaism by Muslims. Apparently many institutes for the study of Islam exist in the Christian world but no institute for the study of Christianity existed in the Muslim world until the Royal Institute was founded. Prince Hassan also wrote a concise book (which the institute published) containing a summary of Christian beliefs and a brief history of Christian churches in the Muslim world. Again, nothing of the sort was available, and the book is being translated into several languages.

The institute has also published works such as *Jerusalem under the Fatimids and the Crusaders; Jesus and Mary in the Koran; the Syriac Christian Community;* and *Christianity in the Modern Ottoman World.* It publishes quarterly and twice-yearly journals and it holds conferences and *conversazioni* on subjects that sound dry in the lingo of academe but are potential dynamite, such as "Religion and Community: Cross-cultural Patterns of Co-existence and Conflict in Contemporary Society".

"It is pure scholarship, geared in one direction," said the director, historian Kamal Salibi, "in whatever bears, directly or indirectly, on religion. We do not preach human understanding. But our work contributes towards it." Contacts with the Institute's counterparts in Israel? "They work very well." Where did the money come from to keep the Institute going? "From His Majesty."

28 GUNS AND BUTTER

Not surprisingly, Jordan had in 1997 a hefty defence budget of about $450m a year (or $100 per head of the population). There seemed to be no immediate threat in the late 1990s, but it would have been tempting fate if King Hussein had lowered his guard.

The Jordanian army (86,000 servicemen and women) is a "highly professional force, well disciplined and with a good *esprit de corps*", says the authoritative *Jane's Sentinel*. "Both officers and NCOs are of high quality."[1]

Many officer-cadets have been trained, like the king, at Sandhurst; many staff officers have been trained at the staff colleges of the American and British armies. Personnel from seven Arab states have trained in Jordan.

By 1997 the army had two mechanized divisions; one "special forces" brigade; two armoured divisions; five artillery brigades; and the Royal Guards, a unit of trusted officers and men mostly made up of Bedouins. Hussein was planning to make the army more mobile and to form a rapid-reaction force. The army had 900 towed howitzers, 340 self-propelled howitzers, some 650 anti-tank missile-launchers as well as 4,800 rocket-launchers and 665 main battle tanks with 50 American M-60/AJs. For air defence, Jordan had 80 long-range Hawks and 790 shorter-range surface-to-air missiles.

The air force had two fighter squadrons equipped with French Mirage F-1s, due to be replaced by American F-16A/Bs (Jordan would like three squadrons of them); three ground-attack squadrons equipped with American F-5s; and two squadrons of 24 American AH/1F Huey and Cobra helicopters. The air force also operates the king's Lockheed Tristar, which he frequently pilots himself.

"Although Jordanian pilots are of very high quality, and although squadrons operate effectively in an attacking role," says *Jane's Sentinel*, "the air force has been affected by a lack of funding and a shortage of spare parts." It also needs equipment for electronic warfare.

The special forces brigade was commanded in 1997 by the king's eldest son, Abdullah, who took command in 1990 and stepped down when he became king. Abdullah is a trained parachutist and has served in a British armoured regiment. The brigade comprises two special forces/counter-terrorism battalions and an airborne brigade. It also has a psychological warfare unit. Their job is to tighten border security because "the police are being out-gunned and out-manoeuvred by a very professional and very well equipped smuggling organization on the Iraqi side and terrorist infiltrations on the Syrian side," said Prince Abdullah in 1997.

The brigade was, however, being subsumed into a wider Special Operations Command also including the police public-security brigade, the Royal Guard, intelligence units and a new airlift wing made up of Huey and Cobra helicopters. Prince Abdullah was to command the new unit; his younger brother, Lieutenant-Colonel Prince Feisal, was to command the airlift wing.[2]

Jordan's armoury, while not massive, is impressive. More important, the armed forces by all accounts know how to use their weapons effectively. This is not the case in certain other Arab states where sometimes hugely expensive military equipment is left without maintenance, accumulating sand. The guiding force behind this undoubted achievement was King Hussein. Had he lived to see it, Glubb Pasha would have been delighted.

Perhaps exaggerating, William Perry, American defence secretary in 1996, said: "We see Jordan as the lynchpin in the security of the Middle East." Times change: only five years earlier, Hussein had been in the international dog-house for his sympathetic attitude towards Saddam Hussein.

It was no coincidence that in March 1996 Hussein had agreed to let an American "air-power expeditionary force" comprising 30 F-15s and F-16s with four tankers be deployed temporarily in the country. The message to any potential adversaries was clear: Hussein had powerful friends. The American aircraft patrolled an air exclusion zone in Iraq where, by UN Security Council order, Iraqi aircraft were not permitted to fly. It also underlined the fact that Hussein's shift away from Iraq was more than cosmetic.[3]

On November 15th 1996, President Clinton declared that Jordan had been accepted as one of America's "major non-NATO allies". This elevated status (shared by Israel and Egypt) was expected to increase the flow of American military aid and equipment to Jordan.

And the economy? Should business people invest in Jordan? At the end of 1997, Jordanians had plunged into a vigorous debate about the country's future as it was becoming more prosperous with the help of free-market policies. The big issue, debated publicly, was over Hussein's agreement, backed by parliament, to normalize relations with Israel in November 1994. Some said it came too quickly – after the PLO signed up for peace with the Jewish state but before Syria and Lebanon did so. On one occasion, some 5,000 people demonstrated against signs that the government was getting too cosy with members of Benjamin Netanyahu's cabinet and Israeli business agents.

Defenders of the peace pact said it would bring a dividend in the form of foreign investment in Jordan. They also claimed that Jordan was now in a better position to use its powers of persuasion on the Israeli government. "If the Arabs want to change Netanyahu, they have to talk to him to change him," said the information minister in 1997, Marwan Muasher. Many Jordanians appeared to favour keeping the peace pact but did not want to go much further in closer co-operation with the Israelis – for the moment.

There was no wave of direct foreign investment. A trade protocol providing for a big increase in sales of Jordanian goods in the "liberated" parts of the West Bank was hampered by Israeli security inspections at bridges over the Jordan. Remittances from Jordanians working abroad had been much reduced since many thousands of workers in the Middle East were sent home in retaliation for Hussein's apparent support for Iraq's invasion of Kuwait. A Western banking source reckons that "a quarter of the population came home". Nonetheless, by 1996 remittances home, worldwide, had picked up dramatically. Trade with Iraq was, however, down to a trickle.

However, Jordan's economy was benefiting from structural changes, starting in 1989, that were putting it on a sound footing. Hitherto, Jordan had been surviving behind high tariff walls, exchange controls with an overvalued dinar, with the government holding stakes of varying sizes in many business enterprises, amounting to 17 per cent of GNP. In 1989, this artificial contraption came tumbling down.

The budget was in deficit; there was a trade deficit; the balance of payments on current account was in deficit; the level of national savings was too low and the foreign debt was too high. There was a run on the dinar, which was devalued by 31 per cent. Surgeons were called in from Washington. The operation by the International Monetary Fund and World Bank was painful. Subsidies on fuel and other basic commodities such as wheat and feedgrains were cut. More free-market economic reforms were implemented. King Hussein accepted the inevitable. His prime minister, Zeid al-Rifai, implemented the changes in a heavy-handed manner.

Riots erupted in the usually loyal south of the country; eight people died and some 50 were injured. Hussein sacked al-Rifai but did not retreat: the new prime minister was the king's cousin, Field Marshal Sharif Zeid bin Shaker. He was conciliatory. The king saw the warning signals clearly: a general election (planned before the troubles) was held in an atmosphere of relative political freedom.

It took time to turn the economy around. Jordan suffered in many ways for its apparent support for Iraq during the war over Iraq's seizure of Kuwait. But it worked. "Jordan has achieved economic stability with strong growth since 1992," said the World Bank in what amounted to an accolade. "The high debt burden and inflation of the late 1980s and the disruptions of the Gulf crisis, including the return of 300,000 Jordanians – almost 10 per cent of the population – were handled with skill and discipline."[4]

Unemployment, which was 25 per cent of the workforce in 1989, had been roughly halved by 1996; inflation was running at an annual rate of 4 per cent; gross domestic product (GDP) was growing by roughly 2.7 per cent in 1997; foreign-exchange reserves reached $800m, high for Jordan but much too low for comfort; the exchange rate was stable; and the current-account deficit was down from 20 per cent of GDP in 1980 to 11 per cent in 1993 and 3 per cent in 1996.

However, there was still a big trade deficit. And there was no noticeable improvement in the standard of living. Indeed, with the elimination of subsidies on irrigation water, municipal water and electricity in 1996, many people were worse off. Income per head of the population was $1,300 in 1988; ten years previously, it was approaching $2,000. According to government statistics, 25 per cent of the population lives in poverty; by another reckoning, 70 per cent of the population lives in poverty, mainly in some southern and northern villages and the suburban town of Zerqa. There is wealth in Jordan, with big hotels being built in prosperous west Amman; there is a housing boom fuelled with money brought home by Palestinians who had been expelled from the Gulf; the roads are excellent.

Telecommunications and electricity supply were opened to private-sector competition. State-owned hotels, the cement company and the railway to Aqaba were to be sold off. Import tariffs were cut from an average of 34 per cent in 1987 to 20 per cent. A liberal exchange-rate regime was maintained in the face of speculation against the dinar. There were ambitious plans to turn Amman into a regional financial centre, complementing its stockmarket.

The workforce is quite well educated. There are 3,600 state schools, often with two shifts a day, over 500 licensed technical and community colleges, and five state and five private universities.

The World Bank describes Jordan as a "regional centre for advanced clinical health care".[5] Improbably, a relatively sophisticated infrastructure of institutions, skills and sound management has been painstakingly established. Hussein could be quite proud of it, even if he had squandered some of the money he was given.

Hussein did not do it all by himself, however. The World Bank, International Monetary Fund and Western aid donors helped. Jordan's government-to-government debt falling due in 1989, 1990, 1994 and 1997 was re-scheduled by the Paris Club of government creditors; commercial-bank debt in 1993 had the same beneficial treatment by the London Club. American, British and French official debt was written off in 1994. Japan lent $215m in 1995 and the European Union made a grant of $125m in 1996. The IMF agreed on a loan of $293m over three years in 1996. The World Bank provided $360m in 1993–96. The International Finance Corporation, the World Bank's private-sector arm, invested $85m in six projects, leveraging a total investment of $420m in pharmaceuticals, paper, tourism and chemicals.

However, the chief reason for the high rates of growth in 1992-95 was the mini-boom generated as a result of the return of some 300,000 Jordanians mainly of Palestinian origin who had been working in the Gulf, mostly Kuwait, and been expelled because of Arafat's support for Iraq in the Gulf War. They have built hundreds of big new houses in West Amman and elsewhere. (Some are elegant but many seem to have been designed by Walt Disney.)

A most encouraging development for the Jordanians came in August 1997 when a new joint venture was revealed. Norsk Hydro, the Norwegian fertiliser and magnesium company, was to build a $500m fertilizer plant in Jordan associated with Jordan Phosphate Mines. "This is a major boost for Jordan," said an analyst at Barings. The plant might also produce magnesium. Israel had already signed a joint venture with the German carmaker Volkswagen to make a magnesium plant using potash deposits on its side of the border.[6]

Had Hussein succeeded in creating that nirvana of economic strategists, a stable business environment? Was there an atmosphere in which cautious business people felt comfortable about investing their money? Yes and no. To be sure, Hussein had made all the right policy reforms and made his peace with Israel. And when Rabin and Peres were in the saddle in Israel, the prospects looked almost limitless.[7] At the first Middle East economic summit after the peace treaties were signed, Jordan confidently presented a portfolio of projects to attract investors. With Netanyahu as prime minister, however, a stable business environment looked like a chimera.

In the circumstances, King Hussein could only concentrate on mending his fences with the rest of the Arab world, which was annoyed with his behaviour over Iraq's invasion of Kuwait. Some expatriate Jordanian workers who were expelled after Kuwait was recaptured went back. Contracts for a few thousand Jordanian workers – mostly teachers and engineers – were signed with Abu Dhabi, Qatar and Oman. Saudi Arabia welcomed skilled labourers from Jordan but its demand for them was low. Kuwait did not take any. Bahrain invited two battalions of Jordanian security forces to help quell Shia insurgents.

The mood in Jordan in 1998 was by one account one of frustration. Many people appeared to be short of cash. The gap between the 'haves' and the 'have-nots' was said by a senior politician to be widening and the usual complaints about corruption and inefficiency persisted. Some economic statistics were found to be inflated to give a good impression. For all the murmuring, however, Jordan remained a fairly open society, within limits, its increasingly free-market economy was growing and its people were better off than in most parts of the non-oil-producing Arab world.

Invest in Jordan? Yes. Saddam Hussein cannot survive forever. After he goes, Iraq's big and vibrant market will reopen: companies operating in next-door Jordan will be in the best position to do business there. Companies banking on a boom in Jordanian trade with Netanyahu's Israel, on the other hand, would have to be patient.

29 THE END OF AN ERA

American presidents, like most politicians, are much given to hyperbole. They also like to make their friends feel at home by telling them how important they are. Even so, making allowances for presidential excess, the welcome that King Hussein received at the White House on April 1st 1997 was little short of remarkable. President Clinton said: "It's always an honour to have His Majesty King Hussein back in the White House. I believe this is our 15th meeting since I became president. I want to have the opportunity to thank him for his continuing devotion to peace and the particularly courageous trip he recently took to Israel [to offer his condolences to the families of Israeli children shot and killed by a crazed Jordanian on the border]. And I want to discuss with him what the next steps are. I think it is clear we would not have gotten the agreement in Hebron had it not been for his leadership, and his leadership is essential as we go forward. This is a difficult time for the peace process, and we have a lot to talk about." This was an accolade indeed for the head of a small and weak state and a tribute to Hussein's ability to intervene, using his acute sense of timing, just when he could be effective.

In November 1997, the king was back again – and forming part of an elaborate presidential snub of Netanyahu, who for weeks had been angling for an invitation to the White House to coincide with a trip to America to talk to American Jewish leaders. But the president's aides just could not find the time on his busy schedule. However, Hussein had been undergoing tests at the same time at the Mayo Clinic, in Minnesota, for cancer, which were said to have given him a clean bill of health. An invitation to the White House arrived, and Hussein stopped in Washington on his way back to Amman.

Clinton compounded the snub by visiting Los Angeles while Netanyahu was there, without seeing him. Adding to the embarrassment, their two airliners were parked side by side at the airport. Clinton also saw Shimon Peres and the widow of Yitzhak Rabin while Netanyahu was in the United States.

Hussein pressed on with his campaign against Netanyahu, apparently after having concluded that he was impossible to deal with. In September 1997 he had been shocked when Netanyahu sent two agents of the Mossad to Amman with orders to kill Khaled Meshal, an Amman-based leader of the radical Palestinian Islamist organization Hamas. The Mossad men tried to spray Meshal's face with a lethal liquid and were caught while running away. Hussein demanded that Netanyahu send the antidote and it was flown to the Jordanian capital only just in time to save Meshal's life.

The king subsequently capitalized on the Mossad's botched job: he swapped the two Mossad men for Sheikh Ahmed Yassin, an elderly radical Palestinian leader and founder of Hamas, a detainee for eight years in an Israeli jail, as well as 23 Jordanians and 50 Palestinians from the West Bank and Gaza, all held in Israeli jails.

The attempted assassination "was an act against Jordan itself, its integrity and its sovereignty, and the results were devastating to the trust we had built so far", Hussein told the *Washington Post* on October 31st. He added that he had run out of ideas for dealing with Netanyahu, whom he accused of repeatedly breaching commitments to his Arab negotiating partners. He also repeated his request for the United States to "move from being a messenger to being actively involved" in the peace process.

The Clinton administration, hitherto viewed as being as pro-Israeli, listened. Madeleine Albright, who had succeeded Warren Christopher as secretary of state, set a December 1997 deadline for Netanyahu to propose an Israeli troop withdrawal from part of the West Bank as required by the Oslo accords. The scope of the withdrawal would have to be acceptable in Washington and to Arafat. However, getting on for a year after the deadline, Netanyahu, pleading divisions in his cabinet, had still not given Albright and Arafat a straight answer. Nor had Netanyahu – backed by the pro-Israel lobby in Congress as well as by AIPAC – made a formal proposal on the percentage of land in the

Occupied Territories from which the Israeli armed forces would withdraw.

The king's role in the West Bank, albeit an indirect one, was as an advocate in Washington for the Palestinians. He also visited London and pressed the same case to Tony Blair: Israel should keep to the Oslo accords.

The king's forthright comments about Netanyahu served a domestic purpose. They protected him from widespread criticism in Jordan that in the Jordan-Israel peace treaty he had gone too far, too fast. He could point to his own blunt language denouncing the Israeli leader and to the close tie he had established with the only power capable of intervening successfully in Israel: the United States.

During this time the domestic scene in Jordan was calm. All in all, the general election results of the previous year were working out well for the king. The boycott of the Muslim Brotherhood robbed the poll of full credibility but he was unmistakably on record as having frequently urged leaders of the Brotherhood to take part. On August 12th 1998, for example, he declared: "The door is open, and has never been slammed in the face of anyone, particularly the Islamist groups which developed and thrived in the care of the late King Abdullah. We hope they will contribute...to the construction of this country by taking part in the elections."

He also confirmed his own popularity in speeches and other appearances around the country, especially in Zaiqa, Ma'an and Aqaba. The result was that the regime had consolidated itself in power with a tame parliament.

By gerrymandering the election constituencies, Hussein had favoured the East Bank conservative establishment and made sure that Jordan's Islamist and Palestinian electors would not win a parliamentary majority. This was welcomed by the old East Bank families, who owed their privileged position to him. When the Brotherhood decided to boycott the vote, the East Bank notables must have thought that it had done them a service. Accustomed as they were to short-term thinking, Hussein and aides such as Zeid al-Rifai will have thought that they had won a few more years of stability. However, Crown Prince Hassan convened a meeting with Brotherhood leaders in August 1998 (when his brother was again in the Mayo Clinic, receiving treatment for cancer) hoping to resume a "dialogue" with them.

As for his former Iraqi friend, President Saddam Hussein, the king had made a break and was fishing in troubled waters. When Saddam Hussein's daughter and her husband, General Hussein Kamel, a cabinet minister, fled the country, Hussein let them stay in Jordan. (Inexplicably, they returned home and the minister was shot dead, apparently by a son of the president.)

Gone was the effusive praise of the Iraqi leader: Hussein had returned to the Western fold. However, the king was guarded. In speeches and interviews he would speak of the need to end the suffering of the Iraqi people without mentioning Saddam Hussein. He spoke in favour of the general principles of democracy and freedom. It was what the Iraqi people wanted to hear. While his words may well have been sincerely meant, they were also an investment in the future of an Iraq without Saddam Hussein.

The king was suspected of having ambitions in Iraq and predictably denied them. However, as the cousin of Iraq's murdered King Feisal, he did say that if the Iraqi people asked him, or the Hashemite family, for help, he would not refuse it. The king was a rank outsider. But who knew? Saddam Hussein would not go on forever. Somebody with a degree of respectability would be needed to take over. Why not a Hashemite?

In February 1998, however, Saddam sent a coded message to the king to keep out. He sent it twice. The first took the form of a professional murder of some Iraqi and Greek businessmen and a senior Iraqi diplomat apparently by Iraqi assassins in Amman. It seemed to be a warning that Iraq, like Israel, could operate freely in Jordan if it so decided.

The second message was Saddam's decision to execute four Jordanian students who were under arrest for smuggling $300-worth of goods. Iraq had picked up clandestine radio messages from Iraqi dissidents in Jordan to allies inside their country and may have wanted to punish Jordan for allowing this to happen. The king protested, to no avail. He also asked for the release of some 70 Jordanian detainees. Saddam agreed – but revealed his intention not to the king but to Laith Shubailat, a leader of the nationalist opposition in Amman who had been detained and subsequently released. It was a calculated Iraqi snub. The Jordanian government did everything possible to prevent Shubailat returning in triumph with the 70 detainees. Journalists covering his arrival were roughed up by the police; relatives of the detainees were told to go home.[1]

The king was using an Iraqi-style hearts-and-minds strategy in his dealings with the Palestinian Authority and its president, Arafat, who looked sick. Formally and officially, Hussein maintained that the PLO was the spokesperson of the Palestinian people, as decided at the Rabat summit. Informally and unofficially, on the other hand, he intervened energetically, sometimes discreetly but at other times on centre stage. He was clearly a force to be reckoned with. Unlike the negotiations for the Oslo agreement between the PLO and Israel, both Israel and the Palestinians would have to take him into consideration.

Before cancer struck him down, Hussein must have speculated about the future of the West Bank after the death or incapacity of Yasser Arafat. There might well have been a role for Hussein and Jordan. There had been talk for years of some sort of Palestinian-Jordanian confederation. It would reassure many Israelis and might secure better terms in the projected permanent settlement. Who would rule out a role for Jordan?

At the same time, the king was prepared to bypass Arafat and deal directly with Israel much as Arafat had bypassed him and dealt with Israel at Oslo. An opportunity arose in October 1998 but it could not be seized because of Israel's attempt to kill Meshal. "It's no secret that 48 hours prior to the painful incident, I sent a message to the Israeli prime minister telling him there was a possibility to discuss holding a dialogue between them and Hamas, to stop the episode of horror and violence," the king said. The proposed talks were to include "discussing all issues that should be dealt with", he added, in a rally speech at Al-Hussein Youth City. "I told them that I was ready to engage in such an endeavour because of our pain...over the loss of...any innocent person's life." But he said he had been told the letter arrived too late.[2]

The Meshal incident allowed the king to seize the initiative. It was followed up by his prime minister, Abdel Salam al-Majali, who dismissed the most recent Israeli peace plan as containing an "unacceptable condition", even though it was up to Arafat as president of the Palestinian Authority to say whether or not a proposal was acceptable.

(The proposal was transparent. Netanyahu suggested eliminating the third stage of Israeli troop withdrawals from Occupied Territories as envisaged in the Oslo agreements, and to move on to negotiations on a final settlement which the Israeli prime minister would string out for as long as possible, as his two Likud mentors, Menachem Begin and Yitzhak Shamir, had done.)

The king was able, at the same time, to defend his peace treaty with Israel. "Some voices were heard saying that Jordan will be swallowed up by Israel economically," he told a rally in Ma'an in October. "But now, after three years, I ask you 'Did anything of this sort happen?' Thank God everything is going the right way, our international borders are recognized for the first time and encroachment on our territory has stopped." He reminded his audience that "the peace treaty was approved by both houses of parliament".[3]

How would the king's relationship with Arafat evolve? In 1998 the two men continued to be rivals, suspicious of each other, engaged in a political chess game. They seemed intent on an unplanned separation of their two administrations and appeared to have little desire to work together. A study published by Chatham House in December 1997 had concluded that "the danger of proceeding without clear goals is that others, not least Israel, may seek to impose an outcome."[4]

Arafat and the Palestinian Authority were busily forming all the institutions of government without consulting Hussein. However, the idea of a confederation was not dead. Less than two years previously, in 1996, an Israeli labour party minister, Yossi Beilin, and the PLO negotiator, Abu Mazen, had drafted a plan for the final settlement of the Israeli-Palestinian dispute for submission to Arafat and to the then Israeli prime minister, Yitzhak Rabin. Part of it said: "Both sides would continue to look favourably at the possibility of establishing a Jordanian-Palestinian confederation, to be agreed upon by the state of Palestine and the Hashemite Kingdom of Jordan." (However, that was agreed when the Labour Party was in power and ready to envisage big territorial concessions on the West Bank and in Gaza to the Palestinian Authority as a contribution to peace, not only in Palestine but also in the region. Under Netanyahu, that prospect had more or less disappeared.)

If Jordan and the Palestinian Authority would not work together, both would inevitably turn to the American-backed regional great power, Israel, for support. Was that what the long struggle and the *intifada* were all about?

The answer was obvious, yet such was the suspicion between Arafat and Hussein that the former would consult the latter only when *in extremis* in his relations with Israel. For his part, Hussein seemed content to place no hindrance in the way of Arafat's efforts to build a separate state, but he did not exactly inundate him with generous offers of money and other forms of assistance. When asked by Arafat for help, however, he invariably gave it.

It was easy for those with suspicious minds to speculate that Hussein was waiting for Arafat to trip up and for the Hashemites to be invited back to the West Bank. By early 1998 there were signs that the Palestinian Authority was in poor shape; Arafat looked ill and exhausted; his parliament resented his autocratic style; his underlings were accused of corruption and incompetence; Israel was breaking its promise to the Palestinians of land for peace, a promise solemnly made in Oslo and on the White House lawn, and getting away with it; and most important of all, three years after the first Oslo agreement in 1993, unemployment in Gaza and the West Bank had nearly doubled at 34 per cent of the workforce, and income per head had shrunk by a fifth.[5] This was mainly due to Israel's closure of its own territory to thousands of Palestinian workers living in Gaza and the West Bank.

Jordan was far better off. It was a well-ordered little kingdom and its currency, the dinar, was still one of the two used in the West Bank and Gaza. If the Palestinian leaders were to be denied a chance of liberating a good part of the East Bank and Gaza through the Oslo agreements, the Chatham House study stated, "Jordan could then come under pressure to step in instead, if only on the grounds that otherwise all would be lost". But it rightly added: "All such approaches would probably fail to sway the king unless they were accompanied by the emergence of a significant

Palestinian constituency for increased Jordanian involvement."[6]

No such constituency among those in power emerged, although those questioned in an opinion poll conducted in mid-1995 in Jordan, in Jordanian refugee camps, the West Bank and the Gaza Strip had overwhelmingly favoured three forms of close collaboration between Palestine and Jordan: confederation, federation or unity.

Which stood most chance? Not unity, however sensible it might appear to outsiders. In Jordan, hardline nationalists would vigorously oppose it for fear of becoming a minority in a Palestinian-dominated country. In the West Bank and Gaza, Palestinian hardliners would oppose it for fear of falling under the sway of the autocratic Hashemites.

Federation, which would involve a central government and two regional ones, as well as a federal budget and foreign policy, was probably also out of the running for the same reasons as unity.

That left confederation, meaning an association of two sovereign states providing shared services and co-ordinating policies while reserving the right to go their own way on specific issues. This arm's-length relationship should calm nerves and suit the suspicious Arafat and Hussein.

There was, however, one snag: Palestine was not a state, and Israel looked on the idea with deep displeasure. Statehood was, nonetheless, not beyond the realms of possibility. If it was tied into an agreement on a confederation with King Hussein, it might have reassured the Israeli public.

A confederation would have given Hussein a strategic foothold on the West Bank, to be used by himself or his successors if called on in the event of the collapse of the Palestinian Authority. It would give Arafat access to Jordanian airspace and the port of Aqaba, thereby evading any limits imposed by Israel.

As a free-trade area, a confederation would provide a new market for both Palestinian and Jordanian entrepreneurs, since bilateral trade in 1997 was severely restricted by Israeli officials at the Allenby Bridge crossing-point. Palestine could have access to the cheap Jordanian electricity grid, which has excess capacity. There was room for joint ventures in many fields and economies of scale. It was an option that

Hussein did not live to try out. (After his death, Arafat surprised the Jordanians and his own people by proposing the adoption of a confederation, implicitly with himself and not the Hashemites in the leading role. The sick Arafat was in a hurry. The cautious Jordanians said No.)

And Israel? Much depended on which party ruled the Jewish state. If it was Likud, the tendency would be to continue turning the country into a Middle Eastern ghetto obsessed with security, isolated, disliked and immobile. It would require a leap of faith, improbable but not impossible, for Netanyahu and his colleagues to entertain the idea of a Palestinian-Jordanian confederation. The fear of the hardliners would be a takeover of Jordan and the Palestinian Authority/state by radical Islamist haters of Israel. But that has seemed to be on the cards in the past and never happened.

In domestic Jordanian affairs, the king was continuing to find his way between the conflicting desires for more democracy and political stability. Thus the need for a free press that was obliged to behave responsibly. Addressing a crowd in Kerak in 1997, the king declared: "Freedom has no ceiling, but it has its own limits when it is exploited to infringe on other people's freedoms or harm the nation or tamper with the national interests and national unity. Once we live up to the required level of awareness, we will not be needing any laws or regulations because then we will be exercising responsible actions and controlling our behaviour in a responsible manner."

And what should journalists do? "Freedom of the press does not mean publishing material that could infringe on morals or promote vice or cause harm to Arab brothers or the country's achievements or offend people, whether they are in public office or otherwise or to practise blackmail."

Hussein wanted a media that was tame yet tough: tame in the sense that journalists accepted as non-negotiable the Hashemite monarchy and the extensive powers of the king, as well as the existence of a regime with members of the royal family scattered through the Amman establishment; tough in the sense that, within the Hashemite context, journalists would challenge the actions of the government of the day, or support them, as a sort of independent loyal opposition, not subsidized by Syria, Saudi Arabia, Egypt or elsewhere.

Unfortunately, the king's list of forbidden actions was much too long and all-inclusive, and was in need of reform. His vision of constitutional democracy was limited to the dominance of the Hashemites over a parliament that would flex its muscles only rarely. The king was *de facto* his own prime minister and foreign minister; those who held the posts in name were mere shadows with little power. By all accounts, the minister whom Hussein liked and respected most was a rare Jordanian, one who stood up to the monarch and gave him, at times, advice which he knew he would not appreciate: Wasfi al-Tall.

There was a subtle shift in the king's attitude to power, according to two members of the establishment. Until the 1990s the king's strategy had been to stay beyond criticism by having his prime minister and his cabinet colleagues propose laws and take the flak if they did not work out as planned. This changed.

Over the moribund peace process in 1998, said a prominent politician, "there is a lot of criticism of the king, not the government, because lately the king has been taking matters into his hands. The government is weaker; he goes public every time there is an issue. The government says that 'According to the wish of the king we are doing so-and-so'.... So the king is ruling directly now, and the people feel it." However, "the majority of the people separate their love for him as a person and his policies".

This applied to politicians too. "If you bring the closest aides to the king and the closest supporters in a room and we discuss the peace process, the level of democracy, the status of civic institutions, I think you will find that most of us, including those who are close to the king, will criticize the policies.... But, if the king comes in, or we are asked to participate in a function, we will defend him, we will salute him, and we will be around him. Nobody because of that criticism is trying to call for the overthrow of the king. Everybody says: 'No, he should stay; he is the safety valve; he is the common denominator between all of us.' This is how it is." A retired general said, emotionally but in all sincerity, that "I do not want live one day longer than my king."

There was also a problem over corruption. When the king sent his instructions to a new government, he talked about corruption. "We have an official committee headed by a general in intelligence, investigating corruption charges against institutions and people," says a well-placed informant. "So corruption reaches to the top, and everybody knows it." One well-known former prime minister, with whom the king worked for many years, is widely rumoured to be corrupt.

What kind of man was Hussein after more than four decades in power? "A courageous character," said an old associate and critic, speaking in 1997. "He likes challenge. He hates weakness. He is a very gentle and soft-spoken person. He believes in a mission vis-à-vis Israel. He also believes that the world has not done justice to him, that he should have been the king of a bigger, more influential country." Did he have wider ambitions? Certainly in the West Bank and in East Jerusalem, part of which as descendant of the Prophet Muhammad he was the guardian until 1967. The loss of East Jerusalem, especially its Holy Places, in that year saddened him. (As the Palestinians see it, Jerusalem has been an Islamic city for 14 centuries and it is a holy city mentioned in the Koran.)

He was a quiet man. "One of our problems in relaying our messages to world leaders is the quietness of the king when he talks to a leader," said the critic. "Sometimes he needs to be more specific to let the other party know what our position is or to ask specifically for the position on the other side.... So many times in the past we used to leave the room and say: 'Why did he not express himself more explicitly? The other leader will not think that the king is passing him a message or asking a question. The king is so general that the other party does not understand.'"

Was he a good listener? "The king has changed," said the critic. "Since four years [that is, in 1993], we don't know if it's because he became sick and less patient, or the peace process, and his eagerness to push for it, before he is too old, I don't know, but the king became less patient and less ready to listen to people... He used to have a 'kitchen cabinet'; he doesn't any more. He used to meet a lot of people and listen to them, no matter how they expressed themselves – sometimes some people would be rude but he would absorb it. Now he doesn't listen, he doesn't see people, and if he sits with someone he doesn't stay long. But if you sit with him and tell jokes, he is ready to stay and reciprocate." Other critics speak of a hot temper. A well-placed diplomat says that the king had a sense of *déjà vu* in talking to politicians, a feeling that he had been there, done that, and that he could do their jobs better than they could. He therefore took more decisions himself.

As he grew older, acts of personal charity which could actually change people's lives for the better assumed greater importance than political wrangles. In one such act of charity, the king took a young Welsh girl, who had been waiting for several months for an operation in a British hospital, to the United States for treatment.

Hussein's life was a long struggle with ailments. There was cancer of the intestine (successfully treated), the removal of a kidney and a testicle, trouble with his prostate, a hearing problem, a sinus problem and, in 1998, inflammation of some lymph glands, often the sign of the spread of cancer.

"I began treatment several months ago for a micro-organism that has agitated my lymph glands and caused occasional fever, weight loss, fatigue and severe exhaustion during that period," the king wrote in an open letter in early 1998 to the then Crown Prince Hassan. The king's doctor in Amman said a biopsy had been taken from a lymph gland in the neck and revealed non-malignant inflammation and, after the same symptoms recurred, a biopsy was taken from an enlarged lymph gland in the armpit with the same result. In July 1998, he visited the Mayo Clinic, for the second time in that year. This time, cancer was discovered and the king began a course of chemotherapy at the Clinic. He would be away in Minnesota for several months.

This did not stop him from firing his prime minister, al-Majali, at long distance after a scandal over polluted tap-water in Amman, or from paying a quick visit to Washington. He had first made the weak al-Majali his prime minister in June 1993 and kept him in office until January 1995 when he was replaced by Sharif Zeid bin Shaker, the king's childhood friend, confidant and former army commander. The ultra-loyal Zeid bin Shaker held the tiller until February 1996, when the king appointed a man who, he hoped, would bring the vigour and ideas of a younger, more liberal generation to the government of Jordan, Abdul Karim Kabariti. To ease his way, the king replaced several high government officials, such as the chief of the *diwan* and the chief of the general intelligence department, with people who Kabariti knew well.

The new prime minister was said to agree with the king on all major policies. It did not work. Kabariti sought publicity, which was usually the preserve of the royal family. He sought to build up his own power base. He tried to enter areas of government that are closed to politicians and prime ministers on military affairs; he took decisions in general without consulting with the king beforehand; he quarrelled with the crown prince; he pressed his own ideas on relations with Israel (which the king regarded as his personal bailiwick). He did not run to do the king's bidding. In short, he began to have ideas above his station. In March 1997 the king fired him, and brought back the compliant al-Majali. So much for Jordanian democracy.

This event provoked some private discussions in Amman about the scarcity of "big men" in Jordanian politics in contrast with the British period. Some analysts pointed to Tawfik Abul Huda, Samir al-Rifai, Said al-Mufti and Wasfi al-Tall. One said: "There is no national figure in Jordan now, aside from the king and Crown Prince Hassan."

In March 1998, Hussein was back in the White House, on a lower-key visit, asking Clinton to use his influence to make Netanyahu carry out the terms of Israel's agreement with the Palestinians at Oslo.

While at the Clinic, the king intervened in stalled talks between Israel's Netanyahu and the Palestinian Authority's Arafat, chaired by Bill Clinton, at the Wye River Plantation outside Washington in October 1998. Hussein, weakened by chemotherapy that had caused him to lose his hair, looked a shadow of his former self.

The king addressed the group, with their aides. He took the long view, saying the details that were holding up agreement had no importance when compared with the significance of an agreement not only for themselves but also for the generations to come. He said the opportunity for making progress towards a wider peace should not be missed. "There has been enough destruction, enough death, enough waste," he added.

Clinton said afterwards that the king "has told us what we should do" and they did it, thereby adding to the esteem for Hussein in the Clinton White House. Subsequently, he flew back to his clinic in Rochester, Minnesota.

During the king's absence at the Mayo Clinic, the succession became the hot topic in Amman. If he succeeded his brother as king, might Hassan be prepared to delegate wider powers to his prime minister than Hussein did?

The king was a special case. He had become identified with Jordan; he was its emblem. Hassan did not enjoy the same status. He would be unable to act as if he were a second Hussein. He would have to adapt, to relinquish a lot of his power to democratic institutions. If he were to resist, he would be in trouble. Did Hassan have it in him to be a more constitutional monarch? Opinions differed sharply. One view was that he recognized political reality and could delegate. Another view was that he might well be a compulsive meddler, a Jack of all trades and master of none.

Would Hassan actually succeed to the Hashemite throne? The constitution gave precedence to the monarch's eldest son (Hussein's and Muna's son Abdullah, who was named crown prince when only three days old). But the constitution was amended to allow the king to nominate his brother as crown prince (in this case Hassan in 1965). If the king was succeeded by the crown prince, then the constitution says Hassan would be succeeded by Hassan's son, and not the king's son.

If the king wanted to change the constitution, and there were in 1998 rumours that he did, there was speculation that he might name Queen Noor's eldest son, Hamzah, as his successor rather than Crown Prince Hassan. There were those who said it was a sensitive matter that Hamzah's mother, Noor, had not been born a Muslim, although the constitution requires both king and queen to be Muslims and both Noor and Muna converted to Islam before marrying Hussein.

It would be even more sensitive, some said, if the king passed over his brother, who had served as regent every time the king had left the country and had been prepared to take over in an emergency for 33 years, and replaced him with young Hamzah, who in 1998 was 18 years old, because his mother was influential. It was said that Noor wanted her son to be king in order to ensure that her influence persisted after Hussein's death. It was said that if Crown Prince Hassan and Sarvath, his wife, were to become king and queen, the strong-willed Noor would leave the country.

Equally, it would be surprising if the English Princess Muna did not harbour ambitions for her and Hussein's first-born son, Abdullah, who bears the name of the king's revered grandfather. Were she alive, Queen Alia would doubtless have been pressing the case of her first-born, Ali, the king's only son of Arab blood.

Not to be forgotten was the elder of Hussein's two brothers, Prince Muhammad, who suffered from a mental illness for some time and was given to making startling gestures such as firing a revolver at an inappropriate moment. He was said to be happily restored to health and substituted for his elder and younger brothers when both were out of the country at the same time. Muhammad was not a contender for the crown but might have had a role to play if the succession issue was not cut and dried before Hussein's death.

The succession was Amman's biggest guessing game. Hassan had not won Jordanians' hearts and minds, for all his earnest endeavour. Abdullah had little support, it was said, presumably because he was half-English. Ali would be popular on the street and in the desert for being all-Arab but did not have a following. Hamzah, even though half-American, was widely regarded as a nice boy and seemed to be the favourite. But would Hussein disappoint his brother and his eldest son? Towards the end of 1998, it seemed unlikely. From the Mayo Clinic, Hussein delegated power to his brother, who was busily holding meetings with leaders of the Muslim Brotherhood and other opposition leaders with the aim of opening a 'dialogue' with them. The Crown Prince also was making pronouncements on regional politics, in response to fears that Jordan was edging into a military pact with Israel and Turkey. Hassan, host to the visiting Turkish prime minister, denied it, but not with great conviction. Hussein's sons did not get a look-in. But Hassan was sowing the seeds of his own downfall.

By his own account, the king had time for reflection during his six-month stay at the Mayo Clinic. He was also well informed by his security services of what was going on in Amman. If his account is accurate, he had cause for concern. On January 19th 1999, the treatment seemed to have succeeded and the king flew home in his private airliner, piloting it himself for part of the journey. He was intent on settling matters. He was given a hero's welcome that once again confirmed that he had won the hearts and minds of his people. But he stood up in the car which took him from the airport to his palace in driving, cold rain and became weakened.

His brother Hassan wrote to him on January 21st, heaping praise on the king and, without saying as much, seeking confirmation of his post of heir-apparent. "Now my father, brother, friend and my magnificent king, after serving as your crown prince since the start of my youth until this day, as my hair starts to grey [he was 51; Hussein was 63], I find myself in a situation where I submit to your will and obey your sublime and kind command," he wrote.

Hassan may have delivered his letter in person if the account in the weekly *al-Majd (Glory)* is accurate. The conversation turned to allegations of disloyalty on the part of Hassan, who asked his brother about rumours that he was about to lose his job as crown prince. At this point, the weekly claims, "Prince Hassan took a gun from his hip, put it on the table in front of the king and called on his brother to shoot him if he doubted his loyalty". If true, this was the action of an unstable man.

Hassan's letter to Hussein read oddly for a brother-to-brother letter and it got short shrift from the king in a letter dated January 25th.

It too was full of circumlocutions. But it was devastating. Hussein asserted, improbably, that he had returned home "deciding to abdicate the throne in your favour despite the differences between us at times". But, he went on, "my small family was affected by slandering and false-hoods, and here I refer to my wife and children". He said he had wanted to "hand the first responsibility to you, but after you I envisioned a role for the family council in which to ensure the unity of the Hashemite family, so that when the time came for you to name your successor, the family would have a great role in naming the most suitable successor".

Hussein went on to say that he wanted the council set up while he was alive but Hassan wanted to set it up only after he became king — when he had accumulated much more power. Hussein said he had given his brother some notes on the issue and asked for his comments, But these comments "did not reflect the spirit of my proposal nor did they meet the needs of the times. We have differed, and we still do, over the succession..."

The king then mentioned in passing that his sister, Basma, and brother, Muhammad, "donated marrow that matches my own. You also volunteered to donate marrow except that yours did not match mine".

He then turned, in what was a rambling letter, to military affairs. "I have intervened from my sickbed," the king wrote, "to prevent meddling in the affairs of the army. This meddling seemed to be meant to settle scores, and included retiring efficient officers whose... bright records are beyond reproach." He added that he had used his authority as supreme commander of the armed forces "to stop any action that would have led to the fragmentation and politicization of the army". The same applied to the "transfer of efficient ambassadors without reason except the reason of age."

Then came his decision. The emergency situation which led to the constitution being amended so that the king could name his brother as his successor no longer existed. "Therefore, His Royal Highness Prince Abdullah would in such a case immediately assume all duties and responsibilities as the crown prince." And assume them he did.

Abdullah became crown prince, and regent during his father's incapacity, partly because of Hassan's manoeuvrings for power (if true) but also for several other reasons. First, it would have been difficult to pass over Abdullah since he bore the name of Hussein's grandfather and hero, King Abdullah, and his son and heir, the king's grandson, was named Prince Hussein. Hussein's own family line was established.

Second, Abdullah's attractive wife, Rania, was a Palestinian and could serve as a rallying point for support for the Hashemite family among the country's majority Palestinian population.

Third, Abdullah commanded units which operated in the desert and it would have been surprising if he had not got to know the Bedouins, many of whom serve in the armed forces and whose legendary loyalty was one of the foundations of the Hashemite dynasty.

Fourth, Abdullah had taken a degree in international relations at Oxford, which seemed likely to help him when he became king, and he was also a pilot, like his father, and he had served with British armed forces in Germany.

However, he remained essentially an unknown quantity. Nobody knew whether the 37-year-old heir-apparent had the spine of steel and the thick skin that was essential for anyone hoping to be a successful practitioner of Middle Eastern politics.

The king's cure from cancer lasted a week. He had returned home in triumph; he returned to the Mayo Clinic in a hurry, looking flushed and leaning on a walking stick. Doctors said he had suffered a relapse of non-Hodgkins lymphoma. First came another bout of chemotherapy and then a bone-marrow transplant. It was a tense time. "The coming stage, lasting for at least two weeks, will not be easy," said Marwan Muasher, Jordanian ambassador to the United States. "Doctors want to make sure that no complications develop." But they did develop: the transplant was unsuccessful.

The king lost consciousness and was flown home to die. By the time that he was taken to an Amman hospital, connected to a life-support machine, almost all the vital signs indicated that he was dead. But there were signs of life and the life-support machine stayed switched on.

Outside the hospital, many ordinary Jordanians prayed for a miracle. Many felt they were losing a father-figure who had ruled over them for 46 years. But there was no miracle. On February 7th 1999, Hussein bin Talal, king of Jordan, died. Black funeral flags flew over Amman. Jordanians sobbed and shouted their grief. The depth of feeling expressed was akin to that after a death in the family.

As might have been expected, the transition was smooth. The funeral took place promptly, as required by Islamic tradition, and was attended by many heads of state and government led by President Clinton, who called the king "a partner and a friend", and Tony Blair. Clinton was accompanied by ex-Presidents Ford, Carter and Bush; Blair was joined by Prince Charles and the two opposition leaders, William Hague and Paddy Ashdown. It was an extraordinary event by any standard. Bitter enemies, such as Assad and Arafat, mingled in the same crowd; both men were adversaries – of sorts – of Hussein. Others among the heads of state and government included the amir of Bahrain, President Hosni Mubarak of Egypt, President Chirac of France, Chancellor Schröder of Germany and the crown princes of Kuwait (which must have pleased the Jordanians) and Saudi Arabia. President Yeltsin flew to Amman in time for the funeral but was not well enough to take part. Israel's delegation was the biggest by far. Saddam Hussein was represented by a deputy prime minister.

The members of each delegation, all of them male in accordance with Islamic tradition, came forward and stood next to the king's coffin, bowed their heads and walked away. They all appeared to receive a handshake and an expression of gratitude for their presence from the new king. No other public figure in the Arab world, and very few elsewhere, could have drawn such a crowd to their funeral.

The next day, King Abdullah showed himself to his people, who waited in a long queue to express their condolences in person, according to Islamic tradition. The new king looked suitably solemn when required and also affable and smiling when out of the spotlight. In the first few days of his reign, he did not put a foot wrong.

Jordan's political class had the experience of two previous transitions – after the assassination of King Abdullah and after the dismissal of King Talal. There was no sign of instability in Abdullah's first few days in power; and in a gesture to unify the family, the new king named Hamzah, Queen Noor's oldest boy and pride and joy, as crown prince.

However, it seemed certain that Abdullah would be challenged. Within the Hashemite family it would be extraordinary if the former crown prince did not become embittered and uncooperative. But to what extent?

Within Jordan, the new king was likely to be challenged by political parties ranging from the Muslim Brothers to the Ba'ath Socialists with the pragmatic notables somewhere in the middle. Modern politicians such as Taher Masri, a former prime minister and foreign minister, could be expected to press for a democratic opening. Would the new king steer a course that avoided collisions?

Outside Jordan, pressures could come from Syria's ailing strongman, Hafez Assad, who, like many compatriots, hankered after a "Greater Syria" including Jordan and Palestine. If he was not old, tired and sick, Yasser Arafat, president of the Palestinian Authority, might have been tempted to try again to create a Palestinian state within a state in Jordan and see if the young king was prepared to counter-attack in a repeat of Black September. And the well-aimed bullet of a madman or the bomb wrapped around a young man destined for death and salvation could never be ruled out.

Enemies of Abdullah might point out that while he spoke perfect English, Arabic was his second language. On the other hand, he had learnt how to use armoured cars (ideal for desert warfare) while serving in the 13th/18th Hussars in the British army, where a fellow-officer described him not only as "a most incredible success" but also as "a tough little bugger". It would also help Jordan's sense of security that it was virtually under America's umbrella.

What might happen if a dispute arose between Israel and the Palestinian Authority that might have been settled by an intervention by King Hussein? Where and how might the new King Abdullah contribute to the stumbling Middle East peace process? Some of these questions would be answered as the new millennium approached.

What were King Hussein's greatest achievements? Almost certainly, stability. A reader of these pages, in which drama follows drama and prime minister follows prime minister, may be surprised at such a judgment. But the king has provided a vital sense of continuity and laid the basis for self-sustaining, non-inflationary, economic growth. Thanks to the king and assorted prime ministers, this improbable country offers investors a stable business environment including a stable currency backed by foreign-exchange reserves. Power is shared by a benevolent strongman and a weak but nonetheless talkative parliament and governments with varying degrees of independent-mindedness. It has hospitals and universities, excellent highways, competent armed forces and peace with all of its neighbours.

Seen from the point of view of the Hashemites, the king's greatest achievement was to consolidate the family's position. The first King Abdullah arrived from Mecca with little money and a small contingent of soldiers which he parlayed into the Emirate of Transjordan and later into the Hashemite Kingdom of Jordan. King Hussein built and consolidated Jordanian institutions – such as the armed forces, the courts, health services, universities and schools. In one way or another, these

institutions serve or employ most Jordanians. They become stakehold-
ers in the Hashemite system and disinclined to overthrow it.

This long list of achievements would not have satisfied the king,
however. What would? Restoration of the West Bank and East
Jerusalem to Jordanian rule, so that successive Hashemite monarchs
can again call themselves keepers of the Holy Places in Jerusalem.

And failures? The six-day war of 1967 and the loss of the West Bank
stand out; the failure, shared with Arafat, to co-ordinate Jordanian and
Palestinian policy in partnership and not in rivalry; the failure to work
out a formula to keep the Islamists in the 1997 general election and
convert them to become Islamic Democrats; and a failure to delegate
power to an elected party leader victorious in a general election.

It is, perhaps, asking too much of a traditional Arab ruler of a frag-
ile Middle Eastern state to turn himself into a constitutional monarch
along European lines. But the fact that high standards have been set
whenever Jordan is assessed – and may be found wanting – is itself an
accolade for a very remarkable king.

NOTES

Chapter 1

1 HM King Hussein of Jordan, *Uneasy Lies the Head*, Heinemann, London, 1962, pp. 1–7.
2 Avi Shlaim, *Collusion Across the Jordan*, Clarendon Press, Oxford, 1988, pp. 604–07.
3 Mark Tessler, *A History of the Israeli-Palestinian Conflict*, Indiana University Press, Bloomington, Ill., 1994, p. 278.

Chapter 2

1 Jerrold Post and Robert Robins, *When Illness Strikes the Leader*, Yale University Press, New Haven, Conn., p. 37.
2 Hussein, *op. cit.*, p. 12.
3 Hussein, *op. cit.*, pp. 16–17.
4 Lieutenant-General Sir John Bagot Glubb, *A Soldier with the Arabs*, Hodder & Stoughton, London, 1957, p. 299.
5 Quoted in James Lunt, *Hussein, a Political Biography*, Macmillan, London, 1989, p. 9.
6 Peter Snow, *Hussein, a Biography*, Barrie & Jenkins, London, 1972, p. 40.
7 Cited in Robert E. Satloff, *From Abdullah to Hussein*, Oxford University Press, New York, NY, and Oxford, p. 17.
8 *Ibid.*, pp. 38–9.
9 Snow, *op. cit.*, p. 44.
10 Satloff, *op. cit.*, p. 50.

Chapter 3

1 F.E. Peters, *A Literary History of the Muslim Holy Land*, Princeton University Press, Princeton, NJ, 1994, p. 348.
2 T.E. Lawrence, *The Seven Pillars of Wisdom*, Penguin Books, London, pp. 100–01.

3   HM King Abdullah, *Memoirs of King Abdullah of Transjordan*, Philosophical Libary, New York, NY, p. 62;

4   Mary C. Wilson, *King Abdullah, Britain and the Making of Jordan*, Cambridge University Press, Cambridge, 1987, p. 19.

5   Peters, *op. cit.*, p. 368.

6   Peters, *op. cit.*, p. 372.

7   M. Brown (ed.), *Letters of T.E. Lawrence*, J.M. Dent, London, 1988.

8   King Abdullah, *op. cit.*, pp 152–3.

9   Quoted in David Holden and Richard Johns, *The House of Saud*, Sidgwick & Jackson, London, 1981, p. 69.

10 Quoted in Peters, *op. cit.*, p. 387.

11 Tessler, *op. cit.*, p. 152.

12 Tessler, *op. cit.*, p. 164.

13 Shlaim, *op. cit.*, p. 28.

14 Peters, *op. cit.*, p. 380.

15 Foreign Office Papers E8118/38/44/91, Public Record Office, Kew.

16 Quoted in David Howarth, *Desert King, a Life of Ibn Saud*, Collins, London, pp. 98–9.

Chapter 4

1   Quoted by Mary C. Wilson, *King Abdullah, Britain and the Making of Jordan*, Cambridge University Press, Cambridge, 1987, p. 65.

2   Glubb, *op. cit.*, p. 26.

3   Kamal Salibi, *The Modern History of Jordan*, I.B. Tauris, London, 1993, p. 129.

4   John P. Richardson, *The West Bank, a Portrait*, Middle East Institute, Washington, DC, 1984, p. 36.

5   *Ibid.*, p. 39.

6   Wilson, *op. cit.*, p. 120.

7   Shlaim, *op. cit.*, p. 61.

8   Wilson, *op. cit.*, p. 148.

9   Glubb, *op. cit.*, p. 63.

10 Golda Meir, *My Life*, Weidenfeld & Nicolson, London, 1975, p. 176.

11 Cited in Shlaim, *op. cit.*, p. 48.

Chapter 5

1   Cited in Shlaim, *op. cit.*, pp. 273–4.

2 Glubb, *op. cit.,* p. 78.
3 Harry S. Truman, *Years of Trial and Hope,* Doubleday, Garden City, NY, 1954, p. 157.
4 Glubb, *op. cit.,* p. 216.
5 Cited in Tessler, *op. cit.,* p. 297.
6 Cited in Shlaim, *op. cit.,* p. 581.
7 Cited in Shlaim, *op. cit.,* p. 584.

Chapter 6
1 Lunt, *op. cit.,* p. 10.
2 Hussein, *op. cit.,* p. 63.
3 Henry Kissinger, *White House Years,* Little, Brown, New York, NY, 1979, p. 362.
4 Glubb, *op. cit.,* pp. 308–09.
5 Glubb, *op. cit.,* p. 384.
6 Satloff, *op. cit.,* p. 93.
7 *Ibid.,* p. 98.

Chapter 7
1 Hussein, *op. cit.,* p. 88.
2 Abba Eban, *Personal Witness,* Jonathan Cape, London, 1992, p. 347.
3 Hussein, *op. cit.,* p. 108.
4 Glubb, *op. cit.,* p. 366.
5 Glubb, *op. cit.,* p. 367.
6 Glubb, *op. cit.,* p. 421.
7 Glubb, *op. cit.,* p. 424.
8 Shlaim, *op. cit.,* p. 31.
9 Dwight D. Eisenhower, *Waging Peace 1956–1961,* Doubleday, Garden City, NY, 1965, pp. 676–7.
10 Stephen Ambrose, *Eisenhower the President,* Simon & Schuster, New York, NY, 1984, pp. 352–3.
11 Keith Kyle, *Suez,* St Martin's Press, New York, NY, pp. 399–400.

Chapter 8
1 Evelyn Shuckburgh, *Descent to Suez,* W.W. Norton, London and New York, NY, 1986, p. 261.
2 Hussein, *op. cit.,* p. 57.

3   Lunt, *op. cit.*, p. 19, and Snow, *op. cit.*, p. 66.

Chapter 9

1   *Washington Post*, February 18th 1977.
2   Hussein, *op. cit.*, p. 136.
3   Eisenhower, *op. cit.*, pp. 194–5.
4   Editorial note, Department of State, Central Files, 785.5-MSP/ 4-2957, p. 108.
5   Department of State, *US Treaties and Other International Agreements*, Vol. 8, Part 1, 1957, p. 1065.

Chapter 10

1   Hussein, *op. cit.*, p. 161.
2   Simon Henderson, *Instant Empire*, Mercury House, San Francisco, CA, 1991, pp. 60–1.
3   Uriel Dann, *King Hussein and the Challenge of Arab Radicalism*, Oxford University Press, 1989, p. 88.
4   Henderson, *op. cit.*, p. 236.
5   Hussein, *op. cit.*, p. 167.
6   Lunt, *op. cit.*, p. 58.

Chapter 11

1   Dann, *op. cit.*, p. 100.
2   Hussein, *op. cit.*, p. 188.
3   Hussein, *op. cit.*, p. 190.

Chapter 12

1   Kissinger, *op. cit.*, p. 362.
2   Snow, *op. cit.*, p. 42.

Chapter 13

1   Asher Susser, *On Both Banks of the Jordan, A Political Biography of Wasfi al-Tall*, Frank Cass & Co, Ilford, UK, 1994, pp. 36–7.
2   Dann, *op. cit.*, p. 133.
3   *Ibid.*, p. 141.
4   FO document EJ 1015/20, Public Record Office, Kew.
5   Cited in FO document EJ 1015/97, Public Record Office, Kew.

6   *Ibid.*
7   FO document 371/186550 EJ 1015/80, Public Record Office, Kew.
8   FO document FO371/186619, Public Record Office, Kew.
9   FO document EJ1015/34, Public Record Office, Kew.
10 Glubb, *op. cit.*, p. 423.

Chapter 14

1   Mahmoud Riad, *The Struggle for Peace in the Middle East,* Quartet Books, London, 1981, p. 17.
2   *Ibid.*
3   Quoted in Samir A. Mutawi, *Jordan and the 1967 war,* Cambridge University Press, Cambridge, p. 87.
4   King Hussein, Vick Vance and Pierre Lauer, *My War with Israel,* Peter Owen, London, 1969, p. 52.
5   *New York Times,* May 29th 1967.
6   Hussein, Vance and Lauer, *op. cit.*, p. 48.
7   Mutawi, *op. cit.*, p. 119.
8   Dean Rusk, *As I Saw It,* I.B. Tauris, London and New York, NY, 1991, p. 331.
9   Shimon Peres, *Battling for Peace,* Orion Books, London, 1995, pp. 122–3.
10 Brian Urquhart, *A Life in Peace and War,* Harper & Row, New York, NY, 1987, p. 214.

Chapter 15

1   Mutawi, *op. cit.*, p. 122.
2   Riad, *op. cit.*, p. 24.
3   Mutawi, *op. cit.*, p.126.
4   Quoted by Snow, *op. cit.*, p. 185.
5   Lunt, *op. cit.*, p. 102.
6   King Hussein, Vance and Lauer, *op. cit.*, p. 113.
7   *Jordan Times,* June 6th 1997.
8   Eban, *op. cit.*, p. 496.

Chapter 16

1   Andrew Gowers and Tony Walker, *Arafat, The Biography,* Virgin Books, London, 1990, p. 30.
2   *Ibid.*, p. 81.

3   Cited by Lunt, *op. cit.*, p. 119.
4   Janet Wallach and John Wallach, *Arafat in the Eyes of the Beholder*, Lyle Stuart, New York, NY, 1990, p. 286.
5   Kissinger, *op. cit.*, p. 609.
6   Kissinger, *op. cit.*, p. 625.
7   Christopher Dobson, *Black September, Its Short, Violent History*, Macmillan, New York, NY, 1974, p. 37.
8   Susser, *op. cit.*, p. 139.
9   Wallach and Wallach, *op. cit.*, p. 291.
10 Amman Radio, June 2nd 1971, cited by Susser, *op. cit.*, p. 152.

Chapter 17
1   Dobson:, *op. cit.*, p. 3.
2   *Ibid.*, p. 13.

Chapter 18
1   Riad, *op. cit.*, p. 230.
2   Riad, *op. cit.*, p. 236.
3   Henry Kissinger, *Years of Upheaval*, Little, Brown, Boston, MA, 1982, p. 461.
4   *Ibid.*, p. 506.
5   Chaim Herzog, *The War of Atonement*, Weidenfeld & Nicolson, London, 1975, p. 140.

Chapter 19
1   Henry Kissinger, *White House Years*, Little, Brown, Boston, MA, 1979, p. 362.
2   Yehuda Lukacs, *The Israeli-Palestinian Conflict: A Documentary Record*, Cambridge University Press, Cambridge, 1992, p. 445.
3   *Ibid*, p. 55.
4   David Hirst and Irene Beeson, *Sadat*, Faber & Faber, London, 1981, p. 182.
5   Madiha Rashid al-Madfai, *Jordan, the United States and the Middle East Peace Process 1974–1991*, Cambridge University Press, Cambridge, 1993, p. 18.
6   Peres, *op. cit.*, p. 349.
7   Gerald Ford, *A Time to Heal*, W.H. Allen, London, 1979, p. 244.

8   *Ibid.*, p. 287.
9   Jimmy Carter, *Keeping Faith*, Bantam Books, New York, NY, 1982, p. 280.
10 *Ibid.*, p. 285.
11 Rashid al-Madfai, *op. cit.*, p. 45.

Chapter 20

1   Rashid al-Madfai, *op. cit.*, p. 49.
2   Carter, *op. cit.*, p. 408.
3   Rashid al-Madfai, *op. cit.*, p. 56.
4   Tessler, *op. cit.*, p. 521.
5   *Ibid.*, pp. 124–6.
6   Jimmy Carter, *The Blood of Abraham*, Houghton Mifflin, Boston, MA, and Sidgwick & Jackson, London, 1985, p.141.
7   Rashid al-Madfai, *op. cit.*, p. 80.
8   Alexander Haig, *Caveat*, Weidenfeld & Nicolson, London, 1984, p. 174.
9   Gowers and Walker, *op. cit.*, p. 261.
10 Tessler, *op. cit.*, p. 590.
11 Gowers and Walker, *op. cit.*, p. 288.
12 George Shultz, *Turmoil and Triumph: My Years as Secretary of State*, Charles Scribner's Sons, New York, NY, 1993, p. 85 ff.
13 *Ibid.*, p. 99.
14 Gowers and Walker, *op. cit.*, p. 294.
15 William B. Quant, *Peace Process*, Brookings Institution, Washington, DC, 1993, p. 347.
16 *New York Times*, April 11th 1983.

Chapter 21

1   http//www.arab.netQNourjo/main/ivmsh.htm.
2   *Ibid.*
3   Interview in *Hello* magazine.
4   *Ibid.*
5   Geraldine Brooks, *Nine Parts of Desire*, Penguin Books, London, 1996, p. 138.
6   *Hello*, November 1st 1997.

Chapter 22

1   Shultz, *op. cit.*, p. 433.

2   Yehuda Lukacs (ed.), *The Israeli-Palestinian Conflict, a Documentary Record,* Cambridge University Press, Cambridge, 1992, p. 487
3   *Ibid.,* p.367.
4   Gowers and Walker, *op. cit.,* p.328 ff.
5   Wallach and Wallach, *op. cit.,* p.318 ff.
6   Lukacs, *op. cit.,* p. 489.
7   Shultz, *op. cit.,* p. 451.
8   Quant, *op. cit.,* pp. 354–5.
9   Shultz, *op. cit.,* p. 457.
10 Shultz, *op. cit.,* p. 458.
11 Lukacs, *op. cit.,* p. 510.
12 Shultz, *op. cit.,* p. 460.

Chapter 23
1   Peres, *op. cit.,* p.356
2   Yitzhak Shamir, *Summing Up,* Weidenfeld & Nicolson, London, 1994, p. 169.
3   Peres, *op. cit.,* pp. 163–5.
4   Gowers and Walker, *op. cit.,* p. 350.
5   *Jordan Times,* April 9th 1988.
6   Asher Susser, *In Through the Out Door: Jordan's Disengagement and the Middle East Peace Process,* Washington Institute for Near East Policy, Washington, DC, 1990, p. 21.
7   HM King Hussein of Jordan, *Collected Speeches,* International Press Centre, Amman, p. 9.
8   Shultz, *op. cit.,* p. 1033.
9   Shultz, *op. cit.,* p. 1043.

Chapter 24
1   James A. Baker III, *The Politics of Diplomacy,* G.P. Putnam's Sons, New York, NY, 1995, p. 121.
2   Shamir, *op. cit.,* p.213.
3   Baker, *op. cit.,* p.128.
4   Gowers and Walker, *op. cit.,* p. 416.
5   HRH General Khaled bin Sultan, *Desert Warrior,* HarperCollins, London, 1995, p. 157.
6   Baker, *op. cit.,* p. 291.

7 Gowers and Walker, *op. cit.*, p. 426.

8 Lawrence Freedman and Efraim Karsh, *The Gulf Conflict 1990–1991,* Faber & Faber, London, 1993, p. 57.

9 Khaled, *op. cit.*, p. 177.

10 Freedman and Karsh, *op. cit.*, p. 60.

11 Khaled, *op. cit.*, p. 181.

12 Freedman and Karsh, *op. cit.*, p. 70.

13 HM King Hussein of Jordan, *Selected Speeches, op. cit.*, p. 28.

14 Freedman and Karsh, *op. cit.*, p. 326.

15 *Middle East International (MEI)*, London, August 31st 1990.

16 Freedman and Karsh, *op. cit.*, p. 379.

17 Baker, *op. cit.*, p. 450.

18 Avi Shlaim, *War and Peace in the Middle East,* Penguin Books, New York, NY, and London, 1994, p. 116.

Chapter 25

1 Peres, *op. cit.*, p. 398.

2 Avi Shlaim, *War and Peace in the Middle East, op. cit.*, p. 123.

3 Mahmoud Abbas (Abu Mazen), *Through Secret Channels,* Garnet Publishing, Reading, UK, 1995, p. 187.

4 Lori Plotkin, *Jordan-Israel Peace: Taking Stock, 1994–1997,* Research Memorandum no. 32, Washington Institute for Near East Policy, Washington, DC, 1997, p. 17.

5 Shlaim, *op. cit.*, p. 123.

6 Plotkin, *op. cit.*, p. 8.

7 *Ibid.*, p. 10.

8 *Ibid.*, p. 12.

9 BBC Summary of Short Wave Broadcasts, ME2866 MED 12, March 13th 1997.

Chapter 26

1 US State Department, *Jordan Country Report on Human Rights Practices for 1996,*Washington, DC, 1997, p. 4.

2 Conversation with William Waldegrave.

3 Conversation with Lord Howe.

4 US State Department, *op. cit.*, p. 8.

5 US State Department, *op. cit.*, pp. 10–13.

Chapter 27

1 Robert Satloff, "They cannot silence our tongues", Policy Paper no. 5, Washington Institute for Near East Policy, Washington, DC, 1986, p. 5.
2 Cited in Satloff, *op. cit.*, p. 12.
3 *MEI*, London, September 22nd 1989.
4 *MEI*, October 20th 1989.
5 Sabah el-Said, *Between Pragmatism and Ideology*, Washington Institute for Near East Policy, Washington DC, 1995, p. 13.
6 *The Economist*, August 30th 1997, p. 49.
7 *The Economist*, November 8th,1997, pp. 79–80.
8 *MEI*, December 5th, 1997, p. 12.
9 BBC Summary of Short Wave Broadcasts, July 16th 1997; monitoring Amman Radio on July 14th.

Chapter 28

1 *Jane's Sentinel*, Jane's Information Group, Coulsdon, Surrey, UK, 1997, p. 4.11.1.
2 *Jane's International Defense Review*, Coulsdon, Surrey, UK, p. 31 ff.
3 *Jane's Sentinel*, *op. cit.*, 44.8.15.
4 World Bank, *Jordan Highlights*, Washington, DC, 1996, p. 2.
5 *Ibid.*, p. 6.
6 *Financial Times*, August 29th 1997.
7 Shimon Peres, *The New Middle East*, Element, Shaftesbury, Dorset, 1993, p. 87.

Chapter 29

1 *The Independent*, January 24th 1998, p. 12.
2 *Jordan Times*, October 9th–10th 1997.
3 *Jordan Times*, August 13th 1997.
4 Mustafa Hamarneh, Rosemary Hollis and Khalil Shikaki, *Jordanian-Palestinian Relations: Where To?* Royal Institute for International Affairs, London, 1997, p. 127.
5 International Monetary Fund, *Recent Economic Developments, Prospects and Progress in Institution Building in the West Bank*, Washington, DC, March 1997.
6 Mustafa Hamarneh *et al.*, *op. cit.*, p. 60.

INDEX